Fabulation and Metafiction

Robert Scholes

University of Illinois Press
Urbana Chicago London

Fabulation
and
Metafiction

ACKNOWLEDGMENTS

Most of the material in this book has appeared in some form or
other in some place or other before the present volume. I am
grateful to the following publishers and publications for per-
mission to recycle these materials:

To the Oxford University Press, for some of the Introduction,
and for material on Durrell, Murdoch, Barth, Vonnegut,
Hawkes, and Southern.

To the *Iowa Review* for material on Borges, experimental fiction,
and metafiction.

To the *Saturday Review* for the eight brief comments collected
here in the section on "The Limits of Metafiction," and the
review of Malamud's *Fidelman*.

To the *Hollins Critic* for the material on John Fowles and orgastic
fiction.

To the *Northwest Review* for the material on Malamud's *Fixer*.

To *Summary* for the material on Vonnegut's college writing.

And to the *New York Times Book Review* for material on Reed and
Vonnegut.

Library of Congress Cataloging in Publication Data

Scholes, Robert E
    Fabulation and metafiction.

    1. Fiction—20th century—History and
criticism. 2. Fiction. I. Title.
PN3503.S32   813'.5'09   78-10776
ISBN 0-252-00704-2

In plain English this time, I dedicate this book to the memory
of that American fabulator who delighted my youth and shaped
my abiding interest in ethically controlled fantasy:

L. Frank Baum
Historian of Oz

Contents

Introduction: Of Fabulators, Fabulation, and Metafiction   1

Fabulation and Reality   5

Fact, Fiction, and Fallibilism   7
The Reality of Borges   9

The Nature of Romance   21

What Good Is Pure Romance?   23
The Orgastic Pattern of Fiction   26
Lawrence Durrell and the Return to Alexandria   29
John Fowles as Romancer   37

Modern Allegory   47

A Fable and Its Gloss   49
Iris Murdoch's *Unicorn*   56
John Barth's *Goat-Boy*   75

Metafiction   103

The Nature of Experimental Fiction   105
The Range of Metafiction: Barth, Barthelme, Coover, Gass   114
The Limits of Metafiction: Warhol, Mosley, Sarraute, Brodeur,
Merwin, Charyn, Dylan, Federman   124

Comedy and Grotesquerie   139

The Comedy of Extremity   141
The Making of a Comedian   150
Vonnegut's *Cat's Cradle* and *Mother Night*   156
Black Humor in Hawkes and Southern   163
John Hawkes's Theory of Fiction   169

The Lime Twig   178

A Portrait of the Artist as "Escape-Goat": Malamud's *Fidelman*   190

Ishmael's Black Art   193

Epilogue   197

History as Fabulation: Malamud and Vonnegut   200

Fabulation as History: Barth, García-Marquez, Fowles, Pynchon, Coover   206

Imagination Dead Imagine: Reflections on Self-Reflexive Fiction   210

Index   219

Introduction: of Fabulators, Fabulation, and Metafiction

This lovely word, "fabulator," dropped out of our language some time ago and was deliberately re-introduced in the first version of the present book, published in 1967 as *The Fabulators*. At that time, over a decade ago, it seemed that a movement of great importance in contemporary fiction was being ignored, misinterpreted, or critically abused because it lacked a name. Many readers, teachers, and professional critics at that time were possessed by notions of fictional propriety derived from a version of realism that had seen its best days and was being perpetuated in a trivial and often mechanical way; while all around us a new and more fabulous kind of fiction was coming into being—a kind of fiction that had much to teach us and many satisfactions to give us.

Wisely or unwisely, I made this new fiction my cause and encumbered it with my enthusiasm, finding the name I felt was needed in one of the first books printed in English. Let us pause for a moment and hear how the word sounded on the lips of William Caxton as he turned the eighth fable of Alfonce into English in 1484:

A disciple was sometime, which took his pleasure to rehearse and tell many fables; the which prayed to his master that he would rehearse unto him a long fable. To whom the master answered, "Keep and beware well that it hap not tô us as it happened to a King and his fabulator." And the disciple answered, "My master, I pray thee to tell to me how it befell." And then the master said to his disciple:

"Sometime was a King which had a fabulator, the which rehearsed to him at every time that he would sleep five fables for to rejoice the King and for to make him fall into a sleep. It befell then on a day that the King was much sorrowful and so heavy that he could in no wise fall asleep. And after that the said fabulator had told and rehearsed his five fables the King desired to hear more. And then the said fabulator recited unto him three fables well short. And the King then said to him, 'I would fain hear one well long, and then shall I sleep.' The fabulator then rehearsed unto him such a fable, of a rich man which went to the market or fair to buy sheep, the which man bought a thousand sheep. And as he was returning from the fair he came unto a river and because of the great waves of the water he could not pass over the bridge. Nevertheless, he went so long to and fro on the rivage [bank] of the said river that at last he found a narrow way upon the which might pass scant enough three sheep at once. And thus he passed and had them over one after another. And hitherto rehearsed of this fable the fabulator fell asleep. And anon after the King awoke the fabulator and said to him in this manner, 'I pray thee that thou wilt make an end of thy fable.' And the fabulator answered to him in this manner: 'Sire, this river is right great, and the ship is little; wherefore, late the merchant do pass over his sheep. And after I shall make an end of my fable.' And then was the King well appeased and pacified.

"And therefor be thou content of that I have rehearsed unto thee; for there is folks superstitious or capacious that they may not be contented with few words."

From the very construction of this fable we can learn something. It is in the form of a tale (about the sheep) within a tale (about king and fabulator) within a tale (about master and disciple). The enclosing or frame tale of master and disciple is not brought completely to an end, but we are led to assume that the tale of king and fabulator must have satisfied the disciple and effectively silenced his request for a long fable. The next tale, of king and fabulator, is neatly rounded off, with the king "well appeased and pacified." The innermost tale, which we might call a shaggy sheep story, is by its nature unending. Though enclosed by the others, it is not shut off, but is allowed to continue in our imaginations toward an "after" that is as vaguely located in the future as the "sometime" which begins the two outer tales is located in the past. This structure tells us a number of things about fabulation. First of all, it reveals an extraordinary delight in design. With its wheels within wheels, rhythms and counterpoints, this shape is partly to be admired for its own sake. A sense of pleasure in form is one characteristic of fabulation.

The structure also, by its very shapeliness, asserts the authority of the shaper, the fabulator behind the fable. (In this case it is Caxton, partly translating, partly reworking a traditional tale introduced into Europe from the East by a Christianized Spanish Jew, who changed his name from Moses to Peter in 1106 and compiled a book of fables for use as exempla in sermons, including this one, *Exemplum XII: De rege et fabulatore suo.*) The authority of the fabulator over his fable is not only asserted by the ingenuity of the fabulation, however; this authority is reinforced by the relations among the characters in the two outer tales. As master is to disciple, so is fabulator to king. The king desperately needs this artist of the story to "rejoice" him and to enable him to relax—especially when the king is "sorrowful" and "heavy." The fabulator is important to the extent that he can rejoice and refresh us. And his ability to produce joy and peace depends on the skill with which he fabulates. Delight in design, and its concur- ᴸ rent emphasis on the art of the designer, will serve in part to distinguish the art of the fabulator from the work of the novelist or the satirist. Of all narrative forms, fabulation puts the highest premium on art and joy.

In using the word "fabulator" to designate certain modern writers of fiction, I meant to emphasize these qualities of art and joy, of course. I also hoped to make the word suggest other, related qualities. Fables traditionally have lent themselves to preaching, either as exempla in medieval sermons or directly through moral tags appended to the tales themselves—or both. This didactic quality is also characteristic of modern fabulation—but in ways which will need considerable qualification as we consider specific authors and instances. For the moment, suffice it to say that modern fabulation, like the ancient fabling of Aesop, tends away from direct representation ³ of the surface of reality but returns toward actual human life by way of ethically controlled fantasy. This whole complex question of the relationship between fabulation and reality requires a fuller discussion—which it will receive below.

Before taking up this question it will be useful to return to the specific situation of fiction in the mid-1960's and reconsider it for a moment. One of the most poignant episodes of that era in the history of fiction was drawing to its close even as I finished writing the first version of this book, though at the time hardly anyone knew of it. For the last decade of his life, one of America's finest writers in realistic/naturalistic tradition was engaged in a serious artistic struggle through which he sought to come to terms with fabulation. Returning to the period of Caxton, John Steinbeck tried, from 1956 until he died in 1968, to produce a modern version of Sir Thomas Malory's *Morte d'Arthur*. The project defeated him, but his unfinished manuscripts were published in 1976 as *The Acts of King Arthur and His Noble Knights*, along with excerpts from the letters which document Steinbeck's long struggle to become a fabulator.

In the fall of 1958 Steinbeck went to Avalon in search of something which he described as follows to his editor, Chase Horton:

It is my profound hope that at Avalon I can make contact with the very old, the older than knowledge, and that this may be a springboard into the newer than knowledge. . . . But in the haunted fields of Cornwall and the mines with the tin and lead pits, in the dunes and the living ghosts of things, I do wish to find a path or a symbol or an approach. . . . And please do know that in turning over the lumber of the past I'm looking for the future. This is no nostalgia for the finished and safe. My looking is not for a dead Arthur but for one sleeping. And if sleeping, he is sleeping everywhere, not alone in a cave in Cornwall. Now there, that's said and done and I've been trying to say it for a long time. [pp. 326–27]

What moved Steinbeck toward fabulation? What but the same impulse that was moving younger writers in the same direction—the sense that the positivistic basis for traditional realism had been eroded, and that reality, if it could be caught at all, would require a whole new set of fictional skills. Surely Steinbeck was right in thinking that these skills would have something to do with the early traditions of fabulation. What he could not quite discover was how these would be transformed. The future he sought was coming into being around him in the works of Barth, Coover, Gardner, Pynchon, Gass, and many, many other young writers. But he could not enter it. As if prevented by enchantment, he sought until his death and died without finding it.

The fabulative movement grew and flourished, however, drawing strength from masters like Borges and Nabokov and finally, in works like *Gravity's Rainbow*, *Ragtime*, and *The Public Burning*, turning back toward the stuff of history itself and reinvigorating it with an imagination tempered by a decade and more of fictional experimentation. For experimental fabulation—or "metafiction" as I have called it, following William Gass's suggestion—has been one of the special and important features of the fabulative movement. Thus, in the present volume, I have tried to attend more thoroughly to the experimental or metafictional dimension of modern fabulation both in short stories, where much experimentation is performed, and in longer works. In doing so, I have also tried to acknowledge the important fact that not all experiments are successful.

What follows, then, is an exploration of the major aspects of fabulation as they manifested themselves in the past decade and a half. It has seemed to me better to consider a few exemplary works, and also to look briefly at a number of minor or peripheral experiments (including some failures), rather than to attempt a complete chronicle of this movement. Its dimensions and its directions, from Borges to Coover and Pynchon, are the subject of this book.

Fabulation and Reality

Fact, Fiction, and Fallibilism

It will be useful to begin by considering the definition of reality offered to us a century ago by the brilliant pragmatist philosopher Charles Saunders Peirce. In an essay called "How to Make Our Ideas Clear" Peirce suggested that we could arrive at a clear notion of the real "by considering the points of difference between reality and its opposite, fiction" (Justus Buchler, ed., *Philosophical Writings of Peirce*, p. 36). The products of imagination are real, said Peirce, in the sense that we really imagine them. If we have a thought or a dream, the thinking and dreaming are themselves real:

> Thus a dream has real existence as a mental phenomenon, if somebody really dreamt it; that he dreamt so and so, does not depend on what anybody thinks was dreamt, but is completely independent of all opinion on the subject. On the other hand, considering not the fact of dreaming, but the thing dreamt, it retains its peculiarities by virtue of no other fact than that it was dreamt to possess them. Thus we may define the real as that whose characters are independent of what anybody may think them to be. [p. 36]

Our fictions are real enough in themselves, but, as signs pointing to any world outside the fiction or the dream, they have no factual status. All thought, being fiction, tends toward this situation. We may think about reality all we please, but we shall never reach it in thought. Reality is absolute for Peirce, but human attempts to signify the truth are relative: "The opinion which is fated to be ultimately agreed to by all who investigate, is what we mean by truth, and the object represented in this opinion is the real" (p. 38).

In life, we do not attain the real. What we reach is a notion of the real which contents us enough so that we can found our behavior upon it. In a word, we arrive at belief. "And what is belief? It is the demi-cadence which closes a musical phrase in the symphony of our intellectual life" (p. 28). To acquiesce in belief would be to end the symphony of life prematurely. Belief is comfortable, but it is in a sense the enemy of truth, because it stifles inquiry. And, since "people cannot attain absolute certainty concerning questions of fact" (p. 50), the appropriate intellectual position for a human being must be what Peirce called "fallibilism," which he expressed in this fashion: "On the whole, then, we cannot in any way reach perfect certitude nor exactitude. We never can be absolutely sure of anything, nor can we with any probability ascertain the exact value of any measure or general ratio" (p. 58).

It is my contention that modern fabulation grows out of an attitude which may be called "fallibilism," just as nineteenth-century realism grew out of an earlier attitude called positivism. Fabulation, then, means not a turning away from reality, but an attempt to find more subtle correspondences between the reality which is fiction and the fiction which is reality. Modern fabulation accepts, even emphasizes, its fallibilism, its inability to reach all the way to the real, but it continues to look toward reality. It aims at telling such truths as fiction may legitimately tell in ways which are appropriately fictional. It will be useful to test that thesis provisionally on a writer who has been one of the major influences on the contemporary fabulative movement, and who is often described as one who has turned his back on reality to play in a purely verbal universe.

The Reality of Borges

"Fame is a form of incomprehension,
perhaps the worst."
—J. L. B.

My argument here is simple. I submit that we have missed the reality
of Borges because we have misunderstood his view of reality and of
the relationship between words and the world. All too often he has
been taken for an extreme formalist, where it would be much more
appropriate to see him as a kind of fallibilist in fiction. It will be
proper, then, to consider what he has had to say about the fact/fic-
tion relationship, beginning in a very humble way by considering
some of the instances of the word "reality" in his texts. Our first
set of illustrations will be taken from his essays on other writers
collected in *Other Inquisitions,* where he takes up this problem on
many occasions, with different emphases that are often quite illuminating.

Writing of Quevedo, Borges introduces a persistent theme in his
critical work. He says of one sonnet, "I shall not say that it is a
transcription of reality, for reality is not verbal. . . ." This opposition between language and reality, the unbridgeable gap between
them, is fundamental to the Borgesian vision, and to much of modern epistemology and poetic theory. In particular, the notion of a lack
of contact between language and world is a characteristic of those
schools of critical thought that are usually called "formalist." In its
extreme form, this view is highly vulnerable to attacks such as that
made by Fredric Jameson in *The Prison-House of Language,* for language is seen in this view as cutting man off from authentic experience by its artificialities and evasions. It is frequently assumed that
Borges is a typical formalist, who holds that language is self-
contained and self-sufficient—self-referential, in fact. But this is
simply not the case. Let us return to that statement about the
Quevedo poem. In presenting it the first time I actually cut it off in
mid-sentence. Here is the whole thing: "I shall not say that it is a

transcription of reality, for reality is not verbal, but I can say that the words are less important than the scene they evoke or the virile accent that seems to inform them" (*Other Inquisitions*, p. 40).

Poems are made of words, and reality is not; yet there is something here between the words and the reality which is important. In this case there are actually two things: a "scene" evoked by the words, and an "accent" that seems to inform them. This scene and this accent, then, are mediations between language and world. Born of words, they have nevertheless moved beyond words toward experiences. The words suggest a speaker with a virile accent; they imply a human being of an order of reality greater than their own. They also present a scene which is more real than language, though it falls short of reality. These fictions or inventions, then, move language *toward* reality, not away from it. Artful writing offers a key that can open the doors of the prison-house of language.

Borges develops this idea further in his philosophic discussion, "Avatars of the Tortoise": "It is hazardous to think that a coordination of words (philosophies are nothing else) can have much resemblance to the universe. It is also hazardous to think that one of those famous coordinations does not resemble it a little more than the others, if only in an infinitesimal way" (p. 114). The term "coordination of words," of course, applies equally well to philosophies and stories. They are all fictions because they are verbal and the universe is not. But again comes the qualifying notion. Some of these coordinations catch more of the universe than others. And Borges adds that, of those he has considered in this context, the only one in which he recognizes "some vestige of the universe" is Schopenhauer's. Reading this, we are permitted, or even obliged, to ask by what faculty Borges or anyone else is capable of recognizing vestiges of the universe in a mere coordination of words. I don't want to pause and consider this question here. Or you might say I can't. But Borges's statement seems to imply that we are in touch with reality in some way, either through valid perceptions or through intuitions which are non-verbal. Considering this further would lead us into philosophical labyrinths darker than the ones Borges himself constructs, so let us avoid them and pick up the thread of his thought.

Twice, when turning to the question of the relationship between language—especially the language of fiction—and reality, Borges has recourse to the same quotation from Chesterton. Summarizing Chesterton's view, he writes, "He reasons that reality is interminably rich and that the language of men does not exhaust that vertiginous treasure" (p. 50). This position is very close to the others we have been considering, but here the solution is a bit more explicit. In both cases the quotation from Chesterton leads to a discussion of allegory, and in both cases Borges is cautious about revealing his own views—or perhaps he is simply uncertain of them. But he clearly entertains the possibility that a certain kind of allegory may serve as the vehicle that links the verbal cosmos with the greater reality. In one discussion he reports that Chesterton considered allegories capable of "somehow" corresponding to "ungraspable reality" (p. 50). And in the other he develops the same notion somewhat more thoroughly, suggesting that allegory may be a useful mediator between language and reality because "it is made up of words but it is not a language of language, a sign of other signs" (p. 155). And he adds, following Chesterton, that Dante's Beatrice, for example, "is not a sign of the word *faith*; she is a sign of the active virtue and the secret illuminations that this word indicates—a more precise sign, a richer and happier sign than the monosyllable *faith*" (p. 155).

In both these discussions of allegory, Borges suggests that allegory fails when its fictions are reducible back to single word-concepts, but succeeds when its fictions function as complex signs moving away from simple concepts toward the "ungraspable reality." For Borges, the language's tendency toward logic is a movement away from reality. The more precise and fixed the terminology, the more inadequate it must become. Thus allegory, at its best, is thinking in images, intuitive and open to truth. Whereas logic is a kind of game, often admirable, but not likely to catch much of the universe in its play. An allegory like Nathaniel Hawthorne's, which at its best is "refractory, so to speak, to reason," may indeed approach the ungraspable. But Borges reproaches Hawthorne for a tendency toward reducing his own allegorical intuitions to mere moral fables. The pointing of a moral at the end of a tale is, of course, an attempt to reduce the complex to the simple, to substitute a concept for an image, and hence is a move away from the possibility of truth. "Better," he says, "are those pure fantasies that do not look for a justification or moral and that seem to have no other substance than an obscure terror" (p. 51).

In discussing the writer to whom he is most justly generous, he elaborates this notion further, making his illustrations concrete and specific. Having discussed the excellence of H. G. Wells as a storyteller, and having recounted with amusement the reaction of Jules Verne to Wells's *The First Men in the Moon* (Verne "exclaimed indignantly, *'Il invente!'* "), Borges suggests that Wells's achievement rests on something even more important than ingenuity:

In my opinion, the excellence of Wells's first novels—*The Island of Dr. Moreau,* for example, or *The Invisible Man*—has a deeper origin. Not only do they tell an ingenious story; but they tell a story symbolic of processes that are somehow inherent in all human destinies. The harassed invisible man who has to sleep as though his eyes were wide open because his eyelids do not exclude light is our solitude and our terror; the conventicle of seated monsters who mouth a servile creed in their night is the Vatican and is Lhasa. Work that endures is always capable of an infinite and plastic ambiguity; it is all things to all men, like the Apostle; it is a mirror that reflects the reader's own features and it is also a map of the world. And it must be ambiguous in an evanescent and modest way, almost in spite of the author; he must appear to be ignorant of all symbolism. Wells displayed that lucid innocence in his first fantastic exercises, which are to me the most admirable part of his admirable work. [p. 87]

This is one of the most perceptive and succinct paragraphs of literary criticism that I have encountered, and it takes us to the heart of Borges's notion of literary reality. Wells's work is a *"mirror* that reflects the reader's own features and it is also a *map* of the world." I wish to suggest that the two images employed here were not chosen lightly. Mirrors and maps are two highly different ways of imaging the world around us. They are also images that Borges returns to again and again in his own fiction. They are, of course, pointedly non-verbal signs of reality, and they are signs of different sorts. Mapping is based on a sign system that is highly arbitrary in its symbols but aspires toward an exact iconicity in its proportions. Mirrors, on the other hand, are superbly iconic in their reflections of reality, but patently artificial in at least three respects. They reduce three dimensions to a plane surface of two, they double distance and reduce size (our face in a mirror is only half its true size), and, most significantly, they reverse right and left.

The distortions of maps and mirrors, because they are visible and comparable with the reality they image, are obvious. With language, however, the distortions are less obvious and therefore more sinister. Thus fiction, which gives us images of human situations and actions, is superior to philosophy, which tries to capture these things in more abstract coordinations of words. Like Sidney, Shelley, and other apologists for literature, Borges is answering Plato's charge that poets falsify the universe. But this is a more total answer, and a stronger one, for two reasons. Unlike the others, it does not weaken itself by accepting the Platonic premise. Borges does *not* argue that literature points toward some eternal realm of perfect ideas. His argument concerns a complex human reality. Furthermore, he uses this complexity as the ground for an attack on philosophy itself. He denies it a privileged position from which to judge the value of literature. His very praise of philosophy robs it of its power of evaluation. Philosophy, he says, "dissolves reality," giving it "a kind of haziness." "I think that people who have no philosophy live a poor kind of life, no? People who are too sure about reality and about themselves. . . . I think that philosophy may give the world a kind of haziness, but that haziness is all to the good" (*Conversations with Borges*, p. 156).

Returning now to the passage on Wells, there is yet another aspect of it that must be considered. The notion that art is a mirror is not a new one. We are all familiar with the classical view that art is a mirror held up to nature, and with Stendhal's more pointed version of this notion—a mirror being carried down a roadway, reflecting the mud below and the sky above. But Borges's mirror is more modest, and does only what ordinary mirrors do. We see in it not nature or the world, but only ourselves: "it is a mirror that reflects the reader's own features." Of the world, art is merely a map, but it is a map that points accurately to things that are there in reality. In Wells's image of the invisible man we recognize "our own solitude and our terror"; and in the "conventicle of seated monsters who mouth a servile creed in their night" we see an image of "the Vatican" and "Lhasa." Such mirroring and such mapping take us deeply into reality, though the images are obviously fabulations rather than transcriptions. And this is a major point. Reality is too subtle for realism to catch it. It cannot be transcribed directly. But by invention, by fabulation, we may open a way toward reality that will come as close to it as human ingenuity may come. We rely on maps and mirrors precisely because we know their limitations and know how to allow for them. But fiction functions as both map and mirror at the same time. Its images are fixed, as the configurations of a map are fixed, and perpetually various, like the features reflected by a mirror, which never gives the same image to the same person. "Work that endures," says Borges, "is capable of an infinite and plastic ambiguity."

The world that Borges maps for us in his own fictions seems at first to be as strange an image of reality as the work of a medieval cartographer. It is a world populated mainly by gauchos and librarians, men of mindless brutality and others of lettered inactivity. These extremes meet, of course, in the figure of the detective, who both acts and ratiocinates. But for the most part the extremes are what Borges chooses to present to us. His map of the world excludes much of the middle ground of life. He concentrates on the fringes, where heroes and monsters, warriors and demigods, meet and interact. And his map abounds in cartographers, busily making their own maps and titling them "Reality." For Borges, the ultimate futility is that of the creature in "The Circular Ruins" who hopes to "dream a man . . . with a minute integrity and insert him into reality"—only to discover that he is himself a fiction in someone else's dream world, and not in "reality" at all. This vertiginous notion that the world may be a dream is perhaps what most people think of when they hear the name Borges. But I am trying to suggest that this notion is not a value held by him, but a fictitious position assumed by him to provoke reality into showing itself. Unlike the figure in "The Circular Ruins," Borges is in reality himself and knows it. The fires of time are consuming him, even as they are consuming us and all we perceive: "Time is the substance I am made of. Time is a river which sweeps me along, but I am the river; it is a tiger which destroys me but I am the tiger; it is a fire which consumes me, but I am the fire. The world, alas, is real; I, alas, am Borges" (*Labyrinths*, p. 234; *Other Inquisitions*, p. 187).

The world in all its awful reality is finally inescapable. When asked whether the writer has a responsibility to the world which he must discharge by writing fiction that is "engaged in the political and social issues of the times," Borges has not answered simply, "No," with formalist disdain, but has spoken as follows:

I think it is engaged all the time. We don't have to worry about that. Being contemporaries, we have to write in the style and mode of our times. If I write a story—even about the man in the moon—it would be an Argentine

story, because I'm an Argentine; and it would fall back on Western civilization because that's the civilization I belong to. I don't think we have to be
conscious about it. Let's take Flaubert's novel *Salammbô* as an example. He
called it a Carthaginian novel, but anyone can see that it was written by a
nineteenth-century French realist. I don't suppose a real Carthaginian would
make anything out of it; for all I know, he might consider it a bad joke. I
don't think you should try to be loyal to your century or your opinions,
because you are being loyal to them all the time. You have a certain voice, a
certain kind of face, a certain way of writing, and you can't run away from
them, even if you want to. So why bother to be modern or contemporary,
since you can't be anything else? [*Borges on Writing*, p 51]

The problem for the writer is not to "represent" ·his own
time. This he cannot help but do. The problem is to be like the
apostle, all things to all men. To reach beyond reality to truth,
beyond the immediate and contemporary to those aspects of the real
which will endure and recur. No dream tiger ever becomes a real
tiger, but the image of a man of letters struggling to capture the
tiger's reality is an image that may still be valid when both men and
tigers are extinct and replaced by other forms of life. The writer seeks
this kind of durability for his work—against great odds: "There is no
exercise of the intellect which is not, in the final analysis, useless. A
philosophical doctrine begins as a plausible description of the universe; with the passage of the years it becomes a mere chapter—if not
a paragraph or a name—in the history of philosophy. In literature
this eventual caducity is even more notorious." (*Labyrinths*, p. 43).

These are the views of Pierre Menard, author of the *Quixote*, who is
in one sense Borges's greatest hero and in another his greatest fool. By
acting on the feelings of futility expressed in this passage, Menard
has refused the possibilities of literary creation. He has sought to
defy time by plunging backward through it toward seventeenth-
century Spain. But his work, because it is *his* and to the extent that it
is *his*, must be read as that of a *fin de siècle* Frenchman affecting an
archaic style. He is as tied to his time as Flaubert, even though he
sought to avoid the curse of temporality by hiding in the past and
assuming the voice of Cervantes. Either he has no reality and is
absorbed into the voice of the dead Spaniard, or he has his own, that
of a contemporary of William James and the friend of Valéry. Readers
will see him as "brazenly pragmatic" or hopelessly relativistic.
Borges is reminding us in this tale that there is no meaning without a
meaner. Language itself always assumes a larger context. It can never

be self-referential, because in order to interpret it we must locate it in a frame of reference which is ineluctably temporal and cultural. The world is real and Menard, alas, is Menard.

There is a further paradox here, which I have only hinted at so far, but which Borges himself has clearly articulated. Reality itself is real, is in time and is subject to the same consuming fires as the creatures and things which constitute it. He has expressed this exquisitely in his "Parable of Cervantes and the Quixote," from which I quote:

> Vanquished by reality, by Spain, Don Quixote died in his native village in the year 1614. He was survived but a short time by Miguel de Cervantes.
>
> For both of them, for the dreamer and the dreamed one, the whole scheme of the work consisted in the opposition of two worlds; the Unreal world of the books of chivalry, the ordinary everyday world of the seventeenth century.
>
> They did not suspect that the years would finally smooth away that discord, they did not suspect that La Mancha and Montiel and the knight's lean figure would be, for posterity, no less poetic than the episodes of Sinbad or the vast geographies of Ariosto.
>
> For in the beginning of literature is the myth, and in the end as well. [p. 242]

Thus reality itself is a thing which fades into mythology with the passage of time. Or rather, most of reality fades into obscurity, and what endures is transformed into mythology. Truth vanishes. Fiction endures if it partakes of that reality beyond reality, which enables it to survive as myth. The real reality is that which has not yet happened but is to come. In one of his finest essays, "The Modesty of History," Borges encourages us to consider this situation. He begins by remarking on the way governments try to manufacture or simulate historical occasions with an "abundance of preconditioning propaganda followed by relentless publicity" (*Other Inquisitions*, p. 167). But behind this fraudulent façade there is a "real history," which is "more modest," he suggests, with "essential dates that may be, for a long time, secret." He cites as one instance an occasion which passed with no chronological marker but certainly altered the world of letters—the date when Aeschylus is said to have changed the shape of drama by introducing a second actor upon the scene. Where only the chorus and a single speaker had appeared, on some "remote spring day, in that honey-colored theater" a second figure took up a position on stage, and with this event "came the dialogue and the infinite possibilities of the reaction of some characters to others. A prophetic spectator would have seen that multitudes of future appearances accompanied him: Hamlet and Faust and Segismundo and Macbeth and Peer Gynt and others our eyes cannot yet discern" (p. 168).

This was a truly historic occasion because the future ratified it and made it such. In the same essay Borges then speaks of another occasion, this one not in the world of letters but in that of heroic action. When the Vikings invaded England in the eleventh century, led by Harald Sigurdarson and Tostig, the brother of England's Saxon King Harold, there occurred a confrontation in which the English king spoke words of great valor and followed them with deeds that led to the death of the two invading chieftains and a great victory for the Saxons. As recorded almost two centuries later by the Icelandic historian Snorri Sturluson, this confrontation has what Borges calls "the fundamental flavor of the heroic," which he considers a value in itself. But he adds,

> Only one thing is more admirable than the admirable reply of the Saxon King: that an Icelander, a man of the lineage of the vanquished, has perpetuated the reply. It is as if a Carthaginian had bequeathed to us the memory of the exploit of Regulus. Saxo Grammaticus wrote with justification in his *Gesta Danorum*: "The men of Thule [Iceland] are very fond of learning and of recording the history of all peoples and they are equally pleased to reveal the excellences of others or of themselves."
> Not the day when the Saxon said the words, but the day when an enemy perpetuated them, was the historic date. A date that is a prophecy of something still in the future: the day when races and nations will be cast into oblivion, and the solidarity of all mankind will be established. The offer owes its virtue to the concept of a fatherland. By relating it, Snorri surmounts and transcends that concept. [pp. 169–70]

Thus politics, wars, exchanges of words and sword thrusts, are saved from oblivion by the historian who turns them into instances of heroic myth, and by doing so offers us a glimpse of a humanity beyond nationalistic pride. The men of heroic action need the men of letters if they and their deeds are to survive. And the men of letters need the heroic actors in order to keep their letters alive. The gaucho on the pampas and the librarian in Buenos Aires are parts of a mythical beast, a kind of centaur, each needing the other for completion.

History, for Borges, is a matter of witnessing as much as a matter of doing. The forms of the past are preserved in frail human vessels which are themselves destined to die—and these deaths, too, are historic, though unrecorded. In his parable of "The Witness" Borges writes, "In time there was a day that extinguished the last eyes to see Christ; the battle of Junín and the love of Helen died with the death of a man. What will die with me when I die, what pathetic or fragile form will the world lose? The voice of Macedonio Fernándes, the image of a red horse in the vacant lot at Serrano and Charcas, a bar of sulphur in the drawer of a mahogany desk?" (*Labyrinths*, p. 243). Here, in accents reminiscent of Pater, Borges reminds us not of the intractability of reality but of the fragility of it. How it resides in little things as well as great, and how they pass away, and how finally even those who have seen them pass away as well. And though Broges can mention the voice of Macedonio Fernándes, his words will never capture that voice. What they will convey, however, is something even more fragile: his feeling about the voice. This, too, is a kind of reality, and not the least kind.

Approaching the end of an essay or a lecture, one's thoughts turn toward conclusions. Speaker and spectator glance surreptitiously at clocks and watches, both, perhaps, looking forward to release from the rigidity of their roles. Still, there is a painful dimension to conclusions; it has animated one of Borge's finest poems, "Límites," which (like much of his literary work) is about something very real indeed. Speaking of that poem to Richard Burgin, he observed,

It's quite easy to write an original poem, let's say, with original thoughts or surprising thoughts. I mean, if you think, that's what the metaphysical poets did in England, no? But in the case of "Límites," I have had the great luck to write a poem about something that everybody has felt or may feel. For example, what I am feeling today in Cambridge—I am going tomorrow to New York and won't be back until Wednesday or Tuesday and I feel that I am doing things for the last time.

And yet, I mean that most common feelings, most human feelings, have found their way into poetry and been worked over and over again, as they should have been for the last thousand years. But here I've been very lucky, because having a long literary past, I mean, having read in many literatures, I seem to have found a subject that is fairly new and yet a subject that is not thought extravagant. Because when I say, especially at a certain age, that we are doing many things for the last time and may not be aware of it—for all I know I may be looking out of this window for the last time, or there are books that I shall never read, books that I have already read for the last time—I think that I have opened, let's say, the door, to a feeling that all men have. [*Conversations with Borges*, pp. 90–91]

The value of the poem is seen by Borges as less in its originality than in its universality: "something that everybody has felt, or may feel"—a sentiment that brings Borges very close to Samuel Johnson. There is a reality of shared human experiences, then, that justifies poems and fictions by their encompassing it. Far from being self-referential or a labyrinthine cul-de-sac, poem and story exist to bridge the gap between people and things—and between one person and another. In this connection it is interesting to observe that Borges's poem bears a startling resemblance to a brief meditation written by Johnson himself—*Idler* 103, the closing paper in the *Idler* series, in which he speculates on the phenomenon of finality:

> Though the Idler and his readers have contracted no close friendship, they are perhaps both unwilling to part. There are few things not purely evil, of which we can say, without some emotion of uneasiness, *this is the last.* Those who never could agree together, shed tears when mutual discontent has determined them to final separation; of a place which has been frequently visited, though without pleasure, the last look is taken with heaviness of heart; and the Idler, with all his chillness of tranquility, is not wholly unaffected by the thought that his last essay is now before him.
>
> This secret horror of the last is inseparable from a thinking being, whose life is limited, and to whom death is dreadful.

I do not mean to suggest that Borges, like Pierre Menard, has been trying to rewrite Dr. Johnson. Quite the opposite. For, though their subjects are quite similar, they are each irrevocably of their time, in style and emphasis, and in those unspoken values that inform style and emphasis. What links them despite these differences is reality itself, and in particular the human condition of that reality. And Johnson, I am sure, would applaud Borges's most succinct statement of his position in this matter. Literature, he has said, "is not a mere juggling of words" (*Borges on Writing*, p. 164). It requires that a writer have what Chesterton called "everything." A notion which Borges glosses in the following way: "To a writer this everything is more than an encompassing word: it is literal. It stands for the chief, for the essential, human experiences. For example, a writer needs loneliness, and he gets his share of it. He needs love, and he gets shared and also unshared love. He needs friendship. In fact, he needs the universe" (p. 163). And the universe—the universe of men and women, at any rate—needs the writer. We need him to say the big things, of course, but also the little ones: things like, "Perhaps a bird was singing and I felt for him a small, birdlike affection" (*Other Inquisitions*, p. 180). And when I say "the writer" I mean specifically the one who is called Jorge Luis Borges, for whom many people in many lands feel a strong human affection, and of whom it is very appropriate to speak in precisely the same language in which he spoke of H. G. Wells. Referring to Wells's early scientific romances, Borges wrote: "I think they will be incorporated, like the fables of Theseus or Ahasuerus, into the general memory of the species and even transcend the fame of their creator or the extinction of the language in which they were written" (p. 88).

Certain fictions, like the fabulations of Wells and Borges, endure because they continue to function for human beings as signs of some unattainable reality, and as emblems of the human struggle to imagine that reality. They are, as Peirce would say, "real dreams."

The Nature of Romance

What Good Is Pure Romance?

A fair question, apparently. Plato asked it and nobody has answered it. Maybe it isn't as fair as it looks. What the question actually meant to him requires a bit of explanation. As I understand it, however, we can approximate Plato's intention by breaking the question into two parts: a) What good effect will listening to stories have on our understanding of the world?, and b) What good effect will listening to stories have on our behavior in the world? Like the good philosopher he was, Plato discovered that philosophy could do both a) and b) better than fiction could. That is, philosophy could tell us more truly both the nature of the cosmos and the attributes of right action. All those apologists for poetry who have accepted Plato's gambit have been reduced to presenting fiction either as sugar coating for the pill of philosophy, or as a handy and accurate shorthand notation of reality—that is, as allegory or as realism.

What Plato was really asking was "What good is poetry *as philosophy?*"—since for him philosophy already had a monopoly on both truth and goodness. Now that science owns truth, and goodness knows where goodness went (religion had it last but seems to have mislaid it), Plato's question has shifted its meaning so far as to expose its underpinnings. Zola tried to answer the question, "What good is fiction *as science?*" and worked himself into the absurd corner of the "experimental" novel, a notion he seems to have had the good sense not to believe but merely to use as journalistic puffery for his own productions, much as his heirs are now crying "phenomenological" novel for similar reasons. Matthew Arnold tried to answer the question, "What good is fiction *as religion?*" and twisted himself around to the point where he could see literature replacing dogma. Now the Marxist asks, "What good is fiction *as politics?*," and the Freudian asks, "What good is fiction *as psychology?*," and so on. But the real question, the one that Plato pretended to be asking, has gotten lost. Probably Plato could not see it himself. Since literary criticism started as a branch of philosophy, it was doubtless necessary to see Plato's question in terms of metaphysics and ethics. Even Aristotle succeeded only in adding a psychological concept, *katharsis*, to his notion of literature, and then returned quickly to its philosophical value as "imitation." But now that we can see criticism as a branch of literature itself, we should be able to set Plato's question in its proper context and make it mean what it should mean: What are the special qualities of fiction for which we value it? In other words, "What good is fiction *as fiction?*"

Not as the "representation of an action," but as an imaginative construct. Not in terms of what it tells us about, even including the imagination itself, but in terms of what makes our experience of fiction a good experience. The Aristotle of *katharsis* is much closer to the mark than the Aristotle of *mimesis*. The students of sleep have discovered that dreaming is necessary to the well-being of the human organism, and perhaps to the higher animals as well. It is not that our dreams teach us anything; they are simply a means of expression for us, a nightly cinema in which we are producer, director, all the actors, and all the audience. And if we are cheated of this imaginative performance in our sleep, we suffer for it during our waking existence in ways still not entirely understood.

I do not think fiction is a substitute for dream, but I think it must work for us in a similar way. It must provide us with an imaginative experience which is necessary to our imaginative well-being. And that is quite enough justification for it. We need all the imagination we have, and we need it exercised and in good condition. The simplest kind of fabling will do this for us to some extent, as long as we can respond to it fully, as long as it can engage our imagination totally. But as our imagination stretches and as we grow more serious (this combination of processes being what we mean, ideally, by the verb "to mature"), we require not fabling but fabulation. Pure romance must be enriched, like skim milk, if it is to sustain a full imaginative life. Allegory is one way of enriching pure romance. On this subject I shall have more to say later. Here, I want to point out only that there is a shadowy allegorical dimension to the *Alexandria Quartet* (an esthetic allegory, mainly, about the ways of story-telling), and that this dimension is, in fact, part of the story.

But once this is said, it should be qualified by observing that

Durrell's story is remarkably independent of its allegorical dimension. It is to the author's credit, I think, that he manages to be so engaging while keeping his narrative so squarely in the tradition of pure romance. He seems to have preserved enough from the tradition of the novel—to have learned enough from Lawrence, Proust, and others—to manage a revival of romance with a minimal amount of allegorizing. This is one important dimension of modern fabulation. In a way it is the simplest: the direct plunge back into the tide of story which rolls through all narrative art. Such a return to story for renewed vigor is a characteristic of the modern fabulators, though the others we shall be considering all add different qualities to their fabulation, which may tend to obscure the revival of romance in fabulation that is so clear in works like Durrell's *Alexandria Quartet* and John Fowles's *Magus*. Both these books return to the Mediterranean locale where Western culture and its first romantic products were born. And both writers emphasize the erotic dimension of the form, which, as we shall see, is a fundamental property of fiction.

The Orgastic Pattern of Fiction

The archetype of all fiction is the sexual act. In saying this I do not mean merely to remind the reader of the connection between all art and the erotic in human nature. Nor do I intend simply to suggest an analogy between fiction and sex. For what connects fiction—and music—with sex is the fundamental orgastic rhythm of tumescence and detumescence, of tension and resolution, of intensification to the point of climax and consummation. In the sophisticated forms of fiction, as in the sophisticated practice of sex, much of the art consists of delaying climax within the framework of desire in order to prolong the pleasurable act itself. When we look at fiction with respect to its form alone, we see a pattern of events designed to move toward climax and resolution, balanced by a counter-pattern of events designed to delay this very climax and resolution.

Fiction which attends mainly to this formal pattern we have learned to call "romance." And it is no accident that the pattern of romance is often used to present a story of sexual consummation delayed by events. Romance structure and romantic situation have a natural affinity for one another. The Greek romances, the Elizabethan romances, and the French romances of Honoré d'Urfé and his followers all share the same orgastic rhythm and the same interest in erotic intrigue. For the novel, as opposed to the romance, the great literary problem has been to adapt what E. M. Forster called this "low atavistic" form, the orgastic story, to the job of spreading the news, telling the truth about man in society. This problem has been much discussed and is still of considerable interest, but here I propose to ignore it and consider more carefully the equally interesting though much less discussed problem of the romance. If the novel is threatened by the inundation of phenomena, overwhelming the fundamental rhythm of fiction, the romance is threatened by emptiness and meaninglessness. Like the sexual act when purged of its possible procreative content and its necessary emotional content, romantic fiction can become a pleasure pursued so narrowly for its own sake that it ceases, finally, even to be a pleasure. The crucial question for the romancer, then, becomes how to avoid emptiness and mere sensationalism. Here I think we need to distinguish between two kinds of content, or rather between the content of the fictional work and the meaning of the fictional act. Content has to do with the ideas and attitudes that are embodied in the language of fiction. But meaning in this special sense has to do with the shared experience of the writer and reader in the fictional act.

Like the sexual act, the act of fiction is a reciprocal relationship. It takes two. Granted, a writer can write for his own amusement, and a reader can read in the same way; but these are acts of mental masturbation, with all the limitations that are involved in narcissistic gratification of the self. In the full fictional act, however, writer and reader share a relationship of mutual dependency. The meaning of the fictional act itself is something like love. The writer, at his best, respects the dignity of the reader. He does this by assuming a sensitivity and intelligence "out there" which will match that of his own best writing self. The reader, at the same time, respects the dignity of the writer. He does not simply try to take *his* pleasure and *his* meaning from the book. He strives to mate with the writer, to share the writer's viewpoint, to come fully to terms with the sensibility and intelligence that have informed this particular work of fiction. When writer and reader make a "marriage of true minds," the act of fiction is perfect and complete.

However, this meaning of the act of fiction—because the act itself is a verbal act, an act of language—is dependent on the meaningfulness of that language which is shared by reader and writer. The two partners in the act reach their mutual understanding *through* the ideas and attitudes which present themselves as the content of the fiction. The things discussed in the fiction are the basis for the deeper meaning of the fictional act. Just as two people may discuss art or politics, not so as to reach conclusions about politics or art but so as to understand one another better, a reader and writer may share a subject matter, a content, in order to establish a relationship. To see this is not to assume that the function of fiction is to lead all readers to Holden Caulfield's position of wanting to call up his favorite authors and talk to them directly. The writer is the person whose being is implied by the book, not necessarily the person you will get on the phone if you call. But Caulfield's impulse is a response to the essential meaning of the act of fiction. The strength of the impulse is a measure of the validity of the experience.

The point I have been making somewhat laboriously here is that the abstractable content is not the meaning of a work of fiction. The meaning is in our experience of it. But the content is important, it is necessary, it is the medium or culture which the real meaning requires in order to grow. The implications of this notion for literary criticism are many. In particular, this view of the relationship between content and meaning clarifies one crucial problem in the criticism of fiction. The real meaning of a work of fiction is something every reader must achieve himself; it must be experienced, it cannot be learned. But the critic, by talking about the book's abstractable content, can perform a useful service. He can facilitate that communication between reader and writer which may lead to a real understanding and a valid experience of a book. That small service is what I hope to accomplish in certain of the following pages.

John Fowles has spoken of the novelist's art as "being able to caress people's imagination." The relevance of this claim to what I have been saying will, I hope, be plain. As should be the relevance of these words by a contemporary American novelist: "My feeling about technique in art is that it has about the same value as technique in love-making. That is to say, heartfelt ineptitude has its appeal and so does heartless skill; but what you want is passionate virtuosity."

This statement was made by John Barth, who, like Iris Murdoch and like John Fowles, has accepted the challenge of writing truly meaningful romances. All three have sought to caress the reader's imagination with passionate virtuosity, with the result that all three have written romances that are rich in philosophical content and unashamedly orgastic in their form.

Lawrence Durrell and the Return to Alexandria

Once upon a time the first words of a story used to be "Once upon a time." But these are the last words, or almost the last words, of Lawrence Durrell's *Alexandria Quartet.* Which suggests that we may have come to the end of a literary cycle, or rather to the beginning of a new loop in the spiral of literary history. You remember the passage which closes *Clea,* the last volume of the *Quartet:*

> Yes, one day I found myself writing down with trembling fingers the four words (four letters! four faces!) with which every storyteller since the world began has staked his slender claim to the attention of his fellow men. Words which presage simply the old story of an artist coming of age. I wrote: "Once upon a time . . ."
> And I felt as if the whole universe had given me a nudge!

In reading the passage we feel very strongly a kind of duality which pervades Durrell's work: we are pulled toward the primitive by those four magical words and by the description of the artist as a mere storyteller, but we are also made aware of the modernity of the work; we are pulled toward the sophisticated by the preoccupation of the passage with the art of story-telling. Like so many modern works, this is a portrait of the artist, a *Künstlerroman,* about a character in a book who is writing a book in which he is a character. And the shades of Proust and Gide, among others, hover between our eyes and the page. What is new in Durrell, however, is neither the primitive nor the sophisticated but his peculiar combination of the two.

Take, for example, the scene in which Pursewarden and Justine visit the house of the child prostitutes. The two visitors are surrounded by these terrible children, who in another scene nearly drive Mountolive out of his wits as they attempt to capture him in the manner of the Lilliputians against Gulliver. Pursewarden describes the way Justine tames the little creatures:

And when the light was brought she suddenly turned herself, crossed her legs under her, and in the ringing words of the street story-teller she intoned: "Now gather about me, all ye blessed of Allah, and hear the wonder of the story I shall tell you . . ."

It was a wild sort of poetry for the place and the time—the little circle of wizened faces, the divan, the flopping light; and the strangely captivating lilt of the Arabic with its heavy damascened imagery, the thick brocade of alliterative repetitions, the nasal twanging accents, gave it a Laic splendour which brought tears to my eyes—gluttonous tears! It was such a rich diet for the soul! It made me aware how thin the fare is which we moderns supply to our hungry readers. The epic contours, that is what her story had. I was envious. How rich those beggar children were. And I was envious too of her audience. Talk of suspended judgment! They sank into the imagery of her story like plummets.

This scene is typical of the book. It is wild, exotic, romantic. Yet its main interest is not life, but art. It is really a little essay in esthetics, presented in the form of a dramatic scene. It reminds us of the moments in *Don Quixote* when there is a pause in the adventures of the Knight of the Mournful Countenance to allow for a literary discussion involving the Bachelor and the Curate or some passing stranger. And the resemblance is not a chance one. Cervantes's work was written as an anti-romance, and became, via Fielding and Smollett in English tradition, a major ancestor of a new literary form—the novel. Durrell's work, as the passage quoted above indicates, is an anti-novel in the same sense as Cervantes's work was an anti-romance. Both men were faced with a constricting literary tradition and revolted against it.

Of course, Pursewarden's point about the thinness of modern literary fare is not meant to be mere literary discussion in a vacuum, any more than the similar discussions in *Don Quixote*. We are meant to apply Pursewarden's theory to Durrell's practice. To do so we must look back, as Pursewarden suggests, to an older literary tradition than the novel. And so we shall. But before we do so we must observe that Durrell's revolt is not an isolated and magnificent gesture of defiance against an entrenched and flourishing literary tradition. The tradition he finds thin and constricting is the very one started by Cervantes—the tradition which begins as anti-romance and gradually insists on more and more scientific treatment of life: the empirical tradition which in its theoretical formulations calls itself first realism and finally naturalism. The naturalism to which

Durrell is reacting is, of course, about as feeble now as the romances were in the time of Cervantes, and the new revolutionary is no more alone in his revolt than the old. A James Joyce can adapt naturalism to allegorical purposes as well as an Edmund Spenser could adapt romance. And a Marcel Proust can destroy empirical notions of characterization as thoroughly as Cervantes himself could destroy the romantic heroes. Just as Samuel Beckett is the heir of Joyce—a somewhat rebellious heir, producing anti-naturalistic anti-allegories—Lawrence Durrell is the heir of Proust. For it is Proust who explodes the empirical notions of characterization so essential to realistic and naturalistic fiction, by demonstrating the artificiality of the real and the reality of the artificial. "Even in the most insignificant details of our daily life," the narrator of *Swann's Way* tells us,

none of us can be said to constitute a material whole, which is identical for everyone, and need only be turned up like a page in an account book or the record of a will; our social personality is created by the thoughts of other people. Even the simple act which we describe as "seeing someone we know" is, to some extent, an intellectual process. We pack the physical outline of the creature we see with all the ideas we have already formed about him . . . so that each time we see the face or hear the voice it is our own ideas of him which we recognize and to which we listen.

Proust emphasizes here the artificiality of reality. We do not see our friends, only our ideas of them. In another passage he develops this paradox further, illustrating the converse principle, the reality of artifice:

None of the feelings which the joys or misfortunes of a "real" person awaken in us can be awakened except through a mental picture of those joys or misfortunes; and the ingenuity of the first novelist lay in his understanding that, as the picture was the one essential element in the complicated structure of our emotions, so, that simplification of it which consisted in the suppression, pure and simple, of "real" people would be a decided improvement. A real person, profoundly as we may sympathize with him, is in great measure perceptible only through our senses, that is to say, he remains opaque, offers a dead weight which our sensibilities have not the strength to lift. . . . The novelist's happy discovery was to think of substituting for those opaque sections, impenetrable by the human spirit, their equivalent in immaterial sections, things, that is, which the spirit can assimilate to itself.

Proust's brilliant exposition of the paradoxical notion that we can truly experience life only through art is the death knell of the realistic-naturalistic movement in fiction, though even today, fifty

years afterward, a small school of neo-naturalists continues to write
frantically, headless chickens unaware of the decapitating axe. For
Durrell, however, Proust's new esthetic is a release and an inspiration. In the following passages from *Justine*, we can observe him
adapting the Proustian view to his own purposes. In the first we find
the narrator, Darley, examining Arnauti's diary, *Moeurs*, in which
Justine is a character called Claudia:

> Nor can it be said that the author's intentions are not full of interest. He
> maintains for example that real people can only exist in the imagination of an
> artist strong enough to contain them and give them form. "Life, the raw
> material, is only lived *in potentia* until the artist deploys it in his work.
> Would that I could do this service for poor Justine."

Like Pursewarden, Arnauti longs for a different kind of fiction. He
wishes to set his ideal book "free to dream." His view is different
from Pursewarden's but complementary, not contradictory; and Durrell's novel embodies both views. Darley finds Arnauti's diary so
vivid that he feels at times like some paper character out of *Moeurs*.
And after Pursewarden's death he writes of him,

> How much of him can I claim to know? I realize that each person can only
> claim one aspect of our character as part of his knowledge. To every one we
> turn a different face of the prism. Over and over again I have found myself
> surprised by observations which brought this home to me. . . . And as for
> Pursewarden, I remember, too, that in the very act of speaking . . . he
> straightened himself and caught sight of his pale reflection in the mirror. The
> glass was raised to his lips, and now, turning his head he squirted out upon
> his own glittering reflection a mouthful of the drink. That remains clearly in
> my mind: a reflection liquifying in the mirror of that shabby, expensive
> room which seems now so appropriate a place for the scene which must have
> followed later that night.

The *Alexandria Quartet* is alive with mirrors. The prismatic facets of
character glitter, unreconciled, in our imaginations. Appearance and
reality are continually confused, and the line between life and art is
continually blurred. Darley feels like a character out of *Moeurs*. But
Darley *is* a character in Durrell's novel. What we took for fact in one
volume is exposed as false in another, and the exposé itself is proved
incorrect in the third. Stendhal could compare his story to a mirror,
strolling down a lane, reflecting the sky and the mud. But for Durrell
fiction is a whirling prism reflected in a liquifying mirror. In the
scene quoted at the beginning of this chapter, in which Justine tells

the child prostitutes a story in Arabic, Pursewarden longs for the opportunity to tell a story of Laic splendor to an audience which is really able to suspend its disbelief. Since the modern reader cannot recapture the esthetic innocence of Justine's audience, Durrell attempts on the one hand to establish in the reader's mind his version of the new, Proustian esthetic, and on the other to blur the line between the real and the artificial in order to make it harder for the reader to begin applying his disbelief, even if he refuses to suspend it. Durrell seeks to confuse and bewilder the reader, to separate him from his habitual reliance on probability and verisimilitude, so as to offer him something better. *Behold,* he as much as tells us, *you thought you could not walk without that crutch of realism. I tell you you can fly!* And he nearly convinces us that we can. Using the modern esthetic of Proust, and a narrative technique which, with its multiple narrators and dislocations of time, seems also typically modern, Durrell takes us on a journey—a magic carpet ride not only through space but through time as well—a return to Alexandria.

For, though Pursewarden says he longs for the old "epic contours," what Durrell gives us is—appropriately enough—more Alexandrian than Attic. As Moses Hadas has observed in his introduction to *Three Greek Romances,* " 'Once upon a time' is not the way the classical Greeks opened a work of literature." But "Once upon a time" does reflect the spirit of Alexandrian literature and of the romances written in the Greek language all over the Mediterranean world in post-Alexandrian times. Alexandria was a Greek city on Egyptian soil. In it the East and West met as they rarely have elsewhere. The old joke has it that when Greek meets Greek, they open a restaurant. But when Greek met Egyptian in ancient Alexandria, they opened a library. From this meeting of cultures developed the first literary critics and a new kind of literature. E. M. Forster has described this literature for us in his *Alexandria, a History and a Guide*—a book Lawrence Durrell frequently alludes to in the *Alexandria Quartet.* Forster points out that the distinguishing characteristic of the new literature was its emphasis on love:

Ancient Greece had also sung of love, but with restraint, regarding it as one activity among many. The Alexandrians seldom sang of anything else: their epigrams, their elegies and their idylls, their one great epic, all turn on the tender passion, and celebrate it in ways that previous ages had never known. . . .

> Who sculptured love and set him by the pool,
> Thinking with water such a fire to cool?

runs a couplet ascribed to one of the early Librarians, and containing in brief
the characteristics of the school—decorative method, mythological allusive-
ness, and the theme of love.

How appropriate, too, that in the twentieth century Durrell's anti-
novel should be set in this romantic spot. It is clear that Durrell's
Alexandria is as much a country of the mind as Poe's Virginia or
Kafka's Germany. Some of the place-names are real, but beyond that
there is little resemblance between the fictional Alexandria of Durrell
and the geographical one. Yet Durrell's work is completely faithful to
the ancient spirit of the place.

As Forster points out, the literature of Alexandria was, unlike the
literature of Greece itself, a literature of love. It was in Alexandria
that love made its way into epic poetry: in the *Argonautica* of the
librarian Apollonius the love of Medea for Jason was presented so
dramatically that it left an indelible mark on poetic fiction. Vergil's
Dido and many of Ovid's love-stricken females are directly derived
from this Alexandrian epic. And the prose romances that were written in Greek around the Mediterranean in the second and third
centuries A.D. (of which Heliodorus' *Ethiopica* and Longus' *Daphnis
and Chloë* are the best-known examples) are also derived, apparently,
from the Alexandrian combination of Greek and Oriental literary
traditions. A papyrus dating from the second century B.C. and called
"The Alexandrian Erotic Fragment" was described by its last editor
as being written in Greek prose similar to the ornate rhyming prose
of Arabic narrative. In its combination of erotic subject matter and
rich prose it also exemplifies the characteristic qualities of Durrell's
work, written over two millennia later.

The *Ethiopica*, richest and most elaborate of the Greek romances,
stands very much in the same relation to the Homeric epics as
Durrell's *Quartet* does to such great realistic novels of the nineteenth
century as *Anna Karenina* and *Middlemarch*. Both the epics and the
great realistic novels present events as ordered by an omniscient
narrator whose controlling mind not only shapes the events but also
colors them and comments on them. But in Heliodorus much of the
narrative is conveyed to us directly by characters in the story. Furthermore, Heliodorus is not content simply to imitate the *Odyssey*
and have one man narrate much of his own tale. In the *Ethiopica* we

have as many narrators as in the *Alexandria Quartet*. Indeed, one of the first stories we are told, a brief résumé of her life by the heroine, turns out to be a tissue of falsehoods designed to deceive her captors (and also the reader, who only afterward learns the truth). In the hands of Heliodorus the romance is characterized by a multiplicity of narrators and tales within tales like a sequence of Chinese boxes; by a consequent dislocation of the time scheme, as the narrative moves backward and forward from its beginning in what George Saintsbury has called a "sort of cat's cradle manner"; and by a fondness for elaborate set pieces of a spectacular nature, involving such things as battles, rituals, necromancy, and celebrations.

Though the general resemblance of the *Alexandria Quartet* to the *Ethiopica* is obvious (some of the action of the ancient story even takes place on the shores of Durrell's beloved Lake Mareotis), the point is not that the resemblance indicates any direct indebtedness; rather, it is that the two works are so similar in spirit. Durrell is not so much a descendant of Heliodorus as a reincarnation of him in the twentieth century. When Durrell speaks of his characters in an interview as "puppets," he reminds us of the way in which Heliodorus manipulates his characters in a virtuoso display of sustained and integrated form. And form, for Durrell, is nearly everything. His early novel, *The Black Book*, displays many of the characteristics of his later work—everything, almost, except form. *The Black Book* was written when Durrell was very much under the influence of D. H. Lawrence and Henry Miller, writers who tend to disdain form, to think of it as a way of distorting reality. In the recently published correspondence between Durrell and Miller we can see him gradually becoming more critical of Miller's work on the grounds of its formlessness. Though traces of Lawrence and Miller remain in Durrell's mature work, there can be little doubt that the spirit which presides over the *Alexandria Quartet* is Proust's. And in turning to Proust, Durrell brought himself into contact with a tradition of sustained form which was fundamentally opposed to the "slice of life" technique characteristic of empirically oriented mimetic fiction. The tradition of elaborate form in fiction leads back through the romances of the seventeenth century to the European rediscovery of Heliodorus in the sixteenth, whose influence on the subsequent development of prose fiction can hardly be exaggerated.

The purely melodramatic side of the Greek romance has, of course,

been greatly modified in its modern reincarnation. In the old romances the characters were mainly highly stylized extremes of virtue
and vice, and the plot was always subservient to the decorum of
poetic justice. In the *Alexandria Quartet* the characters and the prevailing ethos are as elaborate and complicated as the plot and the
setting. The thinness of characterization which, for the modern
reader, relegates the *Ethiopica* to that secondary level of works whose
influence surpasses their interest would be inexcusable in a modern
work of serious intent. But even richness of characterization, which
we think of as a peculiarly modern attribute of fiction, has its roots in
Alexandria. The Alexandrians and their followers, especially Ovid
and the Greek romancers, introduced the arts of rhetoric into narrative literature. The combination of psychology and rhetoric, which
characterizes the crucial monologue of Medea in the Third Book of
the *Argonautica,* works through Dido and the Ovidian lovers into the
mainstream of narrative literature. Lawrence Durrell's rhetoric, rich
and evocative as it is, has been roundly criticized by the English
press as some sort of wild Celtic aberration—not (in the phrase of Mr.
Podsnap) English, and hardly appropriate for a novel. But one of the
glories of our resurgent narrative art has been the rhetoric of Joyce, of
Faulkner, of Conrad, and of Proust; though none of them is (alas)
English, either. The flat prose of sociological fiction is being abandoned to the sociologists, who, God knows, have need of it; and the
rich rhetoric of the Alexandrians, of Ovid and the Greek romancers,
is beginning once again to return narrative literature to the domain
of art. The novel may indeed be dying, but we need not fear for the
future. Durrell and others are generating a renaissance of romance.
The return to Alexandria should be almost as exciting a voyage as the
one described by the city's greatest storyteller, Apollonius; for, like
the voyage of the Argo, it will be an enchanted one. And already, like
the laggard Argonauts on one occasion, we can hear our vehicle itself
admonishing us:

> From Pelian Argo herself came a voice, bidding
>   hasten away:
> For within her a beam divine had been laid, which
>   Athena brought
> From the oak Dodonaean, and into the midst of
>   her stem it was wrought.

John Fowles as Romancer

In his first novel, *The Collector*, John Fowles demonstrated his devotion to the dynamics of story-telling. His second, *The Aristos*, was not a work of narrative fiction at all but a collection of philosophical workpoints—pensées, materials for a tractatus. In the two books which followed *The Aristos*, Fowles has sought a form that can be equally responsive to his fictional and his philosophical concerns. His fourth, *The French Lieutenant's Woman*, has received its due from critics and reviewers, as has his fifth, *Daniel Martin*. But their predecessor, *The Magus*, has been denied the attention it deserves. In his perceptive and laudatory review of *The French Lieutenant's Woman*, on page one of the *New York Times Book Review*, Ian Watt paused to ask, "Was there any deeper commitment than a currently fashionable nastiness behind . . . the mind-blowing manipulations of *The Magus?*" This question can be translated into the terms I have been using here to talk about orgastic fiction. In these terms the question asks whether Fowles's passion in *The Magus* is equal to his virtuosity, whether the book is merely sensational or truly meaningful. It is a fair and important question.

It is interesting that what should be called into question is the presence or absence of ethical commitment to justify the esthetic virtuosity of *The Magus*, because it is precisely the relationship between the ethical and the esthetic which is the central theme in the book's structure of meanings. We are first alerted to this dimension of the novel's content by a passage on the third page of the text. (This is page 13 in the widely available Dell paperback edition, which I will be citing in all further references.) Speaking of his behavior at Oxford the narrator observes,

we argued about essence and existence and called a certain kind of inconsequential behavior existentialist. Less enlightened people would have called it capricious or just plain selfish; but we didn't realize that the heroes, or

anti-heroes, of the French existentialist novels we had read were not supposed to be realistic. We tried to imitate them, mistaking metaphorical
descriptions of complex modes of feeling for straightforward prescriptions of
behavior.

The literary advice offered here is very important. The passage
insists that French existentialist fiction should be treated as metaphor
rather than as description. It implies, by extention, that we should be
careful to take *this* book with *its* "anti-hero" in a metaphorical or
allegorical way. (In the next chapter the question of allegory will be
taken up more explicitly.) And it presents succinctly to us the existential problem of its anti-hero, Nicholas Urfe: he is confused about the
relationship between art and life. Nicholas, of course, is both the
protagonist of the book and its narrator. As narrator he is no longer
confused; in fact, he can present his life to us fictionally, as a meaningful metaphor, precisely because he has learned the difference
between fiction and existence. But the character Nicholas starts in
confusion, and the narrative is the story of his education. The distance between Nicholas as character and Nicholas as narrator is
expressed in the double meaning of the word "enlightened" in the
passage just quoted. Nicholas as character thought of himself as
really enlightened, but as narrator he uses the word to mean something like superficial and dilletantish. Urfe may be related, as he tells
us, to the historical Honoré d'Urfé, the author of the massive
seventeenth-century pastoral romance *Astrée*. Knowing this, we can
see Nicholas-as-character victimized by his romantic vision of life as
art, and we can see Nicholas-as-narrator accepting the conventions of
orgastic romance sufficiently to prevent us from taking his narrative
as a transcript of reality. But Nicholas the character is not merely
confused about how to take his reading. He is also guilty of a more
fundamental error: he uses his misreading of literature as an excuse
for mistreating life as if it were art. In older language, he is a cad, a
Don Juan. He is Kierkegaard's seducer of woman, using them and
discarding them as one might use and discard a drugstore paperback
book: "I mistook the feeling of relief that dropping a girl always
brought," the narrator says of his earlier self, "for a love of freedom."
"Freedom" is a word charged with meaning in the vocabulary of
existentialism, and that word, along with such others as "choice,"
reverberates powerfully throughout the book.

The action of the novel centers around the intrusion of two people into Urfe's selfishly comfortable esthetic world: first Alison, a woman capable of love; and then Conchis, the Magus of the book's title. Alison is, as Nicholas later understands, cast as "reality" in the psychodrama which is his life and our story. Conchis is a teacher, a Prospero who schools his student with masque and magic, playing the "god game" with him until he completes his initiation and achieves his real freedom, his responsibility for himself.

This action commences quietly when Nicholas, at a loss for what to do with himself, accepts the job of teaching English at a boys' school on a Greek island. Before leaving London he lives with Alison for a time. Both Nicholas and Alison are sexually experienced and used to casual affairs, but for Alison this particular affair becomes a matter of love. For Nicholas, it is simply a more pleasant thing than usual. As she tells him later,

> "I think you're so blind you probably don't even know you don't love me. You don't even know you're a filthy selfish bastard who can't, can't like being impotent, can't *ever* think of anything except number one. Because nothing can hurt you, Nicko. Deep down, where it counts. You've built your life so that nothing can ever reach you. So whatever you do you can say, I couldn't help it. You can't lose. You can always have your next adventure. Your next bloody affaire."[p. 260]

Alison diagnoses Nicholas's ailment perfectly, but she cannot cure it herself. Because Nicholas is so insulated in his esthetic world, he can only be reached esthetically, and Alison is too "real" to reach him on this level. This is where Conchis comes in. He is the magician who can break the spell and restore Nicholas to reality. But he must use all his artful magic to do this. Conchis lives on the island of Phraxos, where Nicholas goes to teach but actually becomes a student. Phraxos is derived from the Greek word φραζω, which in one of its forms means to devise or plan for a person, to design or intend something for him. And Conchis tells Nicholas to pronounce his name with the "ch" soft (which would sound like conscious). In one of their talks Conchis presents to Nicholas this version of himself and his activities:

> "Before the war we used to amuse ourselves with my private theatre here. And during the war, when I had a great deal of time to think, and no friends to amuse me, no theatre, I conceived a new kind of drama. One in which the

conventional relations between audience and actors were forgotten. In which the conventional scenic geography, the notions of proscenium, stage, auditorium, were completely discarded. In which continuity of performance, either in time or place, was ignored. And in which the action, the narrative was fluid, with only a point of departure and a fixed point of conclusion." His mesmeric eyes pinned mine. "You will find that Artaud and Pirandello and Brecht were all thinking, in their different ways, along similar lines. But they had neither the money nor the will—and perhaps not the time—to think as I did. The element that they could never bring themselves to discard was the audience." He spread his arms. "Here we are all actors. None of us are as we really are." He raised his hand quickly. "Yes, I know. You think you are not acting. Just pretending a little. But you have much to learn about yourself. You are as far from your true self as that Egyptian mask our American friend wears is from his true face."[p. 366]

By involving Nicholas in a situation in which art and life are really and deliberately confused for an ethical purpose, Conchis succeeds in making Nicholas ultimately hungry for reality. By making the esthetic game painful enough, Conchis teaches Nicholas to accept the pain of life. The primary agent of this education is not Conchis himself, the Prospero of the island, but Lilly, the beautiful girl who plays the role of Miranda to Nicholas's Ferdinand—but with consummate duplicity which leads Nicholas to a richly ironic betrayal. Lilly, in a way, represents ideal beauty—an unattainable ideal. In his pursuit of her, Nicholas turns his back on Alison and reality, for Lilly seems to be what he has always wanted. Her artificiality and unattainability, of course, make it safe for him to want her. She represents a narcissistic gratification, rather than a real engagement with another person. It has been the reality of Alison, her capacity for genuine love, that has prevented Nicholas from wanting her entirely. The news of Alison's suicide after she and Nicholas have met briefly on the mainland of Greece (the episode in which Alison finally confronts Nicholas with his inability to love—in the passage quoted above) is an important stage in the education of Nicholas. One of the results of this news is that Nicholas flees reality even more frenetically, and throws himself desperately into Conchis's masque, both in pursuit of Lilly and in an attempt to fathom Conchis's game:

So I sat at the foot of the ladder and seethed, trying to plumb Conchis's duplicities; to read his palimpsest. His "theatre without an audience" made no sense, it couldn't be the explanation. The one thing all actors and actresses craved was an audience. Perhaps what he was doing sprang from some theory about the theatre—he had said it himself: *The masque is only a metaphor.* A strange and incomprehensible new philosophy? Metaphorism? Perhaps he saw himself as a professor in an impossible faculty of ambiguity, a sort of Empson of the event. I thought and thought, and thought again, and arrived at nothing. [p. 417]

What Nicholas cannot see at this point is that Conchis is playing a "god game" with him for his own sake. And the purpose of this god game is to teach Nicholas to become a magus in his own right. As Lawrence Durrell has put it, "The purpose of art is to grow a personality that will enable one to transcend art." One of the clues left for Nicholas to find in his futile attempt to understand the masque while still enmeshed in it is the manuscript of a fable called "The Prince and the Magician," which is in its way a metaphor for the whole giant fabulation which is the story of Nicholas and the magus. The fable is too long to quote here in its entirety, and too tightly organized to summarize clearly, but in its conclusion the prince learns that "there is no truth beyond magic," and after despairing and being confronted by death he decides, "I can bear it." Whereupon his father, king and magician that he is, declares, "You see, my son . . . you too now begin to be a magician." A magician, finally, is one who accepts the reality of the appearances around him as sufficient. He abandons metaphysics for existence. And by becoming a magician he accepts *responsibility* for those appearances. To be a magician in a world where there is no truth beyond magic, is a fictional metaphor for becoming a responsible individual in a world where there is no truth beyond existence.

It should be emphasized that the kind of existentialist thought which animates the pages of this book and informs its structure is in one crucial respect quite at odds with the variety of existentialist phenomenology which aggravates the nausea and deadens the pages of the French *nouveau roman*. For the French novelists the banality of quotidian existence is an unquestioned first premise. Their work is to capture it in a form that will expose it. But for Fowles reality is not banal. Here is the way Conchis describes it in narrating to Nicholas one of the metaphorical experiences in his life:

"But in a flash of terrible light all our explanations, all our classifications and derivations, our etiologies, suddenly appeared to me like a thin net. That great passive monster, reality, was no longer dead, easy to handle. It was full of a mysterious vigor, new forms, new possibilities. The net was nothing, reality burst through it. . . . That simple phrase, *I do not know*, was my own pillar of fire. An ultimate, a metaphysical, I-do-not-know." [p. 287]

The world is not dead and nauseating. It is alive and unknowable, and therefore invigorating. To accept its unfathomable mystery one must become equally unfathomable; one must accept one's own mystery and become a magician.

While Nicholas works fruitlessly at unraveling Conchis's mysterious masque from inside it, the reality of Alison and her meaning in his existence pursues him:

Staring out to sea, I forced myself to think of her not as someone doing something at that moment, sleeping or breathing or working, somewhere, but as a shovelful of ashes, a futility, a descent out of reality, a dropping object that dwindled, left nothing behind except a smudge like a fallen speck of soot on paper. . . .

I did not pray for her, because prayer has no efficacy; I did not cry for her, because only extroverts cry twice; I sat in the silence of that night, that infinite hostility to man, to permanence, to love, remembering her, remembering her. [p. 400]

But the masque continues, with Lilly leading Nicholas on to that stupefying anticlimax of humiliation which is also a ritual of initiation, capped by the mock trial in which Nicholas is made to face the shame of his existence. After this he begins to understand what Alison was: "what had she called herself? Coarse salt; the candor of salt. I remembered how we had got in the car, how I had talked about my father, had even then only been able to talk to her like that because of *her* honesty; because I knew she was a mirror that did not lie; whose interest in me was real; whose love was real. That had been her supreme virtue: a constant reality" [p. 487]. And he begins to understand what he himself has been:

. . . all my life I had tried to turn life into fiction, to hold reality away; always I had acted as if a third person was watching and listening and giving me marks for good or bad behavior—a god like a novelist, to whom I turned, like a character with the power to feel pleased, the sensitivity to feel slighted, the ability to adapt himself to whatever he believed the novelist-god wanted. This leechlike variation of the superego I had created myself, fostered myself, and because of it I had always been incapable of acting freely. It was not my defense but my despot. And now I saw it, I saw it a death too late. [p. 487]

In this state of mind, carefully led by Conchis to that situation of existential despair which can be the beginning of wisdom, Nicholas sees Alison again in Athens. She is alive; her "suicide" has been a part of the masque. This "betrayal" revives both hope and anger in Nicholas, and he pursues Alison to England, feeling the pangs of love, and its possibilities, for the first time. In London Nicholas reaches his final understanding and accepts the ethical responsibility for his life and the lives of those around him. He now *feels* this responsibility. "Now," he says, "I *felt* it; and by 'feel' I mean that I knew I *had* to choose it, every day, even though I went on failing to keep it, had every day to choose it, every day to try to live by it. And I knew that it was all bound up with Alison; with choosing Alison, and having to go on choosing her every day" (p. 585). The "it" which Nicholas is accepting here is a kind of eleventh commandment which supersedes all the others: "Thou shalt not commit pain." In accepting it and living it, Nicholas is able to accept and respect the human dignity of the clownish females Jojo and Kemp. He can finally treat Jojo in a brotherly fashion, and he can let Kemp mother him, thus assuming his place in the human family. But he has a further lesson to learn. Following a "thou shalt not" is too easy. He must learn finally the necessity of judging as well as choosing, so that ultimately his most loving gesture in the narrative is his striking Alison in the face, accepting the responsibility for causing that pain in violation of the "commandment" and with it the responsibility for Alison herself.

Feeling that Alison has in some sense been captured by Conchis and his masquers, Nicholas sees himself in a new role, that of an Orpheus who must try to rescue Eurydice/Alison from the underworld constituted by Conchis and his friends. Though he is ready to accept responsibility for her in reality, he must convince her of this and persuade her to leave the masque. When he is finally allowed to confront her in Regent's Park, he plays his Orphic role beautifully, assuming that Conchis and his friends are still watching him and Alison. The role, of course, requires that he leave her without looking back, so that she will have the freedom to choose him or not. At this point having declared himself unmistakably, he begins to sense that they are alone:

> I was so sure. It was logical, the characteristic and perfect final touch to the godgame. They had absconded. I was so sure, and yet . . . after so much, how could I be perfectly sure? How could they be so cold? So inhuman? So incurious? So load the dice and yet leave the game? And if I wasn't sure?
> I gave her bowed head one last stare, then I was walking. Firmer than

Orpheus, as firm as Alison herself, that other day of parting, not once looking back. The autumn grass, the autumn sky. People. A blackbird, poor fool, singing out of season from the willows by the lake. A flight of gray pigeons over the houses. Fragments of freedom, an anagram made flesh. And somewhere the stinging smell of burning leaves. [p. 604]

This freedom, the true freedom which Nicholas has finally found not in dropping a girl but in keeping one, also involves his final acceptance of a universe in which no one is watching his gestures and keeping score. The god game is over. Conchis is not there. His own conscience and his own consciousness are his only judges. The fiction is finished, and so is the book. The structure of the book, as we can finally see it looking back from the conclusion, is very similar to the tradition of orgastic romances from Heliodorus to Urfé. Even the interpolated narratives which are a traditional way of delaying and enriching the course of the story are used by Fowles. But these narratives of Conchis's life are integrated into the structure of ideas and images of *The Magus* with extraordinary care and great allegorical skill. For instance, the image of Conchis, gun in hand, confronting the mutilated Cretan terrorist who is still struggling to utter the terrible Greek word for freedom, establishes with extraordinary power the quintessential moment of existentialist choice—a moment which is mirrored (with significant differences) by Nicholas as he holds the cat-o'-nine-tails and faces the tempting back of Lilly, and again as he strikes Alison in the last scene of the book. There are too many images of this sort to trace them all through the book, but this one should serve to illustrate the way Fowles uses the traditional device of the interpolated tale to enrich the content of the book. Finally, we should consider one crucial alteration of the traditional pattern of orgastic romance. In the Greek romances and their imitations, hero and heroine fall in love to begin the story but are prevented from consummating their union until the end. *The Magus* begins with sexual union, and it is love which must wait for consummation until the end of the book.

The French Lieutenant's Woman is neither a more nor a less meaningful book than *The Magus*. In fact, when we encounter in its closing paragraphs the statement that "life, however advantageously Sarah may in some ways seem to fit the role of Sphinx, is not a symbol," we should feel that we are on familiar intellectual ground, encountering an ethical attitude that was advanced, neither more nor less seriously, in the earlier book. *The French Lieutenant's Woman* presents itself more as a novel and less as a romance than *The Magus*. It is, in fact, an imitation of a Victorian novel in much the same way that John Barth's *Sot-Weed Factor* is an imitation of Fielding and Smollett. But beneath the richly documented surface of Fowles's later work the same orgastic rhythm pulsates just as powerfully as in its predecessor. Surprise, reversal, false anti-climax, climax, and even post- or alternate climax—such familiar manipulations as these shape our responses to this more somber fiction. The difference between *The Magus* and *The French Lieutenant's Woman* can be seen as in many ways parallel to the difference between *Giles Goat-Boy* and *The Sot-Weed Factor*. *The Magus* and *Giles* are more fantastic and more philosophical in their orientation than the other two, which share a strong concern for an actual historical past. There are plenty of tonal and other differences between the work of Barth and Fowles, which should make us wary of pushing this comparison too far. But there is enough validity in the comparison to make one notice it. These two men have successfully undertaken some of the most ambitious fictions produced in their countries in recent years. And they have both done so not by turning their backs on the low and atavistic dimension of fictional form, but by embracing it.

> Loves mysteries in soules doo grow,
> But yet the body is his booke.

Modern Allegory

A Fable and Its Gloss

Once there was a country called Fiction, bordered on one side by the mountains of Philosophy and on the other by a great bog called History. The people of Fiction had a great gift, the gift of telling stories which could amuse men. As long as they had no contact with the peoples of the neighboring territories, they were perfectly satisfied with their gift and wanted nothing. But progress, and improved communications, brought them into contact with the strange peoples who lived on their borders and beyond. These peoples were not storytellers like the Fiction people, but they had something called Ideas. And when the Fiction people learned about Ideas they yearned for them terribly and wanted to use them to give their stories more dignity. A story without Ideas, they came to think, was fit only for children. So the Fiction people agreed that they would begin trading with their neighbors to get some Ideas.

This only made things worse. For the people on the Philosophy side of the land of Fiction insisted that Fictional Ideas should come from Philosophy, or from Theology just back in the hills, while the people on the other side said the only Ideas any good for fiction were those of the Historians. For a while those who favored Philosophy and Theology won. They called their part of Fiction "Allegory" and they flourished under leaders like Dante and Spenser. But after a while the Ideas from Philosophy and Theology began to lose their zip, and even the Philosophers started saying that the Historians had a lot of good Ideas. Then the Allegorists grew weak and the other party, who called themselves "Realists," began to grow in size and power. They took Ideas from the Historians and discovered other territories, way back in the bog, peopled by an aggressive breed known as Social Scientists. These fellows had Ideas too, and the Realists took as many as they could get.

Then a strange thing happened. The Historians and Social Scientists got tired of having other folks put their Ideas into stories. They decided to muscle in on the story racket themselves. So they climbed out of the bog and invaded the fertile fields of Fiction, and everybody who stayed on in the territory they occupied had to agree to write non-Fiction novels. At the same time the Philosophers and Theologians got a whole new batch of Ideas called Existentialism and Wittgenstein which frightened them so much that they lit out for the highest peaks leaving Ideas strewn all over the foothills. But some Philosophers had got to like that territory so much that they wouldn't leave. They were still there when the refugees from Realism started to pour in and take over. Finally, in order to stay, they had to agree to show these refugees a new way to do Allegory with all these new Ideas. A few of the refugees had smuggled some Ideas called Jung and Freud with them, and when the leftover Philosophers saw them they said they weren't Social Science Ideas anyway, but things those rascals had stolen from Theology and Philosophy to begin with. So they took all the old and new Ideas they could find and began trying to work out a kind of Allegory. One of the leftover Philosophers who showed the refugees from Fiction the most was a nice lady named Iris Murdoch.

Well. This little exemplum is a pretty feeble fable, just a discursive convenience, really, and not a proper allegory. Its characters and events are too shadowy, of too little interest in themselves, to be thought of as truly allegorical. In the great allegories, tension between the ideas illustrated by the characters and the human qualities in their characterization makes for a much richer and more powerful kind of meaning. The great allegories are never entirely allegorical, just as the great realistic novels are never entirely real. And, in allegory, it is often the tension between the ideational side of a situation and the human side which makes for the power and the meaning—and the power *of* the meaning. Take, for example, the concept of damnation, which is derived from analogies with actual punishment by torture but is referred to an "ideal" eternal world outside the visible universe. And take also a little human situation, a pair of young lovers such as might people a harmless novella of cuckoldry. Put these two things together and you have Francesca da Rimini and her lover Paolo, burning forever in Dante's hell. This is allegory. My fable, on the other hand, was only a nod from criticism in the direction of allegory.

That fable, however, was the shortest and clearest way that I could sketch out my view of the relations of allegory and realism to fiction—both the conceptual relations and the historical ones. Now I must gloss that brief paradigm a bit. Allegory amounts to seeing life through ideational filters provided by philosophy or theology. When realism supplanted allegory as the great form of serious narrative, it claimed to be superior because it looked directly at life—without filters of any kind. The manifestoes of realism are full of terms like "objectivity," "detachment," "experiment," and so on, which suggest a clear and scientific view of life. But we can see now that it is impossible to look directly at life. It is like gazing right into the sun; we see so much that we are blinded.

For a writer, language itself is a great filter which colors his view of life. For the realistic novelist, other filters in the form of concepts of time, space, causality, society, and a whole collection of psychological types and tropes enable him to capture what he calls "life" on paper. He may be unaware of these, simply imitating his predecessors or seeing in the same way his contemporaries see, but the filters are there—and indispensable—whether the novelist knows it or not. As one of realism's great apologists, Georg Lukács, has put it, realism depends on types:

The central category and criterion of realist literature is the type, a peculiar synthesis which organically binds together the general and the particular both in characters and situations. What makes a type a type is not its average quality, not its mere individual being, however profoundly conceived: what makes it a type is that in it all the humanly and socially essential determinants are present on their highest level of development, in the ultimate unfolding of the possibilities latent in them, in extreme presentation of their extremes, rendering concrete the peaks and limits of men and epochs.

Allegory also depends on types, but the types of allegory are referable to a philosophy and theology concerned with ideals and essences; while the types of realism are referable to social sciences concerned with recording and understanding the processes that govern existence. The types of realism are committed to the visible world, while the types of allegory are committed to the invisible. This is why allegory was the great narrative form of the later Middle Ages and early Renaissance. When the Christian cosmos, based on the invisible world of eternity, was challenged by a humanism that put man and his visible world at the cosmic center of things, allegory became the best literary mode for controlling and reconciling these two visions. Francesca da Rimini in Dante's hell is a perfect example of the invisible world controlling the visible, of Christianity acknowledging humanism but mastering it—with difficulty, of course. That is why Dante faints after hearing Francesca. And the faint of the character Dante reflects the effort expended by the author Dante in giving humanism such a fair display and still keeping it subordinate. In a way, the rise of the novel simply reflects the triumph of humanism and the empirical attitudes which came in its train. As the invisible world lost its reality, the visible world became realer. And as dogmatic theology and systematic philosophy lost their control over men's minds, they were supplanted by positivistic or pragmatic and relativistic views of life and conduct. The realistic novel, which presents views of life and conduct in terms of manners and mores, was the appropriate form for serious fiction in the age of Comte.

But that age is ending. Now positivism and realism itself are fading and losing their hold on the minds of men. Instead of being The Way, they now just seem a way. They seem like dogma, and tired old dogma at that. Furthermore, psychology, when it moves away from statistics and experiments with animals and probes into depths of the human psyche, is moving from social science toward philosophy; for the deeps of the psyche are an invisible world also, one which modern men accept with the same unquestioning faith once reserved for the invisible world of Christianity. Freud and Jung together have presented the modern writer with a new scheme of the invisible world which cries out for allegorization. The depths, of course, are murkier than the heavens, and any allegory based on depth psychology will have to be more tentative than an allegory based on the Christian cosmos needed to be. But the archetypal system of Joyce's *Finnegans Wake* is as allegorical as anything in Dante.

Joyce's journey from epiphany to archetype is, like Iris Murdoch's move from philosophy to fiction, a sign of the times. Joyce inherited the notion of epiphany from a romantic/symbolist esthetic of the late nineteenth century. As he worked it out and explained it to himself in the too familiar passages of *Stephen Hero*, an epiphany was the way the world revealed itself and its meaning. At certain times or in certain situations, mundane things and people would reveal their essence to the sensitive observer. The observer, detached and objective, needed only to record what he saw to capture the meaning of an aspect of life.

The artist as sensitive observer and recorder of man in nature is a romantic poet. As sensitive observer and recorder of man in society, he is a realistic novelist. As sensitive observer and recorder of the motions of his own soul, he is the romantic/realistic auto-biographer—a Rousseau. In Joyce a conception of himself based on this romantic/realistic notion of the artist's role in life warred with an older notion of the artist as maker and shaper, organizing the raw material of life so as to display the idea of it already in the creator's mind. Joyce's progress, from the early epiphanies and *Chamber Music* through *Dubliners* and *Stephen Hero, A Portrait, Exiles,* and *Ulysses,* to *Finnegans Wake* is a journey from epiphany to archetype; hence, from symbolism to allegory. This journey was made possible by Joyce's discovery of cyclical theories of history (essentially medieval rather than modern because they are based on a notion of control of events in the visible world by an ideal order outside these events), and his parallel discovery of depth psychology—which modernized this medieval view of history by locating the ideal patterns that control the cycles of human life not in the heavens but in the uncon-scious. The collective unconscious effectively dehumanizes man by de-individualizing him. The social types of Lukács belong to realism. But the archetypes of Jung lead to a new allegory. Jung himself denied this, insisting that "an allegory is a paraphrase of a conscious content, whereas a symbol is the best possible expression for an unconscious content whose nature can only be guessed because still unknown." But once Jung had charted the unconscious and named its symbols, they became available for allegorical use. And this is how Joyce used them.

Finnegans Wake can also serve as the mighty exemplar of another aspect of modern allegorizing. Along with depth psychology, lan-guage theory has developed recently as an important new pseudo-science. I tried to suggest these developments in the little exemplum at the beginning of this chapter, but they too must be glossed a bit here. The modern development of semantics, of structural linguis-tics, and of the philosophy of language in general, has had an im-mense impact on literature. For one thing, it has led philosophy to serious questioning of its linguistic medium, resulting in both the invention of specially pure languages (symbolic logic) for philosophical thought, and a new concentration on language itself as the best mirror of the human mind.

In *Finnegans Wake* Joyce is partly allegorizing along archetypal

lines, using recurrent patterns of birth, fall, death, rebirth, and so on
to organize material drawn from throughout history and pre-history.
But he is also playing a great language game, embracing the duplicity
and ambiguity of his verbal medium, spinning multiplicities of
meaning out of puns and portmanteau words. Just a few sentences
taken from a passage which focuses on the alphabet and language
will illustrate how Joyces's two kinds of allegorizing work together in
that book:

> (Stoop) if you are abcedminded, to this claybook, what curios of signs
> (please stoop), in this allaphbed! Can you rede (since We and Thou had it out
> already) its world? It is the same told of all. Many. Miscegenations on
> miscegenations. Tieckle. They lived and laughed ant loved end left. Forsin.
> Thy thingdome is given to the Meades and Porsons. The meandertale, aloss
> and again, of our old Heidenburgh in the days when Head-in-Clouds
> walked the earth. In the ignorance that implies impression that knits
> knowledge that finds the nameform that whets the wits that convey contacts
> that sweeten sensation that drives desire that adheres to attachment that
> dogs death that bitches birth that entails the ensuance of existentiality. [I, i]

The passage insists that world and word are the same: "Can you
rede . . . its world?" It also insists on cyclical historical process, and
it merges history as process with history as recorded and narrated:
"It is the same told of all." Life is a "meandertale" and all its
possibilities are contained in its beginning—or in the alphabet—"in
this allaphbed." Earth and language make one great "claybook" in
which man's journey from ignorance through knowledge and desire
to procreation and death is written. In the beginning was the word
with a vengeance. Joyce's book certainly is for the "abcedminded."
The passage, in fact, would support a good deal more glossification,
but I do not want to dwell on it any longer. *Finnegans Wake* is
splendidly illustrative of the allegorizing trend of modern fiction.
Illustrative, but not typical. It is too extreme a case. Nor would I call it
exactly a fabulation. It has the playful spirit and delight in language,
but it lacks the purely narrative value that characterizes fabulation;
that delight in story for its own sake which is so marked in Durrell's
Alexandria Quartet is lacking in *Finnegans Wake*. Mind you, this is a
matter of classification only, not of evaluation. But fabulation is my
subject, not the whole range of modern fiction. Joyce is a great
allegorist—well christened "Dublin's Dante" by Oliver Gogarty. But
neither Dublin's nor Florence's Dante cared much for mere story.
They are allegorists but not fabulators. Edmund Spenser and Iris

Murdoch are fabulators as well as allegorists. And fabulation always poses special problems. People will come along who suggest that it should be read for the story only. It can be read in this way, as I suppose Shakespeare can be read for the "beauty of his language." But this is hardly the best way to read them. For in the work of an allegorical fabulator, fiction and ideation are always intertwined. They do not merely depend on one another; they interpenetrate one another. Part of the meaning is *in* the fiction, of course. But so, also, is part of the fiction *in* the meaning. When something happens to a character who is allegorically conceived, the event takes place simultaneously on the level of fiction and the level of ideation. To show how this process works, and to present for serious consideration one of the fine achievements of modern allegorical fabulation, I have chosen to discuss Iris Murdoch's "Gothic" romance, *The Unicorn*.

Iris Murdoch's *Unicorn*

In *The Unicorn* Iris Murdoch is a "Gothic" writer as Isak Dinesen is in *Seven Gothic Tales*. Recently Robert Langbaum, in his exciting study of Dinesen (*The Gaiety of Vision*), has shown us that Dinesen's artificial tales are carefully worked-out romances of ideas—what I would call allegories. The bizarre and artificial elements of her tales are parts of a structure of ideas. This much, I should say, is also true of *The Unicorn*. But, if we can think of these two brilliant ladies as allegorists, Iris Murdoch is "modern" in a way that Isak Dinesen is not. For Isak Dinesen, if Langbaum is right, accepted the romantic view of nature as, in Coleridge's phrase, "the art of God." But modern fabulators are post-realistic and post-romantic as well. They lack that Coleridgean belief in the ultimate order of the world. For the post–World War II fabulators, any order they impose on the world amounts not to a symbol of the divine order that God imposed on the cosmos, but to an allegory of the mind of man with its rage for an order superior to that of nature. It amounts to thumbing their noses at You Know Who. Isak Dinesen seems to have been a genuine romantic esthete, whose work implied a God Who was an artist much like herself. Oscar Wilde was an artist stricken with our kind of modernism when he waspishly observed that Wordsworth "found in stones the sermons he had already hidden there." For the writers of today, nature has been both disenchanted and dehumanized. It is merely alien, other. Their choice is simply whether to try and capture this dehumanization in their art—to be "realistic" as *Nausea*, *The Stranger*, and *Jealousy* are—or to hold up to nature an image not of nature itself but of a human order—as Barth and Iris Murdoch do.

The contemporary allegorist is likely to be both arbitrary and tentative. His world will be idealized but unsystematic, full of meanings but devoid of Meaning. The world of *The Unicorn* is this kind of world. The world of *Seven Gothic Tales*, which includes such perfect allegories as "The Roads Round Pisa" and "The Poet," is no longer available to the serious fabulator. Isak Dinesen was presenting an esthetic answer to the attack on art made by her compatriot Sören Kierkegaard. Iris Murdoch is a critic and interpreter of Jean-Paul Sartre.

Since every scene, every character, and every event in *The Unicorn* contributes to the plot or the meaning—usually to both simultaneously—we must have a firm grip on the structure of character and events in order to deal with the allegorical dimensions of the tale. As I understand the reading process, we read any story by engaging in what Poe called ratiocination. As we start to read, we build up expectations in the form of cloudy and tentative structures, into which we try to fit the details of character and event as they are presented to us. We modify these tentative structures as we are forced to by elements that do not fit, and we seek to perfect them as we move toward the end of the story.

In a work with as much story in it as there is in *The Unicorn* we are given considerable exercise in ratiocination merely in keeping up with events. Take, for example, the opening lines of the book, which begins this way: "How far away is it?" That is the first paragraph. It is ostensibly a single question, but it sets up in our structure of expectations at least eight additional questions: 1) What is *it*? 2) Who wants to know? 3) Why does he want to know? 4) Who is he asking? 5) Does he plan to go to "it"? 6) Will he get there? 7) How? 8) What will he find there? Some of these questions are more important than others, but the reader is not in a position to know which. Some will make themselves felt more consciously than others for different readers. The number of such questions which the reader senses in some way is an indication of the intensity of his response, a measure of his ratiocinative commitment. Some of the eight questions I have listed as probable responses to the opening line actually depend on certain answers to others. Numbers 7 and 8 anticipate a "yes" answer to number 6. The ideal reader, in his structure-building, is probably much like a good chess player, who is always thinking ahead many moves and holding alternative possibilities in mind as structures which the game may actually assume. In the consciousness of such a reader all eight of these questions and others, no doubt, must begin to take shape, along with emotional qualities which make answers to some seem more important than others—all in the few instants it takes him to read those first five words.

As the reading process continues, this reader's consciousness will be filing answers, dismissing apparent irrelevancies, framing new questions—developing a whole structure of intellectual and emotional expectations. Trying deliberately to make this process fully conscious—as it normally is not—we should be able to get some notion of how the opening of *The Unicorn* works on a responsive reader. After the first line the passage continues this way:

"Fifteen miles."
"Is there a bus?"
"There is not."
"Is there a taxi or car I can hire in the village?"
"There is not."
"Then how am I to get there?"
"You might hire a horse hereabouts," someone suggested after a silence.
"I can't ride a horse," she said in exasperation, "and in any case there's my luggage."

From this dialogue we begin inferentially to construct our notion of the situation and its future possibilities. We infer that the questioner is female, alone, in a strange place, come to stay for a while, probably arrived by train, certainly from a more urban place. She may have come to visit or to work. What she is doing in this obviously out-of-the-way place and why she is doing it become our larger tentative questions; exactly where is she going also insists on an answer; how she will get there remains a question but though immediate it does not seem vital, as we begin to assume she will somehow get there and our interest starts to shift toward "there." In context the "it" of the first sentence and the "there" of the seventh refer to something that has been named earlier in the conversation. But since we readers permanently lack that part of the conversation, "it" and "there" are tantalizers that focus our inferential activity toward a place already becoming mysterious for us. The next paragraph gives further impetus to precisely this phase of our ratiocination. In it we learn that the men who have been replying to the questions, "while not exactly hostile, entirely lacked the responsiveness of civilization. They had looked at her a little strangely when she had told them where she was going. Perhaps that was it." By this point we have entered the consciousness of this female visitor, we are sharing her perspective, and are especially alerted by the ominous information in the last two sentences. There is something strange and forbidding about the place where *we* (for now we are incorporated in *her*) are going.

While all this local inferential activity is in progress, the reader is also half-consciously commencing some vague blueprints for the entire structure. Even with no previous knowledge of Iris Murdoch, and with no clues from the jacket or cover, the alert and experienced reader is given enough information in these opening lines so that his first, tentative sketch should derive from his generic knowledge of suspense-mystery fiction. Just as *The Lime Twig* makes use of the conventions of hard-boiled American crime fiction, *The Unicorn* uses the conventions of soft-boiled English mystery fiction. In both works the conventions provide a frame of reference for the reader, helping him orient himself, but they also provide material for ironic or parodic scrutiny by the author, who manipulates the conventions with a certain amount of disdain. In *The Unicorn* Iris Murdoch shows her independence from the conventions of mystery fiction by gradually redirecting the alert reader from inferential activity on the level of who-dun-it and what'll-happen to a more abstract and philosophical level. She also toys with the conventions of comic pairing off of lovers and of tragic destruction of all the characters, and in doing so she transfers the reader's intellectual and emotional interest from the characters themselves to the ideas which have governed their actions. In *The Lime Twig* Hawkes proceeds differently, using his crime-story thread to string psychological rather than philosophical pearls, and letting his plot become clearer and more insistent as he goes along. Interestingly, both these works, in their titles, encourage ideation by naming objects which do not appear in the narratives. There is no lime twig in Hawkes's story and no unicorn in Iris Murdoch's. Both images offer us concepts that help to organize our perceptions into appropriate structures.

The process by which Iris Murdoch encourages us to shift our interest from the fictional to the ideational elements in her narrative is gradual. At certain points we are aware of a greater proportion of commentary to event, and I mean to single out some of these for special attention. But these points are merely climaxes in a structure of ideas which is just as narrative, just as dynamic, as the structure of pure event. For Iris Murdoch is teaching us how to read allegorically in *The Unicorn*, teasing us into this lost way of reading by almost imperceptibly moving from conventional mysteries of motivation and responsibility to the ideational mysteries of philosophy. She starts us building a "Gothic" structure of expectations and then, like a good guide, helps us to see that this fantastic edifice is not just another building with a pleasantly vertiginous view from the top, which gives us a delightful thrill. She allows us to discover that this work is "Gothic" like a cathedral in which every spire and every gargoyle is packed with meaningful allusions to an invisible world.

From "Gothic" action to "Gothic" allegory is the path we follow in this tale. To chart every step of the reader's imaginary journey, to watch in exquisite detail the visions and revisions through which his tentative plan for Strawberry Hill is revised to resemble Notre Dame—this might be worthwhile. It might also be tedious. And it would certainly require a book much longer than *The Unicorn* itself. Thus, in order to deal in some way with the relation between action and allegory in this work, I must indulge in some short-cutting. So I ask my reader to assume the continuation of the inferential processes suggested by the foregoing consideration of the opening lines— through all thirty-five chapters of the book. The properly ratiocinative reader will emerge with a notion of the book's action something like the version I am about to reproduce. The following compact plot-summary should serve to symbolize the process of experiencing the story on the level of action; it should also help to provide that firm grip on the events of the plot which is indispensable for approaching the allegory; and it can function as a handy point of reference for the discussion of the story's meanings to come.

PART I

Ch. 1. Marian Taylor, after an unhappy love affair, arrives at the remote village of Gaze to be a governess at Gaze Castle. She is met at the station by Gerald Scottow and young Jamesie Evercreech. On the ride to the Castle through desolate moors bordering a frightening coastline, she speculates on her exact duties and the positions of her two greeters. She sees the only other dwelling near Gaze Castle—Riders, home of the elderly scholar Max Lejour.

Ch. 2. Marian meets Violet Evercreech, Jamesie's sister, "practically his ma." She meets Denis Nolan, clerk at Gaze and keeper of the fishponds. Finally she meets the mistress of Gaze, Hannah Crean-Smith—an attractive, unkempt woman. Marian learns her "pupil" will be not a child but Hannah.

Ch. 3. Marian tries to swim in the cold sea but is afraid. On the shore she meets Alice Lejour, thirtyish daughter of Max, and learns that Alice's friend Effingham Cooper will be visiting Riders soon.

Ch. 4. Marian begins to teach Hannah French but puzzles over the feudal service Hannah receives from Denis and over Hannah's curiously convalescent and eccentric manner.

Ch. 5. Marian learns from Jamesie that Denis once worked at Riders but was chucked out because he "jumped" upon Alice. She also learns that Hannah's husband is alive, in New York, where he has been for seven years since he fell over a dreadful cliff near Gaze Castle.

Ch. 6. Marian senses and responds to Hannah's need for love.

Ch. 7. Marian meets Denis tending his fish. Denis tells her that seven years ago the brutal Peter Crean-Smith found Hannah in bed with young Philip (Pip) Lejour, and that shortly afterward he fell from the cliff in a struggle with Hannah. Since then Hannah has been a prisoner watched by Scottow and the Evercreeches. Marian sees herself as Gerald's adversary.

PART 2

Ch. 8. Effingham Cooper (who now divides with Marian the role of point-of-view character) comes to visit the Lejours. Max was his tutor at Oxford twenty years before. Alice has been in love with him for years, but he is a successful bureaucrat, with an accommodation with one of his female subordinates. Also, four years before on a visit to Max, he took refuge from a storm at Gaze, where he met Hannah and fell in love with her. His platonic adoration of Hannah has persisted.

Ch. 9. Effingham arrives at Riders, where Pip, Alice, and Max are expecting something to happen because "It's seven years."

Ch. 10. Groups from Gaze and Riders meet while walking and hunting. Effingham meets Marian and agrees to help her learn Greek.

Ch. 11. Effingham pays a visit to Hannah, offers rescue, she declines.

Ch. 12. Effingham and Max talk about Hannah.

Ch. 13. Effingham learns from Pip that Gerald Scottow helped Pip and Hannah consummate their adulterous love seven years ago—and betrayed them to Peter.

Ch. 14. At a Greek lesson Marian tries unsuccessfully to persuade Effingham to rescue Hannah by abducting her.

PART 3

Ch. 15. Marian is asked by Violet Evercreech to "be kind" to Jamesie, who "adores" her. Violet kisses Marian passionately. Marian thinks Jamesie might help rescue Hannah. In his room she finds pictures of Gerald unclothed and in "strange postures." Denis tells her Jamesie tried to rescue Hannah once and was caught by Gerald and whipped, afterward becoming Gerald's "slave."

Ch. 16. At a musical evening Hannah bursts out weeping and Gerald agrees to help Marian rescue her.

Ch. 17. Marian and Effingham attempt the rescue by tricking Hannah into a car. As they near the gates a car driven by Alice drives them off the road. Then Gerald and Jamesie arrive.

Ch. 18. Gerald makes Marian promise not to try again, sealing the promise with a passionate kiss.

Ch. 19. Marian realizes she is now part of the family, the pattern. Alice reports Effingham has wandered into the bog.

PART 4

Ch. 20. Effingham has a metaphysical insight while close to death in the bog. Denis rescues him.

Ch. 21. Effingham, rescued, dressed in Gerald's clothes, and fuddled by medicinal whisky, tries to explain his insight to Hannah and the others. Gerald announces that Peter is returning to Gaze. Hannah pleads with Effingham to stay with her, but Alice drags him away.

Ch. 22. Next evening Effingham returns to Gaze, to find Gerald carrying an apparently willing Hannah to his bedroom.

Ch. 23. The following morning Gerald announces that he is taking Hannah away. Alice reveals that long ago it was she who "sprang" upon Denis—not the reverse. Alice runs out.

Ch. 24. Effingham follows Alice, finds her in a weedy pool. They kiss.

PART 5

Ch. 25. Marian and Denis walk out to a salmon pool and make love.

Ch. 26. Effingham tells Marian he loves Alice. Word arrives that Peter is not coming after all.

Ch. 27. Hannah tells Marian that she (Hannah) has been playing God. Pip arrives at Gaze with a shotgun.

Ch. 28. Pip asks Hannah to come with him into the world. She refuses. He leaves. Gerald is master.

Ch. 29. Gerald, whom Denis says is becoming more like Peter, is killed by Hannah with a shotgun.

PART 6

Ch. 30. Violet and Jamesie take charge of Gaze, looking for Hannah's will and locking her in her room. Alice and Effingham decide to bring Max to Gaze for Peter's arrival.

Ch. 31. Hannah now wants to leave Gaze. Jamesie and Marian unlock her door and see her walk out.

Ch. 32. With rains continuing and flooding beginning Hannah's corpse is brought back to Gaze from "the rocks." Denis, who has gone to meet Peter, announces that Peter was drowned when the coast road flooded as they drove toward Gaze.

PART 7

Ch. 33. With the three bodies laid out in the drawing room, Max arrives and learns he is Hannah's heir.

Ch. 34. Marian and Denis part after he tells her that he caused Peter's death. He goes off through the bog to seek work at a "big house far beyond," taking his favorite fish with him. Alice sends his dog after him. Marian decides to return to the "real" world.

Ch. 35. Effingham parts from Alice and returns to the "real" world on the same train as Marian. Reading a paper he learns that Pip has "accidentally shot and killed himself while cleaning his gun." Effingham and Marian will talk the whole thing over.

From this level of event there are a number of paths leading to the ideational level of the narrative. The significance of the title cries out to be explored as it would not if the book had been called *The Mysterious Affair at Gaze*. Certain chapters in which there is little action indicated in the summary also seem to offer fertile areas for investigation: Chapter 12, for example. And even the simple plot-outline we are using here manages to suggest a significant difference between the worlds presented in the narrative. The world of Gaze and Riders is clearly differentiated from the "real" world outside. I mean to leave none of these avenues unexplored, but I want to begin with this notion of opposing worlds. If we can establish the general significance of these opposed worlds, we should be able to proceed to further refinements of ideation.

This opposition, as I understand it, has much to do with our whole consideration of the uses of romance and fabulation; for Marian and Effingham come from the "real" world into Gaze, just as we readers come into a work of fiction. Just as we do, they make ethical choices and participate in events which leave them unscathed, though the fictional world is strewn with corpses as the curtain is drawn upon it. But they are not entirely unchanged, though they have escaped. Marian, now, will "dance at Geoffrey's wedding." The sorrow and heaviness which drove her into the world of fabulation have been removed by her vicarious existence at Gaze, and she can return rejoiced and refreshed to the confusion and ordinariness in which real people are obliged to exist. All this seems far from accidental.

The Unicorn is, on its esthetic level, a fabulator's manifesto, in which the book itself is seen as fulfilling the purifying function of the traditional scapegoat, by providing a ritual purgation for those initiated into its mysteries.

Marian and Effingham, then, through whose eyes we view the events at Gaze, are representatives of our point of view. They come from the world of realism into a world of romance. They are, like Lockwood in *Wuthering Heights,* necessary intermediaries between these two worlds. (And, like Lockwood, they are both getting away from unsatisfactory erotic relationships in the world they have left.) But in this narrative they also embody certain "modern" ideas and attitudes which collide, in the course of events, with the values prevailing in the world of Gaze and Riders. Marian and Effingham believe in a set of liberal, enlightened virtues: freedom, individual responsibility, personal choice. Like most of us, they have derived their values from a mixture of neo-Freudian hedonism and easygoing utilitarianism. They are for Life and against Death, and they view life as mainly a matter of the senses. These values, to which most enlightened modern citizens subscribe, are met and tested in the story by the events at Gaze. In this castle a more medieval and feudal set of values prevails. Furthermore, a chain of events is in progress—variously referred to by Marian as a "story" or a "pattern"—which seems like something out of a medieval romance. A *princesse lointaine* (as Effingham's devoted friend in the "real" world calls Hannah) is actually being held prisoner as if under a spell maintained by a distant magician. And all these doings are watched from Riders, where a philosopher (Max), a poet (Pip), and a gardener (Alice) live an apparently simple, classical life. Riders, dominated by Max's Platonic or Socratic vision, seems actually to represent a third perspective in the narrative: that of ancient wisdom. Thus we have something like these three basic matrices:

   Marian and Effingham = modern "self-development"
   The Gaze household = feudal Christianity
   The Riders household = classical Platonism.

Deriving from these primary allegorical elements are various individual refinements manifested in the characters, and these refinements of ideation are complicated and qualified by the collisions and couplings of characters as the action proceeds.

At the center of the story is Hannah. The allegory turns mainly on the meaning of her life—the events in it and her reactions to them. Because she is at the center, she is the most remote from us. We see her mainly from the points of view of Marian and Effingham, the outsiders who enter the charmed circle of her love. Marian's perspective on Hannah is widened by Denis, with whom she discusses Hannah's situation. Denis, who serves Hannah with unquestioning feudal devotion, is a religious man, a believer. Our first extended insight into the allegorical implications of the story comes in Chapters 6 and 7, during Marian's talks with Hannah and Denis. Marian is firmly committed to *this* world. In Chapter 6 she and Hannah discuss religion. Marian "never went to church." She is surprised to find Hannah religious. They discuss love, Hannah begging Marian's pardon "for so shamelessly crying out for love." Hannah moves easily from love to religion: "Yet we all need love. Even God needs love. I suppose that's why He created us." Marian's dry comment is, "He made a bad arrangement." Later she questions Hannah's love of God: "But suppose you're loving—something that isn't there?" Hannah's reply leads toward mystical Platonism: "In a way you can't love something that isn't there. I think if you really love, then something *is* there. But I don't understand these things." If Marian is a modern "realist," Hannah is a medieval one. Hannah accepts the reality of universals, the priority of mind over matter.

In Chapter 7, Marian and Denis talk about Hannah. Denis tells Marian that the local people believe Hannah to be under a curse: "They believe that if she comes out of the garden she will die." Moreover, Denis adds, "They think that at the end of seven years something will happen to her." The conversation continues this way:

"Why seven years? Just because that's the time things go on for in fairy tales? But it is the end of seven years now!"
"Yes. But nothing is going to happen."
"Something has happened. I have come."
He was silent, as if shrugging his shoulders.
"Why have I come?" said Marian. Her own place in the story occurred to her for the first time. The ghastly tale had become a reality all about her, it was still going on. And it was a tale in which nothing happened at random.

Several aspects of this passage require attention. The last paragraph presents Marian seeing herself as entering a "tale" which has materialized around her: a tale in which nothing happens at random. This is, of course, strictly true in an ironic way. Marian is a character in a tale by Iris Murdoch, who is certainly the God of this little fictional universe—a very careful God, who will let nothing happen at random. But the passage raises the further question of Marian's role in this tale she has entered. The tale of Hannah is believed to be reaching a crucial stage. And Marian's arrival, her entering the tale at this point, must be significant: "Something has happened. I have come." A few paragraphs later she decides to accept her role in the story. She and Denis have tried unsuccessfully to guess who arranged for Gerald Scottow to hire her in the first place. They do not reach a conclusion about this, but Marian decides to give a meaning of her own to her presence at Gaze: "A prophetic flash of understanding burned her with terrible warmth. That was what she was for; she was for Gerald Scottow: his adversary, his opposite angel. By wrestling with Scottow she would make her way into the story. It was scarcely a coherent thought and it was gone in a moment."

Some of the irony involved in this resolution of Marian's should be apparent from the plot summary. The rest I shall return to later on. Her conversation with Denis continues, however, and we hear her sounding the typical notes of her modern, enlightened view of things. She can domesticate this mystery by reducing it to psychological terms:

> "It sounds to me as if she were really under a spell, I mean a psychological spell, half believing by now that she's somehow *got* to stay here. Oughtn't she to be wakened up? I mean it's all so unhealthy, so unnatural."
>
> "What is spiritual is unnatural. The soul under the burden of sin cannot flee. What is enacted here with her is enacted with all of us in one way or another. You cannot come between her and her suffering, it is too complicated, too precious. We must play her game, whatever it is, and believe her beliefs. That is all we can do for her."
>
> "Well, it's not what I'm going to do," said Marian. "I'm going to talk to her about freedom."

Denis urges Marian not to trouble Hannah with freedom, since she seems to have "made her peace with God" and accepted her punishment.

The other direct perspective we have on Hannah is Effingham's. Like Marian, he tries to take a modern and enlightened view of things. He, too, is in love with Hannah. And just as Denis qualifies Marian's perspective with his feudal and religious view of Hannah, Max Lejour qualifies Effingham's perspective with his Platonic view.

Chapters 11 and 12 parallel 6 and 7 in the structure of the book. In Chapter 11 Effingham has *his* serious interview with Hannah. In Chapter 12 he discusses her with Max. When he sees her she seems "lovelier than ever," but "no younger." He observes that "something was written on that brow, something about suffering: only he could not read the characters." Like Marian, he wants to "break this spell." Hannah responds to his offer of rescue (he would restore her to "ordinary life") by regretting that she has let him into her extraordinary existence: "If it were *now* I think I would send you away, I would not let such a story begin at all." Effingham parts from her, after gazing into "her big golden eyes. She was marvelously strange to him, a fey, almost demonic creature sometimes."

Effingham returns to Riders (Chapter 12) dreading Max's Socratic interrogation. But we, the readers, look forward to it. The mysteriousness of things has been getting intolerable, and we are anxious for more light. Max seems obviously designed to help us, for, unlike Denis, he is not involved in these events. And if we distrust the simple theology of Denis, we hope for more from the philosophy of Max. From a philosopher named Lejour, surely, we are entitled to expect light. And Max provides some: the best and clearest we get in working our way through this dark conceit. But Effingham is a man of intelligence too, and his perceptions undercut some of Max's. Moreover, Max himself declares, "I wish I understood more." Final answers are not going to be provided for us in this book. It is a *modern* allegory.

Max and Effingham first clash over Effingham's attempt to draw a political allegory from his visit to Gaze: the police state of Gaze *vs.* the free society of Riders. Max replies:

"The free society? That rag freedom! Freedom may be a value in politics but it's not a value in morals. Truth, yes. But not freedom. That's a flimsy idea, like happiness. In morals we are all prisoners, but the name of our cure is not freedom."

All prisoners, thought Effingham. Speak for yourself, old man. *You* are a prisoner of books, age, and ill health. It then occurred to him that in some curious way Max might derive consolation from the spectacle, over there in the other house, of another captivity, a distorted mirror image of his own.

It is possible to gloss this passage with the observation that neither Gaze nor Riders is free because they are both devoted to an ideal world: Gaze to a medieval mystery of suffering and obedience; Riders to the Socratic abstractions Goodness, Truth, and Beauty. For the reader, the values of Gaze, Riders, and the "real" world become clearer and clearer as he goes along. But the question of which set is "right" seems to become more and more elusive. Hannah seems to mean something different to everybody, and the reader who carries his mystery-story set of expectations over into the ideational complexities of *The Unicorn* longs for the denouement. Gradually, one realizes that this is just what Iris Murdoch is not going to provide. The relativity of significance emanating from Hannah's suffering is in itself a major dimension of the book's meaning. This book is partly about the difficulty of settling on The Truth in the twentieth century. But if a Truth and a Meaning are elusive, meanings are not. In this discussion between Max and Effingham, Iris Murdoch allows Max to make a number of choral statements which refine our understanding of the meaning attached to Hannah and her suffering. Max says,

"In a way we can't help using her as a scapegoat. In a way that's what she's for, and to recognize it is to do her honour. She is our image of the significance of suffering. But we must also see her as real. And that will make us suffer too."
"I'm not sure that I understand," said Effingham, "I know one mustn't think of her as a legendary creature, a beautiful unicorn—"
"The unicorn is also the image of Christ. But we have to do with an ordinary guilty person."

The book's title makes this passage important. And the passage emphasizes the medieval and allegorical quality of the whole work. Max's statement that the "unicorn is also the image of Christ" is a bit of medieval typology. The medieval bestiaries tell us that "Our Lord Jesus Christ is also a Unicorn spiritually." Specifically, the unicorn's small stature (as the bestiaries describe him) is associated with the humility of the Lord in assuming flesh. The unicorn's curious affinity for maidens (hunters cannot catch one except by leading a virgin girl to where the beast lurks, whereupon it leaps into the girl's lap and embraces her) is associated with the virgin birth of Christ. And finally (in the words of a twelfth-century bestiary translated by T. H. White) "It is like a kid or scapegoat because the Saviour himself was made in the likeness of sinful flesh, and from sin he condemned sin." That Hannah, as the unicorn of the title, is some sort of Christ figure, seems borne out in her name, Crean-Smith, which is an anagram for Christ-name or Christ-mean. But her first name, which reads the same backward as forward, suggests a duplicity or ambiguity in the significance of her life which the connection with Christ does not resolve for modern audiences. This is precisely the point at which the modern allegory is to be distinguished from the medieval. The Hannah = Christ equation in a medieval work would function mainly in one direction, with the character Hannah acquiring an unearthly dignity by means of the allegory. But in this modern work that process, though it operates, is counterbalanced by a flow of ideation in the opposite direction. The ambiguity of Hannah's position works to undercut and make relative the Christian view of the cosmos. The equation of the modern allegory does not say that Hannah's suffering is significant because it is a type of Christ's. It says that Hannah's suffering and Christ's are equally significant, and the significance depends on what we believe about it.

Max, in fact, offers Effingham an interpretation of Hannah's situation which is a pagan parallel to the Christian view. He sees the Greek concept of Ate as relevant to Hannah: "the almost automatic transfer of suffering from one being to another" which "is finally quenched when it encounters a pure being who only suffers and does not attempt to pass the suffering on." But when Effingham asks whether Max really considers Hannah such a being, Max can only reply that she may be, or she may be quite the opposite—a "sort of enchantress, a Circe, a spiritual Penelope keeping her suitors spellbound and enslaved." Then the discussion ranges over Max's own ethics, including his criticism of relativistic "existentialists and linguistic philosophers" who vulgarize the unimaginable nature of the Good by making it "into a mere matter of personal choice." At one point, he comes very close to the view of the absolute expressed by Hannah in Chapter 6, only where she made her formulation in religious terms (God exists if you believe in him) he makes his in ethical, quoting " 'Desire and possession of the Good are one.' " Finally, however, Max admits the subjective limitations of his own view of the situation: " 'Perhaps Hannah is my experiment! I've always had a great theoretical knowledge of morals, but practically speaking I've never done a hand's turn. . . . I don't know the truth either. I just know about it.' " Thus we are given quantities of food for ratiocination in Chapter 12, but no single, clearly acceptable interpretation of events. We are left, with a handful of clues, to continue developing a tentative structure of meanings for ourselves.

Effingham is reluctant to accept Max's view of the possible significance of passive suffering, just as Marian was reluctant to accept
Denis's Christian formulation of the same position. Both Max and
Denis seem to accept the traditional view that though the individual
has not made the world and has little control over its operation, he is
nevertheless responsible for what goes on within his reach. Marian
and Effingham, on the other hand, speak for those modern moralists
who see the individual as hardly responsible for anything but
blessed with all sorts of freedom. Consider the confusions and cross-
purposes implicit in these thoughts of Marian's in Chapter 15: "She
felt above all, as a sort of *categorical imperative,* the desire to set
Hannah free, to smash up all her eerie magical surroundings, *to let
the fresh air in at last:* even if the result should be some dreadful
suffering." I have italicized that Kant phrase of modern morality, the
categorical imperative, to point up its presence in Marian's thought.
The categorical imperative is, as has been observed, an attempt to
generate an absolute and systematic morality without justification
from the invisible world: "old Kant's Tartuffery," Nietzsche called it.
The other phrase I have italicized harks back to Ibsenism, echoing
Lona's ringing curtain speech in Act I of *The Pillars of Society.* It
reminds us that Marian *is* a kind of Ibsenite "new woman," independent, aggressive, free. But she has wandered into a morality play
in which freedom and pleasure contend with such antagonistic virtues as submission and endurance. The categorical command to be
free is itself a paradoxical imperative, because freedom means absence of command; it cannot be imposed. Marian's actions in this
morality play take on allegorical significance, then, as an exploration
of the limitations of this existential paradox. She enlists Effingham
and tries to abduct Hannah. She will end Hannah's expiatory suffering by forcing freedom upon her, "even if the result should be some
dreadful suffering."

Marian herself, of course, is far from free. Not only is she the
servant of her absolute faith in freedom; she is also the instrument of
other powers. She sees herself as Gerald Scottow's adversary. But
after the escape has failed, Gerald rewards her with a lecture, a kiss,
and the nickname of "Maid Marian." In the kiss, she realizes, she has
submitted: "Gerald could have had anything he wanted in that dark
bedroom." In the lecture he offers a stoical and deterministic view of
the world:

"There are things which are appalling to young people because young people think life should be happy and free. But life is never really happy and free in any beautiful sense. Happiness is a weak and paltry thing, and perhaps 'freedom' has no meaning. There are great patterns in which we are all involved, and destinies which belong to us and which we love even in the moment when they destroy us."

He adds that "the pattern" is what has "absolute authority" in the world of Gaze—"here." In the pattern, she and Gerald are not so much adversaries as accomplices. Their opposition is necessary for the ends of the pattern to be accomplished.

Marian's new title, *Maid Marian,* is even more interesting. The bestiaries tell us that the unicorn can be trapped only by a virgin girl used as a lure. And they liken Mary, mother of Jesus, to this virgin because she is the medium through which perfect divinity enters the sinful world of flesh. Our Maid Marian is the virgin lure. Through her intercession Hannah has been entangled in a new web of circumstance which will result in her undertaking a renewed burden of sin and guilt. Maid Marian herself is destined to stain her immaculate innocence in the pattern of events she has entered. When she boldly tells Denis, "Something has happened. I have come," the major irony of her words lies in her ignorance of the role she has been cast for in this mystery play. In Chapter 15, when Denis tells her, "Everyone here is involved in guilt," the reply she murmurs half to herself is, "Except me. Except me. Except me." But by Chapter 19 she is beginning to learn her part: "I have become a part of the pattern," she thinks, later adding that she is "involved now." Finally, when she helps to set Hannah free to die in Chapter 31, she is no longer an innocent maid involved without knowing it in a plot to catch a unicorn. She sees this act as one of "blood guilt which would make its own reckoning." And she has doubts about the rightness of her act. No more easy categorical imperatives absolve her from the difficulties of personal decision:

Had she done right to give Hannah this last thing, the freedom to make her life over in her own way into her own property? When at last Hannah had wanted to break the mirror, to go out through the gate, ought she *then* to have been her jailer? It was not any more the old images of freedom which could move her now. It was Hannah's authority which had moved her, her sense, in the pathetic scene of her final imprisonment, of Hannah's sovereignty, of her royal right to dispose of herself as she would.

Instead of imposing "freedom," Marian is now admitting the divine right of other people to make their own choices. And she is willing to accept the responsibility for allowing Hannah this choice. Recognizing her guilt, she expects her punishment to follow: "And now she stood, as it were, in Hannah's place, and it was perhaps on her that the axe would fall." But in Chapter 34 Marian finds that she will not, after all, be "in Hannah's place." That painful crux is reserved for Denis, whose action in being unfaithful to Hannah (both by making love to Marian and by losing faith in the significance of Hannah's suffering) and in deliberately killing Peter (another breach of faith) has made him the "most guilty." Denis tells Marian that in his guilt lies her "cure."

"I should have loved only and not hated at all. I should have stayed by her and suffered all with her, beside her, becoming her. There was really no other way and I knew that before. But I let myself be driven mad by jealousy, and by her actions, and I was faithless to her and so became mad. I am the most guilty. The guilt passes to me. That is why I must go away by myself."
"But does that leave me—free?"

Denis does not answer Marian's question, but she finally understands that his acceptance of guilt does leave her free. "Yes," she says to him, "you are becoming Hannah now." Denis is the new unicorn, the new scapegoat, the new saviour who takes upon himself the sins of others to atone for them. With the departure of Denis, Marian has a "sense of it all beginning again, the whole tangled business: the violence, the prison house, the guilt. It all still existed. Yet Denis was taking it away with him." Finally, however, she is not sure of the meaning of her experience in this "other world" which she has visited: ". . . she did not know whether the world in which she had been living was a world of good or of evil, a world of significant suffering or a devil's shadow-play, a mere nightmare of violence." And neither do we.

Like Denis and Marian, Max and Effingham have their final views of the matter. And we have our final views of them. Unlike Denis and Marian, Max and Effingham have kept clear of the final action. Effingham has had his metaphysical vision while sinking into the bog—surely an allegory of the absurdity of thought divorced from action. And Max has watched and thought. These two have not become involved in guilt. But they are responsible for their inactions. Max is Hannah's heir, as philosophy is the heir of theology:

"Max will speak her funeral speech, Max will tell the world what she was," thinks Effingham jealously. And Max interprets this gesture of Hannah's as a "romantic decision—if you like, a symbolic decision." He insists that Hannah, "like the rest of us," loved "what wasn't there." And he adds that she "could not really love the people she saw." Here Alice interrupts to tell her father that *he* was the one person she could have loved in presence. To this Max has no response but a shake of the head. But Effingham insists that Max is "her death, and she loved you." Interpretations begin piling up. Max turns Hannah into a symbol, an idea. Earlier Effingham had turned her into a Freudian notion (Chapter 30)—the chaste mother figure desired by the jealous child. Seen this way, Hannah's acceptance of Gerald Scottow as a lover broke the spell of Effingham's "courtly love" for her and freed him to make love to Alice; just as it freed Denis and Marian to perform the act of love. Hannah's "faithlessness" was mirrored by that of those who loved her.

Hannah herself presents an interpretation of her life before its catastrophe. In Chapter 27 she says that she has been playing the part of God but she is really "nothing, a legend." And she adds that

"It was your belief in the significance of my suffering that kept me going. Ah, how much I needed you all! I have battened upon you like a secret vampire. I have even battened on Max Lejour." She sighed. "I needed my audience, I lived in your gaze like a false God. But it is the punishment of a false God to become unreal. I have become unreal. You have made me unreal by thinking about me so much. You made me an object of contemplation. Just like this landscape. I have made it unreal by endlessly looking at it."

This passage must certainly qualify some of the other views presented. It comes, so to speak, from the unicorn's mouth. In particular, the orthodox Christian view of Hannah's death adopted by Denis and Marian, though it follows this speech and Hannah's death, cannot be seen as the last word, the one true interpretation of the events at Gaze. "I lived in your gaze"—says Hannah. The world of Gaze is a place where order, system, and meaning all exist because they are imposed from without. They are in the eyes of the beholders.

In this book, then, we are not entitled to make any final choice among the various metaphysical possibilities offered us. But the book is far from meaningless. There is a meaning in its lesson in relativity. And there is a further meaning, I believe, in our final

views of Marian and Effingham. Hannah's view of herself is echoed
by Effingham's last thoughts of her as he heads back toward "reality"
in the train. He thinks of her as a "strange nun" and agrees that Max
was right in saying that they had all

turned towards her to discover a significance in their own sufferings, to load
their own evil into her to be burned up. It had been fantasy of the spiritual
life, a story, a tragedy. Only the spiritual life has no story and is not tragic.
Hannah had been for them an image of God; and if she was a false God they
had certainly worked hard to make her so. He thought of her now as a
doomed figure, a Lilith, a pale death-dealing enchantress: anything but a
human being.

Finally, he decides that "if what was over had indeed been a fantasy
of the spiritual life, it was its fantastic and not its spiritual quality
which had touched him." Effingham and Marian, as they leave the
world of spiritual fantasy and head toward the "familiar ordinary
world," suggest two kinds of readers and two ways of encountering a
book like The Unicorn, which is itself a "fantasy of the spiritual life":
the reader who, like Marian, becomes engaged in the events and
touches good and evil through imaginative experience; and the reader
who, like Effingham, remains aloof "through egoism, through being
in some sense too small." The Effinghamish reader will find only a
fantasy in the The Unicorn. The Marianite will be touched and moved
spiritually. The Effinghamish critic, in particular, will discourse glibly
about such a book. He will be detached, amusing, skeptical. He will
be more judicious than the Marianite, perhaps. But he will lack one
thing: that experience of the story which can come only to the reader
who commits himself to it imaginatively. Which is the right way? As
in larger issues, Iris Murdoch leaves us to choose. But I think I know
which choice she feels we should make.

John Barth's *Goat-Boy*

Is it true that our air is disturbed, as Mal-
larmé said, by "the trembling of the veil of
the temple" or "that our whole age is seek-
ing to bring forth a sacred book"? Some of
us thought that book near toward the end
of the last century, but the tide sank.
—W. B. Yeats in *The Trembling of the Veil*

The *fin de siècle* was pleasantly titillated by intimations of
Apocalypse. But in our time the holocaust is too real a possibility to
be considered with a *symboliste frisson*. The veil of the temple has
blown away entirely, and we can hear something ticking in there.
The fragmentation Yeats perceived as the curse of modern civilization has continued; the center holds together even less than it did.
But we have got our sacred book now. In the midst of our tribulations
Giles Goat-Boy has slouched toward State College to be born. Hal-
lelujah!

John Barth's fourth work of fiction is a tract for our times, an epic to
end all epics, and a sacred book to end all sacred books. It is not, I
hasten to say, a merely blasphemous work of empty nihilism, though
some reviewers have reacted as if it were. It is a work of genuine epic
vision, a fantastic mosaic constructed from the fragments of our life
and traditions, calculated to startle us into new perceptions of the
epic hero and saviour. It is epic in its scope: in its combination of
myth and history, of the ideal and the actual. And it is a sacred book
because it is concerned with the life of a religious hero and with the
way to salvation. True, it treats these matters comically, even farci-
cally at times; and it is militantly fabulative, insisting on its fabulous
dimension, its unreality. But this insistence is part of the book's
point: In our time any sacred book must be a work of fiction.

Barth's choice of comic allegory as the method of his fiction should
come as no surprise to anyone who has read this book from the
beginning. The vision of fabulation is essentially comic because it is
an instrument of reason; and it is frankly allegorical because it has

not the naïve faith in the possibility of capturing the actual world on the printed page which realism requires of its practitioners. Barth has observed that "If you are a novelist of a certain type of temperament, then what you really want to do is re-invent the world. God wasn't too bad a novelist, except he was a Realist." Realism, in this view, is a game that only God can play. Man is not in a position to re-create God's world on paper. The old realistic novel has always assumed that a readily ascertainable thing called reality exists, and that we all live in it; therefore, it is the only thing to write about. But Barth says that he doesn't "know much about Reality." He declines the realistic gambit, refuses to accept the notion that the truth can be captured just by reporting the way things are. Barth insists on an inevitable "discrepancy between art and the Real Thing." His comment on the French *nouveau roman* is enlightening:

From what I know of Robbe-Grillet and his pals, their aesthetic is finally a more up-to-date kind of psychological realism: a higher fi to human consciousness and unconsciousness. Well, that's nice. A different way to come to terms with the discrepancy between art and the Real Thing is to *affirm* the artificial element in art (you can't get rid of it anyhow), and make the artifice part of your point instead of working for higher and higher fi with a lot of literary woofers and tweeters. That would be my way. Scheherazade's my *avant-gardiste*.

The Real Thing, then, is God's world. The world of the fabulator is different. And the difference, the artifice, is "part of your point." The fabulator's attitude toward life is elliptical. By presenting something that is like life but markedly different from it, he helps us to define life by indirection. Fabulation is a tricky business for both reader and writer—a matter of delicate control on the one hand and intelligent inference on the other. Any reader of *Giles Goat-Boy*, then, will be put on his mettle. The demands on his learning and ingenuity will be strenuous.

In *Giles Goat-Boy*, John Barth has forged an allegorical instrument that enables him to piece together our fragmented world and explore the possible ways of living in it. To understand the vision of this book, the reader must come to terms with its allegory. He must learn its workings—its facets and their relations; in fact, he must discover how to play his part in the interpretation of the events of the story. Thus, for the bulk of this chapter I shall be concerned with mastery of the allegorical dimensions of the story. But before trying to thread the entire labyrinth of the allegory, I think it advisable to make a sort of preliminary sortie to determine whether the game is worth the candle. We can begin to assess the value of a literary work by considering closely some representative passages. This is a dangerous business, and can be grossly unfair, especially in dealing with a work like this one, which is highly structured and depends for its cumulative effect upon the careful dovetailing of many thematic and narrative elements. But Barth is asking a good deal of his readers in the way of a commitment of time and energy, so he must be ready to let us do a bit of preliminary examining before making the big plunge.

The passages I have selected for investigation should provide some sense of the texture of Barth's prose, and the way his vision is related to his use of language. Moreover, since they are thematically related, they should reveal something of the book's structure as well. Each passage is concerned directly with vision, and with the use of scopes or lenses as visual aids. Just as the ubiquitous mirrors of the *Alexandria Quartet* emphasized that work's cubist perspectivism, so does a bizarre collection of scopes and lenses underscore the motifs of quest and perception in *Giles Goat-Boy*. The first passage is a description of a tender moment. After many trials and tribulations, the hero holds the heroine in his arms:

"Anastasia . . ." The name seemed strange to me now, and her hair's rich smell. What was it I held called *Anastasia*? A slender bagful of meaty pipes and pouches, grown upon with hairs, soaked through with juices, strung up on jointed sticks, the whole thing pulsing, squirting, bubbling, flexing, combusting, and respiring in my arms; doomed soon enough to decompose into its elements, yet afflicted in the brief meanwhile with mad imaginings, so that, not content to jelly through the night and meld, ingest, divide, it troubled its sleep with dreams of passèdness, of *love*. . . .

Obviously, this is no ordinary love scene. The hero has some excuse for his anatomical ruminations, however, since he has just finished gazing at the lady's innards through a fluoroscope. The scene continues:

She squeezed more tightly; I felt the blood-muscle pumping behind her teat, through no governance of *Anastasia*. My penis rose unbid by *George*;

was it a George of its own? A quarter-billion beasties were set to swarm therefrom and thrash like salmon up the mucous of her womb; were they little Georges all?

I groaned: "I don't understand anything!" [p. 616]

We might call the vision here fluoroscopic. It penetrates the skin to the meaty pipes and pouches within. But it also looks at the outsides of the human anatomy. And it listens as well, even noting chemical processes such as the combustion which turns fodder into energy, warming the human frame. This embrace in a doctor's office is presented in appropriately clinical terminology, but the language is not merely clinical. In particular the verbal drive of the passage is remarkable. Consider these verbal forms from a single sentence: "grown up . . . soaked through . . . strung up . . . pulsing, squirting, bubbling, flexing, combusting, and respiring . . . doomed . . . to decompose . . . afflicted . . . to jelly . . . meld . . . ingest . . . divide . . . troubled." These verbs form alone, excerpted from the sentence in which they function, illustrate the range and precision of Barth's vocabulary. Together they emphasize the complexity of mere organic existence, the multifariousness of the life process. And all the participles and infinitives which describe this complexity weigh against the main verb of the sentence, which comes at the end—"troubled." Despite its ineluctably physical mechanisms, described so richly and fully, this organism, this human body, this Anastasia *troubles* its mere mechanical existence with ideals—notions that no fluoroscope or microscope can locate or justify, dreams of blessedness and love. Moreover, in addition to these ideals, which trouble the organism and keep it from merely jellying along like an amoeba, the body is swayed and governed by all sorts of corporeal activity beyond its control and beyond that necessary for its untroubled existence—the heart pounding, where it need only beat; the penis rising, yearning toward another. Where in all this mixture of activity and purpose does the identity of Anastasia or of George begin and end, the passage asks. And the quarter-billion spermatozoa ready to thrash salmon-like about their master's business—who are they? And who is their master?

One of George's mysterious tasks, which he must achieve in order to complete his heroic quest, is to "see through your ladyship." The fluoroscopic method reveals some things, but it provides no final illumination, only riddles—especially riddles of the sphincter. This

passage must be contrasted with the act of love later performed by
George and Anastasia in the belly of the great computer, which is the
true fulfillment of the task. (And this act itself must be contrasted
with George's first non-human "servicing" of Anastasia—the tele-
vised Sunrise Service performed in Stoker's Living Room as the
climax to his great vernal orgy.) The act of love is the necessary act of
vision for George, because when we simply look, no matter how fine
our scope, we merely (like Max Lejour in *The Unicorn*) "know about"
the things we gaze at. When we act, and engage ourselves with
things, we come to know them. In WESCAC's belly George knows
Anastasia as Adam knew Eve. And she conceives. In a way Barth is
exploring the truth in the linguistic riddles posed by words like
"know" and "conceive." And he is using the action of his fiction to
expound a philosophy of action which cannot properly be presented
discursively. Any commentary on this fictional action—such as
mine, here—amounts to reducing "knowing" to "knowing about."
All interpretive criticism amounts to this. That is the limitation of
such criticism. And one of its virtues—clarification—is a function of
this limitation. It clarifies, at the expense of reducing the experience
of fiction through which we "know" a work, to a discussion through
which we "know about" it. Thus its only use is to prepare us to
encounter or re-enter the primary material, the work itself.

Having looked at a passage of fluoroscopic vision, and considered
briefly its place in the whole scheme, we may now turn to a passage
which connects the limited sphere of proctoscopy to a more cosmic
view of things. This passage, from early in the book, presents the
achievement of George's tutor, Max Spielman. In it we can find the
same disposition in Barth to explore the riddle of language, to shake
the hidden meanings out of metaphors, and to use puns and other
devices of language as ways to generate new meanings:

In three words Max Spielman synthesized all the fields which thitherto he'd
browsed in brilliantly one by one—showed the "sphincter's riddle" and
the mystery of the University to be the same. *Ontogeny recapitulates
cosmogeny*—what is it but to say that proctoscopy repeats hagiography? That
our Founder on Founder's Hill and the rawest freshman on his first *mons
veneris* are father and son? That my day, my year, my life, and the history of
the West Campus are wheels within wheels? [p. 7]

Like Joyce in *Finnegans Wake*, Barth is playing with archetypes
here, and playing with words. It was Oedipus who solved the sphinx's

riddle and became the saviour of his city. And it was Oedipus who killed his father, married his mother, and finally saved his city once again by becoming a scapegoat, suffering expulsion and blindness to atone for his lack of vision. By the punning alteration of "sphinx's" to "sphincter's," Barth unites these two actions more firmly than Freud himself, and in doing so he brings whole mansions of philosophy into the place of excrement. The sphincter's riddle involves the mysteries of creation and of love. That portion of feminine anatomy so beautifully named the mount of Venus provides both linguistic and archetypal connections to those mountains of mythology where the high god performs his creative act, making a cosmos out of chaos. Barth has taken the Darwinian "ontogeny recapitulates philogeny"—the life of the individual organism in its growth stages repeats the evolutionary cycle of its species—he has taken this and substituted "cosmogeny" for "philogeny," turning biology into archetypology. The mystery of the universe and the sphincter's riddle are the same because the genesis of the individual and the genesis of the cosmos are aspects of the same process. The proctoscope examining fundamental human anatomy will tell us the same thing as the lives of the saints: because saints, too, have fundaments, and because—though the place *is* the place of excrement—the mansions of love and creative power are indubitably there. The greatness of Max Spielman is in seeing the connection. That is epic vision.

The fluoroscope of Dr. Sear, the proctoscope of Max Spielman— these fallible gadgets are closer to seeing into the mystery of the universe than the telescopes and other lenses of Eblis Eierkopf. According to Eierkopf, Spielman "thinks with his ventricles." And Sear's main locus of thought seems even lower in the human anatomy than the heart. But Eierkopf, as his name suggests, is all eye and head. He is so much the man of "reason," in fact, that he cannot perform the simplest bodily functions without aid from the nearly brainless but superbly physical Croaker. When Eierkopf is mounted on Croaker's shoulders, together they make something like a whole man. But Eierkopf by himself presents a purely scientific and positivistic approach to the mystery of the universe. All his lenses— from his great telescope down to his eyeglasses—are designed by Barth to expose the limits of this kind of vision. He watches coeds undress with an infrared telescope in his frivolous moments, but this is not so much wicked as it is revealing: revealing of Eierkopf, that is, for he watches nature in the same way: "*I try to take nature by surprise.*" And what he is looking for is a miracle. He denies the world of spirit in this way: "'. . . You want spooks and spirits? Bah, George Goat-Boy! We look with our microscopes and our telescopes, and what do we see? Order! Number! Energies and Elements! Where's any Founder or Grand Tutor?' He tapped his gleaming skull. 'In here, no place else . . .'" But in his weaker moments he hopes with his gazing and peering to find something else:

"*. . . I try to take nature by surprise!* I try to catch her napping once!" He laughed at his own folly, which it nevertheless plainly excited him to confess. He would sometimes stare at the furniture of his observatory for hours on end, he declared, at the familiar books and instruments in their accustomed places, and contemplate the inexorable laws of nature that held them fast, determined their appearance and relations, and governed his perception of them. And he would find himself first fretting that the brown pencil-jar on his desk, for example, could not suddenly turn green, or stir of its own volition; from a fret that such wonders could not be, he would come to a wish that just once they might, thence to a vain and gruntsome willing that they be—as if by concentration he could bring a miracle to pass. [pp. 335–36]

In the final dramatic scene at Max's shafting, Eierkopf becomes a believer in the matter of Grand Tutoriality: "'I'm *Übertrittig*, Goat-Boy!' he cried, 'My eyes have been opened!' . . . For he had seen with his own two eyes (abetted, to be sure, by corrective lenses) wonders unexplainable by natural law and student reason."

The wonders he has seen, however, have been performed by George's devilish adversary, Harold Bray. Eierkopf's positivistic science has led him to embrace evil as the supreme good. The devil cannot only quote scripture if he needs to. He can also appear to defy natural law in such a way as to make those who demand only ocular evidence of divinity take him for a god. Which is just what Eblis Eierkopf does. The eyeball, too, is a lens, and vision is not just a matter of eyeballs. That is one of the lessons of the Oedipus myth. Oedipus sees truly only after he is blind. This myth, and Dante's mythic trip through Hell and Purgatory to Paradise, have contributed heavily to Barth's vision in *Giles Goat-Boy*. Just as Dante must learn to abandon reason for revelation when reason has taken him as far as it can, leaving his old guide, Vergil, for his new one, Beatrice; so George, separated from his mentor, Max, gains his greatest insight when he sees through his ladyship: in the dark of WESCAC's belly, his head covered by his mother's purse and his body united with Anastasia's in conjugal embrace, he sees: "In the darkness, blinding light! The end of the University! Commencement Day!"

The allegorist acknowledges the visionary power of his linguistic medium. He sees through his language. Metaphor, the vital principle of language, is also the animating force in allegory. It is because life can be seen as a journey, a quest, or a voyage that Dante, the Redcross Knight, or Gulliver can serve as examples of human behavior, even though they exist for us in imaginary and non-realistic realms. John Barth has chosen two basic metaphors for his fabulative epic, which combine to make a dominant image from which many metaphorical consequences flow. He has chosen to see the universe as a university, and he has chosen to make his hero a man whose formative years were spent as a goat among goats. Before discussing the workings of the allegory itself, I want to consider the appropriateness of these two choices as metaphors for the human condition, and their effectiveness as basic materials for an allegorical narrative.

First, appropriateness. Language has provided the key to the first of these basic metaphors in the similarity of the words universe and university. The words are identical for three syllables, and then— worlds apart. But there is a meaningful connection between these two worlds. If the universe means *everything*—our whole world from the innermost piece of the smallest particle, outward to the ends of space, including those heavenly and hellish realms discerned only by poets and prophets—then the university means the place where *everything* is present as an object of inquiry and concern. For the thoughtful person, the world *is* a university, and his education always in process. For Barth, the university must have had the great virtue of including everything, already organized in terms of inquiry and quest. And beyond that, the American university of the present, though it strives to preserve an atmosphere of critical scrutiny and contemplation, is by no means an Arcadia studded with ivory towers where detached mandarins think beautiful thoughts. Despite its heritage from pagan academies and Christian cloisters, the modern American university is a brawling marketplace where CIA men mingle with student leftists, and careering business majors jostle with poets and painters. Not only is a university involved in the study and practice of politics in the statewide, national, and international spheres; it has its own internal politics, too. At some points, in fact, the two begin to merge. Men move back and forth between university posts and positions in government with increasing freedom. Concepts like the "multiversity" emphasize this particular penetration. And when a recent governor of our most populous state, a man with presidential aspiration, made his first significant official act the firing of the head of that state's university system, who could say the world is not in the university and the university in the world? It is precisely because the directors of universities, foundations, and corporations have become virtually interchangeable with high government officials—many of them serving Caesar and Socrates almost simultaneously—that Barth is able to get so much allegorical leverage from his selection of the university as his universe.

The appropriateness of his other fundamental metaphor should be equally evident. Again, language has provided the key. The connection between man and goat begins with the metaphorical application of the word for young goat to the young human. We all begin as kids. But if any particular kid should grow up to become a religious leader, the bringer of a new dispensation, a saviour who can expect ultimately that martyrdom with which mankind habitually reward their saints—then a whole new range of metaphorical materials comes into play; for we touch here on the connection between pastoral imagery and the religious life. This is the connection Milton exploited so powerfully in "Lycidas" by taking advantage of all the metaphorical implications of the word *pastoral*. Barth proceeds similarly. From goat-boy to scapegoat, the pilgrimage of George Giles ranges over the same metaphorical ground, only in comic and satyric fashion. From the traditional description of Christian judgment as a matter of separating "the sheep from the goats" Barth draws metaphoric strength. By making his "hero" a "goat" (an expression which in our idiom is paradoxical) he has chosen to upset the traditional Christian view of salvation. In tradition Christ, the Lamb of God, drove the pagan gods out of Europe and stilled forever the voice of the goatish Pan. Barth's *Revised New Syllabus* comically but seriously reinstates the goatish side of man. George is, as Stoker jokingly remarks, "Enos Enoch with balls"—a saviour who will restore sexuality to an honored place in human existence. In this respect Barth joins Yeats, Lawrence, Swinburne, and other artists who have rebelled against the puritanical and ascetic side of the religion founded by the "Pale Galilean." There should be nothing shocking in this. In a post-Freudian world, even the traditional celibacy of the Roman Catholic priesthood is being seriously challenged from within the Church. Barth's *Revised New Syllabus* simply reflects this new attitude.

If we grant the appropriateness of Barth's choice of basic metaphors, we may go on to consider their effectiveness, which is largely a matter of the interaction of the two metaphors. The metaphors of goat/man and university/universe merge when George the Goat-Boy leaves the *pasture* to enter the *campus,* metaphorically exchanging one *field* for another. His curious upbringing as a Goat-Boy and his potential as a possible saviour or "Grand Tutor" make this journey especially poignant. Having been brought up as a kid, an animal, George seeks to reach the highest possible level of human development. The enormity of this quest reflects the enormity of human existence, for we all begin as kids, faced with the problem of becoming as fully human as possible. The university becomes the proper sphere for George's quest because it is the place where life is studied and questioned. This enables Barth to use terms like "commencement," "failure," and "passage" as ways of talking about the whole development of human beings. Because universities were originally church oriented, with holy orders normally the object of a university degree, there is a theological implication in this system which Barth can exploit. And because the system combines this theocratic and authoritarian machinery with an antipathetic spirit of inquiry and skepticism, it provides the appropriate arena for the drama of George's search for Answers, as well as the proper test for his ecclesiastical aspirations.

Universities function now, all too often, as mere trade schools for aspirants to various technical positions. But at their center we still can find the notion that the unexamined life is not worth living, and that the university is a place where life may be examined. Ethical philosophy, which shares, or ought to share, with literature the central position in university education—frequently begins with the old choice between being a happy animal or an unhappy man. We begin to learn the rudiments of ethics by accepting our humanity and exploring its implications. George the Goat-Boy makes this choice literally, having actually experienced the pleasures of happy animal existence. Some of the implications of the choice are explored in the following passage, which is not—as at least one critic has suggested—Barth's own view of life, but only the point of departure from which a man with aspirations to full humanity must leave, and which no man can leave without some nostalgic backward glances. Here George presents the goatish view of life:

Who neglects his appetites suffers their pangs; Who presumes incautiously may well be butted; Who fouls his stall must sleep in filth. Cleave to him, I learned, who does you kindness; Avoid him who does you hurt; Stay inside the fence; Take of what's offered as much as you can for as long as you may; Don't exchange the certain for the possible; Boss when you're able, be bossed when you aren't, but don't forsake the herd. Simple lessons, instinct with wisdom, that grant to him who heeds them afternoons of browsy bliss and dreamless nights. Thirteen years they fenced my soul's pasture; I romped without a care. In the fourteenth I slipped their gate—as I have since many another—looked over my shoulder, and saw that what I'd said bye-bye to was my happiness. [pp. 8–9]

It should be obvious that neither Barth nor his spokesman George is offering a recipe for the good life here; the speaker is commemorating his passage from kidship to manhood, his departure from the world of animal happiness for the troubled world of men. This typical, this archetypal journey is simply rescued by Barth from the realm of matter-of-course and given new life by his literalizing of the metaphor of child as kid and the consequent dramatization of the choice between animal simplicity and human complication. But to explore Barth's vision in any way approaching thoroughness, we must move beyond these basic metaphors to their operation in the whole allegorical structure of the book.

Allegory is notoriously an affair of "levels," but I should like to discard that notion—which implies more of a fixed hierarchy among kinds of meaning and a stricter separation among them than I believe exists, even in the great traditional allegories. Yet there are different meanings and different kinds of meaning in any richly imagined allegory. To encompass this variety of meaning without the unwelcome implications of "levels," I should like to consider the varieties of meaning in *Giles Goat-Boy* as facets or dimensions which become discernible to us when we consider the narrative from different angles of vision. This fabulation has, for example, its element of pure story or pure romance, the meanings of which are visceral rather than intellectual. These romance elements, however, are intimately connected with Barth's deliberate employment of myths and archetypes—dimensions of narrative that modern criticism is equipped to measure and understand. At the same time, the central events in the story of the hero's progress involve his adaptation of certain distinct ethical attitudes and his action according to those attitudes. The consequences of George's acting according to these different ethical attitudes lead him (and us) to evaluations of them, giving the book a philosophical dimension which is structurally central to the narrative. There are also important facets of *Giles Goat-Boy* that we might call sociological, psychological, and historical. We are used to thinking of matters of these latter kinds as the domain of realistic fiction rather than as allegorical facets of a work which is not essentially a piece of realism. This may make it hard for us to accept the validity of this dimension in a work of fabulation. Yet this is just what we must do in order to come to terms with Barth's narrative. Or, rather, it is one of a number of things we must do to grasp the whole narrative with full awareness of all its dimensions. For our reading of multi-dimensional allegory depends not only on our apprehending all the dimensions of the narrative, but also, even mainly, on our being aware of the interaction among them. In treating this sort of work, the critic must huff and puff along in an attempt to deal separately and statically with materials that function as a complex dynamic process in the work. Accordingly, I shall consider the allegory of *Giles Goat-Boy* under three main headings which reflect the three principal facets of the work. These rubrics (inevitably) are analogous to the main geographical divisions sketched out in the little fable that began this chapter: history (including social science), fiction (including myth), and philosophy (including theology).

I mean the term "history" in this sense to include every aspect of *Giles Goat-Boy* which points directly to the visible world as we know it. It will include, then, specific facts and individuals referred to—as Enos Enoch in *Giles* refers to Jesus Christ—and will also include the more general aspects of life as they are rendered intelligible for us by psychology and sociology. In terms of the book's historical frame of reference, we can distinguish between a simple sort of allusion to a specific person or event under another name—as in the case of Enos Enoch—and a more complicated sort of allegorical allusion, through which a character or event in *Giles* acquires a discernible reference to a corresponding person or event in actuality without becoming entirely governed by or explainable in terms of that actuality. Max Spielman, for example, has overtones of Einstein and Oppenheimer specifically, but points more dimly to other figures, mainly Jewish, who have shaped modern life: Freud and Jung certainly, Marx possibly. Spielman also operates in a more general frame of reference, where he figures as a stereotypical Jew, and as the kind of scientist who retains his full humanity—compared to Eierkopf, whose narrow scientism is inhumane. Spielman, of course, is not merely historical in his allegorical dimensions. Seen in terms of myth, he is George's Mentor, the Chiron who sees to his education in a secluded retreat, the Vergil who guides him as far as reason can. In Eierkopf, on the other hand, the general references—positivistic scientist—seem to outweigh any specific historical reference, and the ethical implications of his views are more evident than any mythic implications derived from his role in the narrative. Peter Greene and Leonid Andreich, also, are far too complex to refer to any single individual. Lucky Rexford, however, alludes strongly to John F. Kennedy in the specific frame of reference, but just as strongly represents a type: the type of the good administrator, by which Rexford is connected to fictional figures like Melville's Captain Vere or historical personages like Pontius Pilate. Rexford and George are set to re-enact the archetypal confrontation between Pilate and prophet when *Giles Goat-Boy* comes to an end.

This dimension of historical allusions also includes such non-personal aspects as the way New Tammany refers to the United States, Nikolay to Russia, and so on. This aspect of the allegory is actually quite superficial. It functions merely to remind us that this is *not* a literal transcript of Reality, and to cause us to re-see the countries referred to in the new perspective provided by the allegory. All of these specific references—the national and the personal—have received some attention from the book's first reviewers. In fact, for many of them, these constituted the entire allegorical aspect of the narrative. This is unfortunate, because this dimension is actually the least amusing and the least significant in the whole fabulation, taken by itself. Its main importance is that it leads toward the other dimensions. It is essential that we take Lucky Rexford, for example, beyond the Kennedy reference to the larger historical and mythic references his character and actions generate. While it is true that Rexford's equivocal brother, Stoker, can be seen as a Kennedy brother doing the necessary dirty work behind the scenes to keep his sibling in power, Stoker must also be seen as a force necessarily opposed to Rexford's, and vital to Rexford's definition of himself and to his functioning: a parallel to Bray's opposition to George Giles.

These opposed pairs lead to the book's philosophical dimension, where the question of the relationship and purpose of Good and Evil is a principal concern, along with the implications of this relationship in the sphere of practical ethics. Rexford and Stoker, like Eierkopf and Croaker, or George and Bray, become a variant on the oriental symbol for necessary opposition: the balanced curvilinear forms of Yang and Yin. This symbol in black and white is echoed by the pairs mentioned here, but is also specifically invoked by the narrator to describe the positions of George and Anastasia descending in the elevator to WESCAC's belly. The struggle and necessary opposition of sexual embrace, thus finally embodies this same law of necessary opposition which is the guiding principle of the university as George learns to see it. Creation involves the kind of necessary and fruitful conflict symbolized by Yang and Yin and manifested in the sexual embrace. That is why proctoscopy repeats hagiography, why the freshman on his first *mons Veneris* and God creating the universe are archetypally related; and why, in fact, ontogeny recapitulates cosmogeny. The dimension of historical allusion, rightly understood, leads inevitably to the dimensions of philosophy and myth.

Some other characters will also serve to illustrate this principle of inter-connectedness among the allegorical dimensions of this tale. I am not sure whether Dr. Sear has any specific reference or not. But his name, suggesting a brownish-yellow color (see his description on page 188) and the sound of the name, taken with the more general references to contemporary life that he seems to incorporate, suggest that he may be a composite caricature of Norman O. Brown and Timothy Leary. That decadent Freudianism which led to the cult of sensation and an infantile reveling in polymorphous perversity was frequently combined on our campuses with a solemnly ritualized indulgence in hallucinogens. Dr. Sear certainly points to the indulgence of the senses, whether or not he refers as well to the high priests usually invoked by the masters of such reveling. And Sear's wasting disease, along with the change in his attitude generated by the events of the narrative, point just as clearly to Barth's condemnation of these forms of self-indulgence.

Anastasia the heroine, like George the hero, alludes to no particular person. Her Russian-sounding name reminds us of Dostoevsky's Sonya, that prototype of the generous-minded whore. But Barth locates Anastasia's generosity inside her sexual psychology, rather than separate from it. She is generous with herself because she is a masochist, because she is a frigid, nymphomaniacal type—if we regard her from the angle of clinical psychology. Yet she loves, and this provides a different perspective on the same activities. Which is the true view? Leonid Andreich, Dostoevsky's countryman, sees her as a generous spirit. Peter Greene, sentimental in a more Anglo-Saxon way, must separate her into two women—the chaste Stacey and the promiscuous Lacey. Dr. Sear regards her as an object or instrument. For George, who is obliged to see through her, she becomes the *other* person, who in the intimacy of sexual embrace helps to complete and define him. And he urges her to return to Stoker for the same reason. He needs her, she him. Anastasia also figures in the mythic dimension of the tale as a Beatrice figure, providing the revelation which completes George's education in humanity. But this revelation has not been spiritualized, as in the *Commedia;* it is a matter of the flesh. This is not, I should emphasize, a mere parody or burlesque of Dante, any more than D. H. Lawrence's *The Man Who Died* is just a joke on Jesus. Lawrence and Barth reject equally the medieval notion of an ideal future life: What is the best man can achieve in the flesh?, they ask.

The sociological dimension of the narrative functions in ways similar to the historical and psychological. The university metaphor operates here more restrictively perhaps than in other areas, for the life presented frequently takes its outward forms from college mores. The various student protesters, the lovemaking of the Be-ist in the buckwheat and his Chickie, the considerations of teaching methods and their computerization, as well as the treatment of academic minds in the persons of librarians and philosophers—all these are somewhat narrowly focused; but even here, in the few pointedly academic passages in the book, some extra-curricular things are going on. Consider this excerpt from Harold Bray's orientation lecture:

> *"For those with eyes to see New Tammany abounds with voiceless admonitions to humility. Not for nothing are 'Staff' and 'Faculty' equally privileged, so that groundskeepers and dormitory-cooks are affluent as new professors; not for nothing does custom decree that our trustees be unlettered folk, and that our chancellor be selected not from the intelligentsia but by ballot, from the lower percentiles: tinkers and tillers and keepers of shops. For the same reason one observes among the faculty not graybeard scholars only, their cowls ablaze with exotic marks of honor, but men of the people: former business majors, public-relations clerks, gentle carpenters and husbandmen. It is fit that our libraries be more modest than our cow-barns, our cow-barns than our skating-rinks, our skating-rinks than our stadiums. Was not Enos Enoch, the Founder's Boy, by nature an outdoor type, a do-it-Himselfer who chose as his original Tutees the first dozen people He met; Who never took degree or published monograph or stood behind lectern, but gathered about him whoever would listen, in the buckwheat valleys or the wild rhododendron of the slope, and taught them by simple fictions and maxims proof against time, which are now graved in the limestone friezes of our halls?"* [pp. 403–4]

Harold Bray is being serious and straightforward here. And the state of affairs he depicts is a recognizable view of the land-grant university as we encounter it in the United States today. But the voice, as we listen to it, becomes more and more familiar, the final description of Enos Enoch reminding us of Bruce Barton's portrait of Jesus as a businessman. This is the rhetoric of hucksterism, designed by Barth to be ironically seen through. Earlier, Bray (the voice and name go together) has insisted, cynically, that the undergraduate's only task is to *"Get the Answers, by any means at all,"* adding that there is no such thing as cheating, because *"To cheat can only mean to Pass in ignorance of the Answers, which is impossible."* Bray's emphasis on ends rather than means leads to a view of the educational process in terms of the acquisition of a degree, rather than in terms of giving shape to a life. It is oriented to appearances only, and salvation is not in it. The clever peroration of the same speech, a prayer which shrewdly talks down to the audience by merging the religious and the collegiate perspectives, is tainted with the same "practical" ideology. The conflict between Bray and George, which has its mythic and philosophical dimensions, here takes its shape in terms of educational policy, as George listens helplessly, dazzled by Bray's rhetorical display. The professor's prayer, as Bray formulates it, is firmly grounded in the sociology of the academy, from backseat to podium. But its fundamental attitude is at odds with George's, and its notion of salvation is opposed to the one George learns to value. Consider the clever close of the prayer:

". . . Be keg and tap behind the bar of every order, that the brothers may chug-a-lug Thy lore, see Truth in the bottom of their steins, and find their heads a-crack with insight. Be with each co-ed at the evening's close: paw her with facts, make vain her protests against learning's advances; take her to Thy mind's backseat, strip off preconceptions, let down illusions, unharness her from error— that she may ere the curfew be infused with Knowledge. Above all, Sir, stand by me at my lectern; be chalk and notes to me; silence the mowers and stay the traffic that I may speak; awaken the drowsy, confound the heckler; bring him to naught who would digress when I would not, and would not when I would; take my words from his mouth who would take them from mine; save me from slip of tongue and lapse of memory, from twice-told joke and unzippered fly. Doctor of doctors, vouchsafe unto me examples of the Unexampled, words to speak the Wordless; be now and ever my visual aid, that upon the empty slate of these young minds I may inscribe, bold and squeaklessly, the Answers!" [pp. 408–9]

This is, in a way, every professor's prayer, but it also exposes the absurdity of the professorial position, especially the position of the lecturer who seeks not to stimulate thought but to inculcate lessons—to brainwash. The infusion of knowledge can be seen as a backseat operation, only because one thinks of knowledge as a thing to be infused. Bray is successful in the academic sphere, much more so than George, because he gives the students what they want. But answers dispensed in such a way never turn out to be The Answers; these can never be given, only found. Bray's backseat image must be contrasted with George and Anastasia's lovemaking. In the difference between the furtive pleasure of a petting party gone the limit and the full and fertile union of two committed lovers, can be seen the difference between Bray's answers and those George finds with so much difficulty.

As he listens to Bray's speech, George himself is not experienced enough to see quite through it. But he learns from it that such an educational process is not for him: "Matriculation yes, class-attendance no; I must wrest my answers like swede-roots by main strength from their holes." Later, after experience has educated him, he sees the whole problem of Answers differently. In his final years, when twice interviewed by the journalism majors, he has replied,

> yes, I was the Grand Tutor, for better or worse, there was no help for it; yes, I knew what studentdom was pleased to call "The Answer" though that term—indeed the whole proposition—was as misleading as any other (and thus as satisfactory), since what I "knew" neither "I" nor anyone else could "teach," not even to my own Tutees. [p. 703]

Thus the sociology of the academy is connected by metaphoric strands to the philosophical dimension of the book through the notion of man's search for answers. By seeing the search too academically, Bray trivializes it. By seeing the limitations of any instructional apparatus, and beyond them the conceptual limitations of the whole notion of Answers, George reminds us of the feebleness of academic guideposts in a mysterious cosmos. The pedagogue on his podium is somewhat between Founder and freshman, related to both.

The whole range of social and historical data in *Giles Goat-Boy* is impossible to trace without glossing virtually every page. Barth's employment of psychological perspectives similarly ranges from direct attention to the debauched Freudianism of Dr. Sear to the Jungian notion of archetypes which animates the cyclological theory of Max Spielman and the mythic structure of the story itself. And beyond this there is the vague but crucial dimension of psychological "rightness" in the responses of characters to situations. One might expect Anastasia, a creature fabricated from odds and ends of myth and psychoanalysis, to move as woodenly as Dr. Frankenstein's crude monster. But from her first siren-like appearance in the gorge to our last glimpse of her as the hard-eyed, nagging promoter of her kind of Gilesianism (keeping George at work on the Syllabus he does not want to record) she moves with a convincingness that is a tribute to Barth's perception of the way men and women actually behave. Effective allegory is never *merely* allegorical in its presentation of character and action.

Barth's insistence on "using stock figures, stereotype Jews and Negroes, just for fun" (as he said of *The Sot-Weed Factor*) is carried even further in *Giles Goat-Boy*. Spielman talks an absurd stage-Yiddish kind of English, for example, and the Peter Greene-Leonid Andreich duo are distinguished by equally blatant tricks of speech.

These thick crusts of type-characterization certainly obliterate any potential for profoundly developed individual personalities. Such characters are closer to pre-novelistic kinds of characterization than to the deep individuality of the realists. Their vitality is mainly a matter of accumulated facets and functions, rather than an accretion of telling idiosyncracies. Yet Barth has learned enough from the realists—as his first two novels show—to make stereotypes like Greene and Spielman behave with psychological rightness, even when their behavior is heavily burdened with mythic or ethical implications. The loss of each of Greene's eyes, for example, is a bizarre and improbable event, important in its ethical implications, comic and pathetic in its immediate narration, and presented with an emotional appropriateness that justifies the improbability of the actual event and the weight of allegory that it supports. Greene's innocent narration of the loss of his first eye (pp. 233–35) is too long to quote and to fine to summarize, but I offer it as evidence of the astonishing way Barth can move his narrative along, invent bizarrely symbolic events, and generate in the reader amusement, pity, sympathy, derision, and all manner of high and low thoughts—carrying conviction on all levels from the immediate to the remotest reaches of the allegory. Greene's whole narrative, the archetypal history of the American WASP, complete with triumphs and the neuroses appropriate to them, failures and the faults responsible for them, is a masterful job in the dimensions of history, sociology, and psychology. It is probably Barth's strongest performance in this dimension in *Giles Goat-Boy*. I urge the reader to see it for himself.

This fabulation has other aspects which must be explored, even at the expense of leaving much unsaid about its historical dimension. The story of George the Goat-Boy, which is at the heart of the narrative, itself points in two major directions: outward toward the mythic area which correlates all experience in terms of great archetypal patterns, and inward toward a single philosophical position which may be regarded as the moral of this great fabulation. (If I have understood rightly the meaning of Henry James's esthetic parable "The Figure in the Carpet," James sees the literary artist and the critic as totally separate in their functions. The writer must have his entire say about the meaning of his work through the work itself. Those words once said, he must remain mute and rely on his audience to understand. The critic functions simply as the spearhead of that audience. It is his job, above all, to understand, to see the figure in the carpet and perhaps even to expound it—a thing he can do and the author cannot, precisely because his words have no claim to authority beyond their more or less convincing exposition of the text. I accept James's view—as I understand it—and will try to present here an interpretation of the central figure in Barth's great Arabian rug.)

Such aspects of this figure as belong mainly to myth, I set aside for the moment, to touch on them later. The philosophical dimension of the narrative is my concern here. And in dealing with it I must confess that I am not a philosopher. I cannot go quite so far as Barth himself, who says, "I don't know anything about philosophy. I've never even studied it, much less learned it." But I do have only the slenderest experience of formal philosophical discipline. Barth's own disclaimer I am inclined to take with some grains of salt. He is certainly an amateur of philosophy, and a professional at dealing with philosophical materials in narrative form (an art that few professional philosophers master—see Iris Murdoch's criticisms of Sartre in her *Sartre, Romantic Rationalist,* for example).

The moral of this fabulation emerges from the events of George's life, and in particular from his dialectical progress in trying to work out a Grand Tutorial philosophy. I call this process dialectical because its three main phases—thesis, antithesis, and synthesis—are unmistakable. They are correlated in the narrative with George's three descents to WESCAC's belly, and all the actions and advice associated with those three descents.

George's first Grand Tutorial posture, which I call Thesis, is formulated on page 420 and repeated in the form of advice up through his first descent (pp. 507ff.). This view—"that the first reality of life on campus must be the clear distinction between Passage and Failure"—leads George to a posture of fundamentalist righteousness. The advice which follows from it, in every sphere from personal relations to the boundary dispute between the East and West Campuses, is disastrous. This Thesis, in fact, is so intolerable that we shall do well to look into the way it is fashioned. George first formulates it in a dispute with Stoker ("more in hopes of unsettling my adversary than of instructing either him or myself"). It is a debating point originally, a mere piece of rhetoric, but, as so often happens in life and in fiction, George becomes a prisoner of his rhetoric and finally begins to believe it; even though in this early phase of his acceptance of the Thesis he feels that there is "some murky valid *point* in Stoker's life, which I could not as yet assimilate." It is no wonder that, when he emerges from WESCAC's belly, he wears the mask of Harold Bray. Like Bray, he has not Answers to offer, but empty rhetoric. But unlike Bray, he believes his own formulations. And the reader, wishing George well and wanting him to succeed in his quest, inevitably grants George's Thesis some degree of empathetic assent, thus entangling himself emotionally and intellectually in the dialectical process.

George's second Grand Tutorial posture is the Antithesis of the first. He arrives at this Antithesis while munching pages of the original New Syllabus—Enos Enoch's Testament. The passage illustrates so well the convincingness with which Barth renders such a bizarre episode—the rightness of the attitudes involved, the solidity of the detail—that I quote it at some length. The incident takes place in Main Detention, where George is temporarily imprisoned. In the excitement after Leonid has attempted suicide, George is left with his demented mother, who used to feed him in this manner when he was a kid:

Crosslegged on the floor, black-shawled and -dressed, the New Syllabus on her lap as always, she flapped at me her thrice-weekly peanut-butter sandwich and crooned, "Come, Billy! Come, love! Come!"

Anxious as I was for my Nikolayan cellmate, I laid my head in her lap, pretended to hunger for the ritual food, and chewed the pages of antique wisdom she tore out for me, though they tasted sourly of much thumbing.

"Now then, love, let me see . . ." She adjusted her spectacles, brightly licked her forefingertip, and opened the book to a dogeared page. "People ought to use bookmarks!" she fussed. "And there's a verse marked, too. People *shouldn't* mark in library-books." Her tone softened. "Oh, but look what it is, Billikins: I'm *so* proud of the things you write!"

Such was her gentle madness, she thought me at once Billy Bocksfuss in the hemlock-grove, the baby GILES she'd bellied—and, alas, the long-commencèd Enos Enoch.

"*Passèd are the flunked,*" she read, very formally. "My, but that's a nice thought. Don't you think?"

I didn't answer, not alone because my tongue was peanut-buttered, but because those dark and famous words from the Seminar-on-the-Hill brought

me upright. As lightning might a man bewildered, they showed me in one
flash the source and nature of my fall, the way to the Way, and, so I
imagined, the far gold flicker of Commencement Gate. [p. 551]

This moment of illumination leads George to formulate his new
View that *"failure is passage."* This new answer, with its beguiling
paradoxes, proves finally to be as rhetorical as the first, though the
rhetoric this time is not that of fundamentalist preaching but of
semantic philosophizing. The absurd wordiness associated with this
posture is exposed not only by the horrible results of the new advice
founded on it (total anarchy, the dangerously insane set "free," etc.)
but directly in a passage in which George has a one-way conversation with the Living Sakhyan, with choral commentary from a group
of student protesters. This audience affects George much the same
way that Stoker did in the formulation of his original Thesis. He
shows off verbally for their appreciation. But the approval of these
lads is, in the full context, a criticism. Their readiness to "go limp" is
an outward sign of their spiritual flabbiness. All too easily they can
verbalize themselves into a state of wordless apathy based on their
knowledge of the arbitrariness of categories. Since everything is
arbitrary, nothing matters. Limpness is all.

The final absurdity of the limp view of life is exposed in George's
second descent to WESCAC's belly. There, called upon to designate
his sex, he reasons thus: "what were *male* and *female* if not the most
invidious of the false polarities into which undergraduate reason was
wont to sunder Truth." This denial of sex, already rendered absurd
by the floroscopic episode (quoted above, p. 77), is an attempt to
deny the principle of creation through division, upon which all
higher life is founded. These categories, which George would
abolish, are not merely WESCAC's, they are life's. In denying them,
George denies the very dialectical process he is involved in, denies
his separation from and attraction to Anastasia. If failure is passage,
then death is life.

George persists in this fatal view until, with the University
crumbling into chaos around him, he is confronted with the now
completely blinded Peter and Leonid, handcuffed together in
Stoker's sidecar. Stoker asks him, "So there they sit, Goat-Boy: two
blind bats! Are they passed or failed?" This question drives George

once again over the questions he has thought settled, fetching him "from apathy into the intensest concentration" of his life:

Indeed it was not I concentrating, but something concentrating upon me, taking me over, like the spasms of defecation or labor pains. Leonid Andreich and Peter Greene—their estates were rather the occasion than the object of this concentration, whose real substance was the fundamental contradictions of failure and passage. Truly now those paradoxes became paroxysms . . . That circular device on my assignment sheet—beginningless, endless, infinite equivalence . . . constricted my reason like a torture tool from the Age of Faith. Passage *was* Failure, and Failure Passage; yet Passage was Passage, Failure Failure! Equally true, none was the Answer; the two were not different, neither were they the same; and *true* and *false*, and *same* and *different*—Unspeakable! Unnamable! Unimaginable! Surely my mind must crack! [pp. 649–50]

At this moment, as George strains to face and subdue the questions he has dodged around with rhetorical gimmicks, the tension mounts and Stoker shouts a warning to his prisoners:

"Don't try to get loose!" No doubt it was Leonid Stoker warned, but his words struck my heart, and I gave myself up utterly to that which bound, possessed, and bore me. I let go, I let all go; relief went through me like a purge. And as if in signal of my freedom, over the reaches of the campus the bells of Tower Clock suddenly rang out, somehow unjammed: their first full striking since the day I'd passed through Scrapegoat Grate. As I listened astonished, the strokes mounted—*one, two, three, four*—each bringing from my pressèd eyes the only tears they'd spilled since a fateful late June morn many terms past, out in the barns. *Sol, la, ti,* each a tone higher than its predecessor, unbinding, releasing me—then *do:* my eyes were opened; I was delivered. [pp. 650–51]

The last note, musically the octave-completing *do,* stands also for the simple imperative urging action: do!

This is Synthesis. Passage and failure are distinct but interdependent. They define one another and are as necessary as north and south or male and female to the functioning of the universe. Action by each individual, appropriate to himself and his situation, discovered by the dialectic process of trial and error, is the only way to salvation. Thus there are no formulas. The *Revised New Syllabus* is not a catechism, but the story of one man's heroic attempt to work out his own life and find his own truth. The philosophical dimension of this book emphasizes the isolation of the individual and the loneliness of his way. We are left finally without a moral. We are given only the story of a life to imitate, with the qualification that to imitate it we must diverge from it, since George's life is his; ours, ours. But because this life itself resembles other lives that we know through fiction and history, we know that we shall have companions in our loneliness. What philosophy sunders, myth unites, and philosophy is only one facet of this fabulation.

The moral evaporates in our hands; the story remains with us. And since the moral urges the advantages of action over ratiocination, this is appropriate enough. Actually, the philosophical dimension of the narrative functions mainly as a story within the larger story of George's adventures. It is appropriately concerned with the academic side of George's experience—from matriculation to graduation. It is an intellectual episode in a sequence of more physical adventures to which it is connected in many ways—most importantly as the pivotal achievement which releases George from intellectual concerns so that he can complete his other tasks. In effect, by defining "himself," George prepares for true recognition of the "other" in Anastasia. Their union in WESCAC's belly is the physical ratification of George's intellectual achievement. This act of love, and the idyllic interlude at the farm which follows it, end the erotic romance plot of the narrative. This consummation in turn frees George for his final work. Having found himself and won the lady, he must slay the dragon. That is, he must drive Harold Bray off the face of the campus. Bray is his work, as necessary to his completion in the realm of action as Anastasia is to his personal completion.

In the world of this book there are no loose ends, because *its* creator is not a realist. The world we live in is another matter. Though we can learn from the world of George and Anastasia, we cannot enter that world. It is resolutely fictional—the world of the fabulator. Barth insists on the non-reality of his world in many ways, of which I wish to point out just one, before turning to a consideration of the way the mythic and philosophical dimensions of the narrative are interrelated. The eposode I have in mind occurs on George's last trip to the Belfry. After refusing to answer the scholars' request for a gloss on the crucial *lacuna* in the Founder's Scroll ("*Flunkèd who would Pass* or *Passèd are the Flunked*"), George approaches a librarian to ask if there is a way up beside the guarded elevator:

The pimpled maid, thin and udderless as Mrs. Rexford but infinitely less prepossessing, looked over her spectacles from the large novel she was involved in and said with careful clarity—as if that question, from a fleecèd goat-boy at just that moment were exactly what she'd expected—"Yes. A stairway goes up to the Clockworks from this floor. You may enter it through the little door behind me."

All the while she marked with her finger her place in the book, to which she returned at once upon delivering her line. Mild, undistinguished creature, never seen before or since, whose homely face I forgot in two seconds; whose name, if she bore one, I never knew; whose history and fate, if any she had, must be *lacunae* till the end of the terms of my life's story—Passage be yours, for that in your moment of my time you did announce, clearly as from a written text, your modest information. Simple answer to a simple question, but lacking which this tale were as truncate as the Founder's Scroll, an endless fragment!

"*-less fragment,*" I thought I heard her murmur as I stooped through the little door she'd pointed out. I paused and frowned; but though her lips moved on, as did her finger across the page, her words were drowned by the bells of Tower Clock. [p. 666]

This girl "delivers her line" so perfectly because she is reading it out of the book in front of her. In fact she is reading this particular book: *Giles Goat-Boy*. She is where she is; the staircase is where it is; everything in this tale is where it is because it was made that way by its fabricator. This "tale" would indeed be "truncate" if she and her staircase were not there. They are in place because Barth is a fabulator, and he is gently and wittily reminding us of that, reminding us that our world and this one are different, different. But at the same time he is working toward mythic connections through which we can perceive the dimensions of our own lives that transcend the individual and personal to partake of something universal.

The mythic dimension of *Giles Goat-Boy* has necessarily impinged on every aspect of my discussion in this chapter. Yet more remains to be done with it than I can do. It would be possible to trace through all the Oedipal allusions in the book, from the exuberant parody, *Taliped Decanus*, through the Freudian implications of the myth as they relate to George's own behavior or that of the other central characters, to its connection with the theme of blindness and vision in the tale. Such a glossing would reveal the astonishing interconnectedness of the narrative itself, and at the same time would illuminate one passage of connection between the mythic and the experiential worlds. Similarly, one could trace through the Dantesque, the Quixotic, the Ulyssean, the Mosaic allusions, showing how the human truth embodied in these myths is reinvigorated by the new combinations of them assembled in this chronicle of heroic action. All this, given world enough and time, one could do. But I believe the alert reader picks up many of these threads without assistance, some consciously and others subliminally, so that such glossing is not really necessary. And besides, to take the mythography of *Giles Goat-Boy* in too heavy a way would do the story violence. Barth's vision, like Joyce's, holds myth and comedy in a precarious balance. There are reasons beyond any question of affinity or influence why two such gifted writers treat mythic materials comically; and before returning for a last look at myth and philosophy in *Giles Goat-Boy*, I should like to consider these reasons, since they bear importantly on the whole matter of fabulation as a modern mode of fiction.

The mythic and archetypal dimension of literature, fundamental as it is, has only recently begun to be understood. That is, a criticism and understanding of fiction based upon an awareness of the archetypal patterns of mythology and their relationship to the human psyche is a fairly recent development. As a result of this new understanding and the proliferation of literary studies based upon it, some influential critics have been ready to proclaim a new age of myth as the most likely literary development of the immediate future. But this, it seems to me, is the least likely of literary developments. Once so much is known *about* myths and archetypes, they can no longer be used innocently. Even their connection to the unconscious finally becomes attenuated as the mythic materials are used more consciously. All symbols become allegorical to the extent that we understand them. Thus the really perceptive writer is not merely conscious that he is using mythic materials: He is conscious that he is using them consciously. He *knows,* finally, that he is allegorizing. Such a writer, aware of the nature of categories, is not likely to believe that his own mythic lenses really capture the truth. Thus his use of myth will inevitably partake of the comic.

Every one of the fabulators considered here can be called a comic writer, even John Hawkes, whose vision is the darkest. Fabulation, then, seems to partake inevitably of the comic. It derives, I would suggest, from the fabulator's awareness of the limits of fabulation. He knows too much—that is the modern writer's predicament, and that is precisely what prevents his perspective from being seriously mythic. This quotation from Barth's interview in *Wisconsin Studies* bears on the point I am trying to make:

Somebody told me I must have had in mind Lord Raglan's twenty-five prerequisites for ritual heroes when I created the character of Ebenezer Cooke in *The Sot-Weed Factor*. I hadn't read Raglan so I bought *The Hero*, and Ebenezer scored on twenty-three of the twenty-five, which is higher than anybody else except Oedipus. If I hadn't lied about Ebenezer's grave, I would have scored twenty-four. Nobody knows where the real chap is buried; I made up a grave for Ebenezer because I wanted to write his epitaph. Well, subsequently I got excited over Raglan and Joseph Campbell, who may be a crank for all I know or care, and I really haven't been able to get that business off my mind—the tradition of the wandering hero. The only way I could use it would be to make it comic, and there will be some of that in *Giles Goat-Boy*.

There is, of course, more than a little of "that" in *Giles Goat-Boy*. From George's mysterious birth to his anticipated disappearance, his life falls into Lord Raglan's pattern, which is to say into the great patterns of primitive myth and the major literary treatments of myth. And so, up to a point, do all our lives. Insofar as Spielman's Law is valid in the experiential world, all our lives have archetypal significance: myth tells us that we are all part of a great story. But the fabulators, so clearly aware of the difference between fact and fiction, are unwilling to accept the mythic view of life as completely valid. Against this view they balance one which I am calling the philosophical, which tells us that every man is unique, alone, poised over chaos. In *Giles Goat-Boy*, for example, the great computer WESCAC functions mythically as the father-god engaged in the archetypal struggle with the son who seeks to displace him. But George's final view specifically repudiates this mythic perspective on his father: "I had been wrong, I said, to think it Troll. Black cap and gown of naked Truth, it screened from the general eye what only a few, Truth's lovers and tutees, might look on bare and not be blinded" (p. 676). Here the philosophical view dominates. But myth prevails in George's struggle with Bray, his proper adversary. Throughout *Giles Goat-Boy* and throughout modern fabulation, these two perspectives on experience engage like Yang and Yin in equal struggle for control. This mighty tension is at the heart of Barth's great fabulation and all the rest. Just as the realistic novel was rooted in the conflict between the individual and society, fabulation springs from the collision between the philosophical and mythic perspectives on the meaning and value of existence, with their opposed dogmas of struggle and acquiescence. If existence *is* mythic, then man may accept his role with equanimity. If not, then he must struggle through part after part trying to create one uniquely his own. Barth and the other fabulators build on the interinanimation of these two views. All our assignment sheets, they tell us, are stamped like George's: Pass All/Fail All.

Metafiction

The Nature of Experimental Fiction

> Many of the so-called anti-novels are really
> metafictions.   —W. H. Gass

> And it is above all to the need for new
> modes of perception and fictional forms
> able to contain them that I, barber's basin
> on my head, address these stories.
>   —Robert Coover

> . . . the sentence itself is a man-made ob-
> ject, not the one we wanted of course, but
> still a construction of man, a structure to be
> treasured for its weakness, as opposed to
> the strength of stones. . .
>   —Donald Barthelme

> We tend to think of experiments as cold
> exercises in technique. My feeling about
> technique in art is that it has about the
> same value as technique in lovemaking.
> That is to say, heartfelt ineptitude has its
> appeal and so does heartless skill; but what
> you want is passionate virtuosity.
>   —John Barth

To approach the nature of contemporary experimental fiction, to understand why and how it is experimental, we must first adopt an appropriate view of the whole order of fiction and its relation to the conditions of being in which we find ourselves. Thus I must begin this consideration of experimental fiction with what may seem an over-elaborate discussion of fictional theory, and I ask the reader interested mainly in specifics to bear with me. In this discussion I will be trying not so much to present a new and startling view of fiction as to organize a group of assumptions which seem to inform much modern fiction and much of the fiction of the past as well. Once organized, these assumptions should make it possible to "place" certain fictional and critical activities so as to understand better both their capabilities and their limitations.

One assumption I must make is that both the conditions of being and the order of fiction partake of a duality which distinguishes existence from essence. My notion of fiction is incomplete without a concept of essential values, and so is my notion of life. Like many modern novelists—in fact, like most poets and artists in Western culture, ancient and modern—I am something of a Platonist. One other assumption necessary to the view I am going to present is that the order of fiction somehow reflects the conditions of being which make man what he is. And if this be Aristotelianism, I intend to make the most of it. These conditions of being, both existential and essential, are reflected in all human activity, especially in the human use of language for esthetic ends, as in the making of fictions. Imagine, then, the conditions of being, divided into existence and essence, along with the order of fiction, similarly divided. This simple scheme can be displayed in a simple diagram:

Fiction	Being
forms	existence
ideas	essence

Figure 1

The forms of fiction and the behavioral patterns of human existence both exist in time, above the horizontal line in the diagram. All human actions take place in time, in existence, yet these actions are tied to the essential nature of man, which is unchanging or changing so slowly as to make no difference to men caught up in time. Forms of behavior change, but man does not, without becoming more or less than man, angel or ape, superman or beast. Forms of fiction change too, but the ideas of fiction are an aspect of the essence of man, and will not change until the conditions of being a man change. The ideas of fiction are those essential qualities which define and characterize it. They are aspects of the essence of being human. To the extent that fiction fills a human need in all cultures, at all times, it is governed by these ideas. But the ideas themselves, like the causes of events in nature, always retreat beyond the range of our analytical instruments.

   Both the forms of existence and the forms of fiction are most
satisfying when they are in harmony with their essential qualities.
But because these forms exist in time, they cannot persist unchanged
without losing their harmonious relationship to the essence of being
and the ideas of fiction. In the world of existence, we see how social
and political modes of behavior lose their vitality in time as they
persist to a point where, instead of connecting man to the roots of his
being, they cut him off from this deep reality. All revolutionary
crises, including the present one, can be seen as caused by the
profound malaise that attacks men when the forms of human behavior lose touch with the essence of human nature. It is similar with
fiction. Forms atrophy and lose touch with the vital ideas of fiction.
Originality in fiction, rightly understood, is the successful attempt to
find new forms that are capable of tapping once again the sources of
fictional vitality. Because, as John Barth has observed, both time and
history "apparently" are real, it is only by being original that we can
establish a harmonious relationship with the origins of our being.
   Now every individual work of fiction takes its place in the whole
body of fictional forms designated by the upper left-hand quadrant
in Figure 1. Among all these works we can trace the various diachronic relationships of literary genres as they evolve in time, and the
synchronic relations of literary modes as they exist across time. As a
way of reducing all these relationships to manageable order, I propose that we see the various emphases that fiction allows as reflections of the two aspects of fiction and the two aspects of being
already described. Diagrammatically this could be represented by
subdividing the whole body of fictional forms (the upper left-hand
quadrant of Figure 1) into four subquadrants, in this manner:

fiction of forms (romance)	fiction of existence (novel)
fiction of ideas (myth)	fiction of essence (allegory)

Figure 2

Most significant works of fiction attend to all four of these dimensions of fictional form, though they may select an emphasis among them. But for convenience and clarity I will begin this discussion by speaking as if individual works existed to define each of these four fictional categories.

The fiction of ideas needs to be discussed first because the terminology is misleading on this point. By fiction of ideas in this system is meant not the "novel of ideas" or some such thing, but that fiction which is most directly animated by the essential ideas of fiction. The fiction of ideas is mythic fiction as we find it in folktales, where fiction springs most directly from human deeds and desires. In mythic fiction the ideas of fiction are most obviously in control, are closest to the surface, where, among other things, they can be studied by the analytical instruments of self-conscious ages that can no longer produce myths precisely because of the increase in consciousness that has come with time. Existing in time, the history of fiction shows a continual movement away from the pure expression of fictional ideas. Which brings us to the next dimension, the fiction of forms.

The fiction of forms is fiction that imitates other fiction. After the first myth, all fiction became imitative in this sense and remains so. The history of the form he works in lies between every writer and the pure ideas of fiction. It is his legacy, his opportunity, and his problem. The fiction of forms at one level simply accepts the legacy and repeats the form bequeathed it, satisfying an audience that wants this familiarity. But the movement of time carries such derivative forms further and further from the ideas of fiction until they atrophy and decay. At another level, the fiction of forms is aware of the problem of imitating the forms of the past and seeks to deal with it by elaboration, by developing and extending the implications of the form. This process in time follows an inexorable curve to the point where elaboration reaches its most efficient extension, where it reaches the limits of tolerable complexity. Sometimes a form like euphuistic fiction or the romances of the Scudéry family may carry a particular audience beyond what later eras will find to be a tolerable complexity. Some of our most cherished modern works may share this fate. The fiction of forms is usually labeled "romance" in English criticism, quite properly, for the distinguishing characteristic of romance is that it concentrates on the elaboration of previous fictions.

There is also a dimension of the fiction of forms which is aware of the problem of literary legacy and chooses the opposite response to elaboration. This is the surgical response of parody. But parody exists in a parasitic relationship to romance. It feeds off the organism it attacks and precipitates their mutual destruction. From this decay new growth may spring. But all of the forms of fiction, existing in time, are bound to decay, leaving behind the noble ruins of certain great individual works to excite the admiration and envy of the future—to the extent that the future can climb backward down the ladder of history and understand the past.

The fiction of existence seeks to imitate not the forms of fiction but the forms of human behavior. It is mimetic in the sense that Erich Auerbach has given to the term "mimesis." It seeks to "represent reality." But "reality" for the fiction of existence is a behavioristically observable reality. This behavioral fiction is a report on manners, customs, institutions, habits. It differs from history only, as Henry Fielding (and Aristotle) insisted, in that its truth is general and typical, rather than factual and unique. The most typical form of behavioral fiction is the realistic novel (and henceforth in this discussion the term "novel" will imply a behavioristic realism). The novel is doubly involved in time: as fiction in the evolution of fictional forms, and as a report on changing patterns of behavior. In a sense, the continual development of its material offers it a solution to the problem of formal change. If it succeeds in capturing changes in behavior, it will have succeeded in changing its form: discovery will have created its appropriate technique. But as Mark Schorer has persuasively argued, it may be rather that new techniques in fiction enable new discoveries about human behavior to be made. So the great formal problem remains, even for behavioristic fiction. A further problem for the novel lies in the non-fictional adjuncts to its apprehension of behavior. How does the novelist perceive his reality? In general, he perceives it with the aid of non-fictional systems of apprehension and evaluation. Notions like the control of personality by angels and devils, by humors in the body, by abstract "ruling passions," by phrenological or physiognomical characteristics, by hereditary gifts and failings, by environmental shapings and twistings, by psychological needs—all these have been indispensable to the novelist as ways of making human behavior manageable. Tracing the history of the novel, we trace the shift from religious perspectives on behavior through pseudo-scientific views toward a behavioral science which is perhaps close to achievement at last. If the study of human behavior should become truly scientific, it might limit the activities of novelists drastically. Currently, this danger seems to be driving writers of fiction away from behaviorism into other dimensions of narrative art, one of which is the fiction of essence.

The fiction of essence is concerned with the deep structure of being, just as the fiction of behavior is concerned with its surface structure. One route from behavior to essence is via depth psychology, and many novelists have taken that route, but there is some doubt whether it gets to the heart of the matter. The fiction of essence is characterized by an act of faith, by a leap beyond behavior toward ultimate values. This is a leap from behavioral realism to what Auerbach has called the "figural realism" of Dante. In effect, it is the distinguishing characteristic of allegorical fiction. This is not to be confused with the petty allegory by which a character with a fictional name is used to point coyly at a historical personage with another. The fiction of essence is that allegory which probes and develops metaphysical questions and ideals. It is concerned most with ethical ideas and absolutes of value, where behavioral fiction emphasizes the relative values of action in practice. One of the great strengths of fiction has been its ability to be both allegorical and behavioral, to test ideals by giving them behavioristic embodiment, and to test conduct against the ideals of being. The problems of the allegorist lie partly in his management of the complex interrelations among the formal, behavioral, and essential dimensions of his art. They lie also, however, in his dependence on theological and philosophical systems of thought as approaches to the essence of being. These systems, of course, exist in time, and tend in time to lose whatever they may have captured of the essence of being.

The current retreat of philosophy into existential and behavioral postures presents special problems for the allegorist. Existentialism, for instance, in one of its aspects seeks to become purely active and situational. It is a theory which argues against theory. Thus the existential allegorist must often give us narratives of characters who make a discovery which cannot be communicated. They discover the truth, and in discovering it find that it is true for them only. Thus the best of contemporary allegorists (writers like Barth, Fowles, and Iris

Murdoch—who work closely with existentialist ideas) often find themselves moving through the fiction of essence and back into the fiction of forms, producing, instead of romances which turn into allegories, allegories which turn into romances. The allegorist struggles with fictional form, trying to make it express ultimate truth, just as the realist tries to make it capture behavioral truth. In a symposium published in *Novel* (Spring, 1970), John Barth compared both of these struggles to the myth of Proteus: "The depressing thing about the myth is that he turns back into Proteus again. If the shifting of forms is thought of [in terms of] literary forms, what's particularly depressing is that he doesn't talk until he's turned back into old Proteus again, the thing that you seized in the first place, a dead end in a way." It is the ideas of fiction which render Proteus mute except in his own fictional form. The myth of Proteus symbolizes the unchanging laws that govern that myth and all others, the ideas which exert their power whenever man seeks to create in fictional form.

The fourfold perspective on fiction presented here is intended to clarify certain aspects of fictional creation. It should also serve to clarify the relationship between certain kinds of criticism and certain kinds of fiction. We can see the criticism of fiction as having four dimensions which correspond to the four dimensions of fiction in a way described by Figure 3:

formal criticism	behavioral criticism
structural criticism	philosophical criticism

Figure 3

Both formal criticism and structural criticism are concerned with the way fiction works. But structural criticism is directed toward the essential ideas of fiction. It treats the individual works as instances of the ideas or principles that inform them. Both the French Structuralists of today and the Russian Formalists of yesterday may be called structural critics in this sense. (Which makes, alas, for an unfortunate terminological overlap.) Because of their structural

orientation, some of the most successful and influential work of the
Russian Formalists has been based on myths and folktales, where the
ideas of fiction exist in their purest form. Propp's *Morphology of the
Folk Tale* is typical of the achievement of structural criticism in
general. Formal criticism is closely related to structural criticism, but
it is more concerned with individual works than with the ideas that
inform them. Formal criticism is also concerned with the formal
relationships among literary works as they exist in time. Where the
structuralist looks for the ideas common to all fiction, as they relate to
the human use of language and to other human activities, the formalist looks for the way fictional forms change in time to create
generic patterns within which individual works take shape. The
structuralist is mainly synchronic in his orientation; the formalist is
diachronic. The ends of formal criticism are esthetic: what the artist
has achieved in a particular work. The ends of structural criticism are
scientific: the laws of fictional construction as they reveal themselves
in many works. The self-conscious work which shows its awareness
of fictional form by elaboration or parody is the particular delight of
the formal critic: Fielding or Sterne, James or Joyce. This esthetically
oriented criticism works best with esthetically oriented fiction—
which is to say romance and anti-romance.

   The formal and structural critics are concerned to explain how
fiction works. The behavioral and philosophical critics are more
interested in interpreting what fiction means. The behavioral critic in
particular comes to fiction with strong convictions about the nature
of existence. The rigid values of critics as different as Lukács and
Leavis are characteristic of the social consciousness of behavioral
criticism. The behavioral critic pronounces true those works which
agree with his ideological perspective and damns as false those
which see behavior differently or emphasize some dimension of
fiction other than behavior. More than other literary critics, the
behaviorists are in the world and aware of the world. The great
behavioral critics have all been, in the broadest sense of the word,
socialists. Marxist, Liberal, or Tory Radical, they have tended to see
society as evolving in time toward a better life for all men, and have
looked at literature in terms of its contribution to that evolution.

   One would expect philosophical critics to be more detached and
contemplative than the behaviorists, but it would be more correct to
say that such philosophical criticism as we have had in recent years

has been merely feeble and derivative. Too often our philosophical critics have been concerned with exegesis alone. W. H. Gass has made the case against this sort of criticism in an essay called "Philosophy and the Form of Fiction":

> Still, the philosophical analysis of fiction has scarcely taken its first steps. Philosophers continue to interpret novels as if they were philosophies themselves, platforms to speak from, middens from which may be scratched important messages for mankind; they have predictably looked for content, not form, they have regarded fictions as ways of viewing reality and not as additions to it. There are many ways of refusing experience. This is one of them.

Yet the kind of truly philosophical criticism Gass calls for in this essay does in fact exist—in the work of the "Geneva" critics, sometimes called phenomenological critics or "critics of consciousness." Their work parallels that of the structuralists, but is quite distinct from it. As the structuralist looks for the ideas that inform fictional structure and the laws that preside over the order of fiction, the critic of consciousness looks for the essential values that inhere in the experience of fiction. Clearly these two activities are connected, and language is the bridge that connects them. At any rate, it is fair to say that in recent years the most vigorous and important work in the criticism of fiction, which used to be done by formal and behavioral critics, has passed into the hands of structural and philosophical critics. The fact that much of this work has been done in French is perhaps to the shame of British and American criticism. But at the same time it must be said that criticism seems to have stifled fiction in France, while in the chaos and confusion of American critical thought a vigorous new fiction has developed.

The Range of Metafiction: Barth, Barthelme, Coover, Gass

Metafiction assimilates all the perspectives of criticism into the fictional process itself. It may emphasize structural, formal, behavioral, or philosophical qualities, but most writers of metafiction are thoroughly aware of all these possibilities and are likely to have experimented with all of them. In the following pages I will be considering four works of metafiction by four American writers: John Barth's *Lost in the Funhouse,* Donald Barthelme's *City Life,* Robert Coover's *Pricksongs and Descants,* and W. H. Gass's *In the Heart of the Heart of the Country.* All four of these books are collections of short pieces. This is not merely a matter of symmetry. When extended, metafiction must either lapse into a more fundamental mode of fiction or risk losing all fictional interest in order to maintain its intellectual perspectives. The ideas that govern fiction assert themselves more powerfully in direct proportion to the length of a fictional work. Metafiction, then, tends toward brevity because it attempts, among other things, to assault or transcend the laws of fiction—an undertaking which can only be achieved from within fictional form.

The four works chosen here are impressive in themselves: the products of active intelligence grappling with the problems of living and writing in the second half of the twentieth century. Any one of them might provide fruit for extended explication—and probably will. But that is not my intention here. I will do justice to no author, no book, not even any single story. Rather, I will use these four books to illustrate the range and vigor of contemporary metafiction, and the depth of the problems confronted by it. Each of the four books, taken as a whole, emphasizes one aspect of metafiction which may be related to one of the aspects of fiction and criticism as I presented them in the previous essay. This emphasis is displayed diagrammatically in Figure 4.

Lost in the Funhouse (formal)	*City Life* (behavioral)
Pricksongs and Descants (structural)	*In the Heart of the Heart of the Country* (philosophical)

Figure 4

These four books, of course, do not fit into the four categories described above like pigeons into pigeonholes. Their metafictional resourcefulness alone would ensure that. But each one does take a distinct direction, which can be designated initially and tentatively by the above diagram. The special emphasis of each work can be seen even in its title and the selection and arrangement of the pieces included. *City Life,* for instance, *sounds* behavioral—a book about life in the city. And in a sense that is exactly what the book is, slices of life, but not cut in the old naturalistic way of behavioral fiction. Oh no. Still, the book is dominated by a Dadaist impulse to make funny art-objects out of found pieces of junk. The found pieces in this case are mainly bits of intellectual and psychological debris, worn and battered fragments of old insights and frustrations, "tastefully" arranged like a toilet-rim halo perched jauntily on a bust of Freud.

In the Heart of the Heart of the Country sounds behavioral, too, only directed toward midwestern farms and villages rather than toward the urban east. But there is one heart too many in that title, which gives us pause. Gass *is* interested in behavior, but he is always trying to see through it, philosophically, to an essential order behind it: "the quantity in the action, the principle in the thing"—the heart of the heart. He rightly says that Barthelme "has managed to place himself in the center of modern consciousness," and Barthelme has done so by adopting a relentlessly ironic vision which will tolerate no notion of essences, as he explains, ironically, in "Kierkegaard Unfair to Schlegel." But there is a difference between the center of consciousness and the heart of the heart. The woman who narrates in "Order of Insects" speaks with Gass's voice:

I had always thought that love knew nothing of order and that life itself was turmoil and confusion. Let us leap, let us shout! I have leaped, and to my shame I have wrestled. But this bug that I hold in my hand and know to be

dead is beautiful, and there is a fierce joy in its composition that beggars
every other, for its joy is the joy of stone, and it lives in its tomb like a lion.

I don't know which is more surprising: to find such order in a roach or
such ideas in a woman. [p. 170]

The difference between the approaches of Gass and Barthelme to
the phenomena of behavior appear clearly when we see them both
looking at the same object, like a basketball:

Why do they always applaud the man who makes the shot?
Why don't they applaud the ball?
It is the ball that actually goes into the net.
The man doesn't go into the net.
Never have I seen a man going into the net. [*City Life*, p. 54]

Only the ball moves serenely through this dazzling din. Obedient to law it
scarcely speaks but caroms quietly and lives at peace. [*In the Heart*, p. 206]

Barthelme's ironic voice, with its remorseless Dick-and-Jane rhythms
and its equally remorseless pseudo-logic, moves toward the absurdity of existence by generating a ridiculous vision of a man going
through the net—man as object. Gass, using pronounced alliteration
in a sentence which divides into an assonant iambic couplet—

Obedient to law it scarcely speaks
But caroms quietly and lives at peace—

works in the opposite direction, raising the object to the level of
sentient, harmonious life. Gass reaches for the poetic order behind
prose. Barthelme exposes the banality of prosaic statement. The two
writers share a view of modern behavior, but Gass's vision is enabled
by his metaphysical idea of order, while Barthelme includes any idea
of a metaphysical order within the irony of his behavioral perspective.

In "Brain Damage" Barthelme's voice mentions the "brain damage
caused by art. I could describe it better if I weren't afflicted with it."
And concludes with the parodic vision of brain damage falling like
the snow that descends on the living and the dead in the last paragraph of another volume of stories of city life—Joyce's *Dubliners:*

And there is brain damage in Arizona, and brain damage in Maine, and
little towns in Idaho are in the grip of it, and my blue heaven is black with it,
brain damage covering everything like an unbreakable lease—

Skiing along on the soft surface of brain damage, never to sink, because we
don't understand the danger— [*City Life*, p. 146]

This is not simply a parody of Joyce and the quasi-religious perspective of the end of "The Dead." It is also a measure of how far we have come since *Dubliners*. This snow-like fallout of brain damage is not just a reminder of the pollution of our physical atmosphere, it is the crust of phenomenal existence which has covered our mental landscape, cutting us off from the essence of our being, afflicting even the artists. For Barthelme, man has become a phenomenon among phenomena. "WHAT RECOURSE?" ask the bold-type headlines of "Brain Damage." In "Kierkegaard Unfair to Schlegel" Q and A discuss two possibilities, which are the two principal resources of metafiction: fantasy and irony.

Q: That's a very common fantasy.
A: All my fantasies are extremely ordinary.
Q: Does it give you pleasure?
A: A poor . . . A rather unsatisfactory. . . . [p. 84]

A: But I love my irony.
Q: Does it give you pleasure?
A: A poor . . . A rather unsatisfactory. . . . [p. 92]

What recourse, indeed, for those gripped by phenomenological brain damage? They are beyond good and evil, beyond being, barely existing, snowed under.

For Gass, this phenomenological despair is a tempting refuge which he cannot quite accept: "I would rather it were the weather that was to blame for what I am and what my friends and neighbors are—we who live here in the heart of the country. Better the weather, the wind, the pale dying snow . . . the snow—why not the snow?" (*In the Heart*, p. 191) But it is not the snow, the weather. Though the speaker tries to convince himself that "body equals being, and if your weight goes down you are the less," at the end of the title story (and of the volume) he is straining to hear "through the boughs of falling snow" the "twisted and metallic strains of a tune" that may or may not be "Joy to the World." Gass's world is full of snow, but there is always something active within it, like the mysterious killer in the black stocking-cap who haunts the blizzard in "The Pedersen Kid." Gass's snow is not a crust that will support a man, but a curtain that man must penetrate. It is not phenomenal, but apocalyptic: "He was in the thick snow now. More was coming. More was blowing down. He was in it now and could go on and he could come through it because he had before. Maybe he belonged in the snow. Maybe he lived there, like a fish does in a lake. Spring didn't have anything like him" (p. 72). After the purgation of this snowborne violence, there may be a new life, peace, even joy:

It was pleasant not to have to stamp the snow off my boots, and the fire was speaking pleasantly and the kettle was sounding softly. There was no need for me to grieve. I had been the brave one and now I was free. The snow would keep me. I would bury pa and the Pedersens and Hans and even ma if I wanted to bother. I hadn't wanted to come but now I didn't mind. The kid and me, we'd done brave things well worth remembering. The way that fellow had come so mysteriously through the snow and done us such a glorious turn—well it made me think how I was told to feel in church. The winter time had finally got them all, and I really did hope the kid was as warm as I was now, warm inside and out, burning up, inside and out, with joy. [pp. 78–79]

In *Pricksongs and Descants* and *Lost in the Funhouse* Coover and Barth are less directly concerned with the conditions of being than are Gass and Barthelme, and more immediately interested in the order of fiction itself. This difference of emphasis is proclaimed in the titles of the works and developed in each collection. Both descants and pricksongs are contrapuntal music. They run counter to the *cantus firmus* of behavior. But to run counter is not to run free. These songs must speak to us finally about reality, however roundabout their approach. There are also some puns in Coover's title which can be looked at later. The title of Barth's *Lost in the Funhouse* is taken from a story about a boy who "actually" gets lost in a "real" funhouse. But the story is also about the difficulty of writing a story about that "real" experience, as the book is about the difficulty of the writer whose position in existence is distorted by his desire to find fictional equivalents for the conditions of being. For Barth, nature and Homer have a fearful symmetry—and they had it especially for Homer, he would add. "For whom is the funhouse fun? Perhaps for lovers." But not for artists and thinkers who alternate between making pricksongs and shouting, Stop the music. Trapped in life like a boy lost in a funhouse, this kind of man—intellectual man—seeks to maintain control over his being by *imagining* that he is lost in a funhouse, like Sartre's waiter in *Being and Nothingness* who seeks to control the problem of being a waiter by pretending to be a waiter. Barth's Ambrose is lost in a funhouse, so he "pretends that it is not so bad after all in the funhouse." The boy Ambrose, figure of thinking man, treats the problem of being lost in a "real" funhouse by constructing an imaginary one:

How long will it last? He envisions a truly astonishing funhouse, incredibly complex yet utterly controlled from a great central switchboard like the console of a pipe organ. Nobody had enough imagination. He could design such a place himself, wiring and all, and he's only thirteen years old. He would be its operator: panel lights would show what was up in every cranny of its cunning of its multifarious vastness; a switch-flick would ease this fellow's way, complicate that's, to balance things out; if anyone seemed lost or frightened, all the operator had to do was. [*Lost in the Funhouse*, p. 97]

Was what? Was what Ambrose can't think of without remembering that the funhouse he's in is not so well planned, so neatly equipped, is in fact "real." But he does remember. "He wishes he had not entered the funhouse. But he has. Then he wishes he were dead. But he's not. Therefore he will construct funhouses for others and be their secret operator—though he would rather be among the lovers for whom funhouses are designed" (p. 97).

Because life is a rather badly made funhouse, the artist tries to imagine a better one. Because God was a realist, man must be a fabulator. The energizing power of Barth's universe is the tension between the imagination of man and the conditions of being which actually prevail. After the "Frame-Tale" (a moebius strip which reads, endlessly, "ONCE UPON A TIME THERE WAS A STORY THAT BEGAN"), *Lost in the Funhouse* begins with "Night-Sea Journey," the tiny epic voyage of a spermatozoan caught in the inexorable motion of life, sex, and art. And it ends with the tale of an anonymous Greek writer (figure of Homer, father of fiction) who gets his inspiration by draining wine from nine amphorae (named after the Muses) which he then fills with sperm and fiction written on goatskin in a mixture of wine, blood, and squid ink. He casts these creations upon the waters to float like spermatozoa on some night-sea journey of impregnation. *Lost in the Funhouse* is concerned with philosophical questions, but its metaphysics is inside its esthetics (life is bad art); just as Barthelme's concern for essential values is lost in the "Brain Damage" and "Bone Bubbles" of *City Life*. For Barthelme, language is inside behavior and cannot get outside it to establish a perspective beyond the disordered wanderings of damaged brains. For Barth, behavior is inside language. Life is tantalizingly fictitious, a rough draft of what might be perfected as a supreme fiction. For Gass, there is a deep reality behind behavior, beyond the walls of the funhouse. "Against the mechanical flutter of appearance" he places "the glacial movement of reality." To approach this inner truth is difficult, because the path through human behavior leads into ultimate falsehood as well as ultimate truth. The fear of this falsehood haunts the truth-seeking narrator of "Mrs. Mean": "Indeed I am not myself. This is not the world. I have gone too far. It is the way fairy tales begin—with a sudden slip over the rim of reality" (*In the Heart*, p. 117).

For Robert Coover, the way to truth leads precisely over the rim of reality and through the gingerbread house. He sees contemporary man as living in a contracting universe, forced to re-assume "cosmic, eternal, supernatural (in its soberest sense) and pessimistic" perspectives. In such a world the writer must use

the fabulous to probe beyond the phenomenological, beyond appearances, beyond randomly perceived events, beyond mere history. But these probes are above all—like [Don Quixote's] sallies—challenges to the assumptions of a dying age, exemplary adventures of the Poetic Imagination, high-minded journeys toward the New World and never mind that the nag's a pile of bones. [*Pricksongs*, p. 78]

Barth minds very much that the nag's a pile of bones. He feels that "the narrator has narrated himself into a corner . . . and because his position is absurd he calls the world absurd" (*Lost in the Funhouse*, p. 112). He feels as imprisoned in the funhouse of fiction as Barthelme does in the brain damage of phenomena. But Coover, like Gass, senses an order beyond fiction and beyond phenomena, which may be discovered. But where Gass seeks to move through behavior to essence, Coover makes the parallel move through form to idea. This is why some of the most successful things in *Pricksongs* are reworkings of fairy tales which probe into the human needs behind them.

Gass thinks of a "real" Hansel and Gretel "who went for a walk in a real forest but they walked too far in the forest and suddenly the forest was a forest of story with the loveliest little gingerbread house in it" (*In the Heart*, p. 117). But Coover thinks of a fictional Hansel and Gretel who find in a gingerbread house the door to reality:

The children approach the gingerbread house through a garden of candied fruits and all-day suckers, hopping along on flagstones of variegated wafers. They sample the gingerbread weatherboarding with its carmel coating, lick at the meringue on the windowsills, kiss each other's sweetened lips. The boy climbs up on the chocolate roof to break off a peppermint-stick chimney, comes sliding down into a rainbarrel of vanilla pudding. The girl, reaching out to catch him in his fall, slips on a sugarplum and tumbles into a sticky garden of candied chestnuts. Laughing gaily they lick each other clean. And how grand is the red-and-white striped chimney the boy holds up for her! how bright! how sweet! But the door: here they pause and catch their breath. It is heart-shaped and blood-stone red, its burnished surface gleaming in the sunlight. Oh what a thing is that door! Shining like a ruby, like hard cherry candy, and pulsing softly, radiantly. Yes, marvelous! delicious! insuperable! but beyond: what is that sound of black rags flapping? [*Pricksongs,* p. 75]

This gingerbread house is a garden of sexuality, with its phallic chimney and cherry-red door. Sex itself is the door that connects fictional form and mythic idea: which is why these tales are called pricksongs and descants, or "death-cunt-and-prick songs," as Granny calls them in the opening story, "The Door." Apertures and orifices are as dominant in *Pricksongs* as mirrors and containers are in the *Funhouse.* Coover's technique is to take the motifs of folk litera-ture and explode them into motivations and revelations, as the energy might be released from a packed atomic structure. "The Door" itself is a critical mass obtained by the fusion of "Jack the Giant-Killer," "Beauty and the Beast," "Little Red Riding Hood," and other mythic fictions. In the heavy water of this mixture there is more truth than in many surface phenomena. Granny is aware of this as she ruminates on the younger generation's preoccupation with epidermal existence:

whose nose does she think she's twistin the little cow? bit of new fuzz on her pubes and juice in the little bubbies and off she prances into that world of hers that ain't got forests nor prodigies a dippy smile on her face and her skirts up around her ears well I'll give her a mystery today I will if I'm not too late already and so what if I am? let her go tippytoin through the flux and tedium and trip on her dropped drawers a few times and see if she don't come runnin back to old Granny God preserve me whistlin a different tune! don't understand! hah! for ain't I the old Beauty who married the Beast? [p. 16]

Granny is witch and wolf, wife and mother; she is the old Beauty who married the Beast—"only my Beast never became a prince"— she is temptress and artist, a Scheherazade who has "veils to lift and tales to tell"; she is initatrix into the mysteries of her own degrada-tion and transfiguration:

for I have mated with the monster my love and listened to him lap clean his lolly after. . . . I have been split with the pain and terrible haste of his thick quick cock and then still itchin and bleedin have gazed on as he lept other bitches at random and I have watched my own beauty decline my love and still no Prince no Prince and yet you doubt that I understand? and loved him my child loved the damned Beast after all. [p. 17]

The "flux and tedium" of phenomenal existence is not reality but the thing which hides it. For Coover, reality is mythic, and the myths are the doors of perception. Like a mind-blown Lévi-Strauss, he is concerned to open those doors.

Coover's mythic vision can be defined partly by its distance from Barthelme's perspective on myth. Usually a fabricator of assemblages of "flux and tedium," in "The Glass Mountain" Barthelme gives us a fairy tale of sorts. It seems there is this man climbing—grasping in each hand "a sturdy plumber's friend"—a glass mountain "at the corner of Thirteenth Street and Eighth Avenue." In one hundred numbered sentences and fragments he reaches the top with its "beautiful enchanted symbol."

97. I approached the symbol, with its layers of meaning, but when I touched it, it changed into only a beautiful princess.
98. I threw the beautiful princess headfirst down the mountain. . . . [City Life, p. 65]

This is myth enmeshed in phenomena. The "symbol" in the story symbolizes symbolism, reducing it to absurdity. It becomes an object with a sign on it that says "beautiful enchanted symbol." The magical transformation of "symbol" into "princess" is simply a change of signs. Barthelme is like a comic magician who removes a sign labeled "rabbit" from behind a sign labeled "hat" in a parody of all magic. But when Coover gives us a magician putting a lady in a hat in the last story of Pricksongs, she is a real lady in a real hat:

Pockets handkerchief. Is becoming rather frantic. Grasps hat and thumps it vigorously, shakes it. Places it once more on table, brim up. Closes eyes as though in incantations, hands extended over hat. Snaps fingers several times, reaches in tenuously. Fumbles. Loud slap. Withdraws hand hastily in angry astonishment. Grasps hat. Gritting teeth, infuriated, hurls hat to floor, leaps on it with both feet. Something crunches. Hideous piercing shriek. [Pricksongs, p. 255]

Magic is real. The fairy tales are true. Beast and princess are not phony symbols for Coover but fictional ideas of human essences. Barth and Barthelme are the chroniclers of our despair: despair over the exhausted forms of our thought and our existence. No wonder they laugh so much. Coover and Gass are reaching through form and behavior for some ultimate values, some true truth. No wonder they come on so strong. All four are working in that rarefied air of metafiction, trying to climb beyond Beckett and Borges, toward things that no critic—not even a metacritic, if there were such a thing—can discern.

The Limits of Metafiction: Warhol, Mosley, Sarraute, Brodeur, Merwin, Charyn, Dylan, Federman, Le Clezio

Experiments in fiction reached a kind of peak around 1970. Not that their achievement was necessarily the greatest in that year, but there were more experimental fictions published in the years around 1970 than before or since. The Nixon recession, which hit publishers as well as others, is partly responsible for the decline in published experimental fiction after 1970; but so, I suspect, was the relatively low number of successes—either critical or commercial—that experiments in fiction achieved during those years. In the pages that follow may be found a kind of chronicle of the period, in the form of eight reviews which were published in the *Saturday Review* from December, 1968, to January, 1972. The books, all clearly experiments in fiction, were chosen by the editors for review and sent to me because the earlier publication of *The Fabulators* suggested my interest in the field and, probably, my sympathy with such experimentation. As you will see, the expected sympathy is not always in evidence. The reviews appear here in chronological sequence, unedited.

Andy Warhol's *a* (December, 1968)

Long before the author became famous, zoologists had heard tales of a mythical beast called a Warhol. The creature was said to feed on the refuse of a civilized society (long since decadent and destroyed) and to pass the material easily through its system, finally ejecting it completely undigested but neatly packaged in colored containers. The bored denizens of this doomed society valued the beast's droppings highly and collected them avidly, vying with one another to assemble the largest heaps. The zoologists, naturally, rejected these tales as unscientific nonsense.

As near as I can make out, the 451 pages in this volume were printed without correction from inaccurate transcriptions made by various typists from poorly recorded tapes, which in turn had been assembled by following one of Andy Warhol's friends around with a tape recorder. I have tried hard to read it all, and nearly succeeded. No words except those contained in the book can adequately convey the dullness of the experience.

This might be enough said. But since the one-upmen of "In" will no doubt provide ingenious slogans purporting to demonstrate the importance of this "ultimate realism," I will add a few words of my own. First of all, the book is not important. It is not ultimate. It is not real. It is not even a failure, since nothing is really attempted. It is simply hours of dull conversation, haphazardly recorded, sloppily typed, irresponsibly printed, and greedily published.

Reality—bless its heart—is not to be captured so easily; but we did not require *a* to make that discovery. The whole lesson of literary history is that reality is elusive, not to be caught in verbal traps except by the most powerfully imaginative writers—people who feel, think, care, and work. Warhol does none of this. His book is not a "novel," and it is not by Andy Warhol. He has neither edited nor written it; he has merely marketed it. The tapes it purports to represent are censored, misunderstood fragments of talk among the pathetic creatures who inhabit Warhol's Underground. Tolkien's Hobbits have greater reality.

Nicholas Mosley's *Impossible Object* (January, 1969)

I note with shame that *Impossible Object* is Nicholas Mosley's seventh novel. With shame, because he is so good and this is the first of his books I have read, though I saw the Pinterized film version of his *Accident*. And I wonder, has he always been this good, hidden among the unappreciative English? Or has he developed from book to book the mastery he exhibits in *Impossible Object*? All I know is that he now has under full control four of the novelist's priceless gifts. He knows how to exploit the metaphoric possibilities of language. He has a shrewd grasp of the dynamics of emotional and sexual relationships. He has a developed sense of the philosophical, which lends resonance to the situations and people he presents. And he knows how to handle the storyteller's fundamental tools: suspense and revelation.

Certainly no one is born with all these gifts. But I, for one, mean to look into Mr. Mosley's earlier work to find out just what was going on back there. At the moment, however, I must try to describe *Impossible Object*—no easy task. This quotation from the epilogue points to the difficulty: "I wanted to write you something impossible, like a staircase climbing a spiral to come out where it started or a cube with a vertical line at the back overlapping a horizontal one in front. These cannot exist in three dimensions but can be drawn in two; by cutting out one dimension a fourth is created. The object is that life is impossible; one cuts out fabrication and creates reality." Mr. Mosley's book is an impossible object in that it is constructed of eight separate stories, all fairly straightforward and realistic in presentation, which cannot be brought into three-dimensional congruity. The same characters—or characters with many of the same attributes—reappear frequently, but it is hard to sort their lives into any single story. The central characters seem to be a woman with a daughter and a man with three sons, who love one another and labor furiously to keep their love and their lives from becoming ordinary. For the man in particular this is a major goal in life, almost an obsession. He knows that "love flourishes in time of war" and that life dwindles unless we "make impossibilities." Love itself, conceivable as an idea, is impossible as an object. It exists in two or four dimensions and cannot be brought into three; it cannot be realized and made permanent. And neither can life. The essence of life is that it is transitory yet repetitious. If we seek by an act of will to freeze certain recurring moments into the permanence of art, we engage in a heroic but doomed struggle. That is what Mr. Mosley's book is about.

In *Impossible Object* the struggle takes the form of various attempts by the man to keep his life and the lives of those connected with him at the most intense possible pitch. He is successful. He is also destructive of strangers, family, himself. He leaves a trail of dead and wounded behind him in his pursuit of "ecstasy." And we are not allowed the luxury of condemnation. After all, we are paying to observe all this. And destruction—even the culminating death of a love-child—is not the whole story: "You used to dislike happy endings, feeling it is better to have your heart cut out like an Aztec rather than suffer the prevarications of Spaniards. So I have given you an unhappy end like those of your favorite films—the girl shot over and over in snow like a rabbit, the car drowning in a few inches of water. There is also a happy end, though this is less explicit."

The narrator is talking to someone here. Perhaps it is the man, who is a writer, talking to his lover, or to his wife. But it is also the author talking to us, making a last attempt to prevent our response from being commonplace.

Interpolated among the eight stories, and standing as prologue and epilogue to the larger sequence, are nine little fables on related themes. These are brilliant prose constructions, combining images and perspectives with a vigor and control reminiscent of the later work of Picasso. The scenes they present are grotesque and bizarre, but always rooted in life and returning to life. These little pieces frame the "real" action, but the word "frame" is too inactive to convey how they really operate. Mosley uses his perspectivist parables as a way of generating an emotionally charged field of ideas and attitudes which then cluster around the situations in the "real" stories, illuminating them with a fabulous phosphorescence.

After John Fowles's *Magus* (a very different kind of novel), this is the best book by a young Englishman that I have read in recent years.

Nathalie Sarraute's *Between Life and Death* (May, 1969)

This is Nathalie Sarraute's sixth work of fiction. She is also, of course, the author of a really important collection of essays on the novel, *The Age of Suspicion*, wherein she undermined the fictional giants of the past, on whose grandiose ruins she and other postmodern French writers proposed to construct a "new" novel. Alain Robbe-Grillet's critical volume, *For a New Novel*, is in many respects simply a more polemical version of Mme Sarraute's quiet pronouncements.

Now no one seriously interested in the future of fiction can afford to ignore these two books. Yet the question remains whether the fictional achievements of the "new" novelists have been equal to the brilliance and the promise of their critical manifestos. I, for one, am not yet ready to attempt the resolution of that question; I have not read widely enough in the *nouveau roman* nor thought long enough about it for that undertaking. But I wish to consider Mme Sarraute's latest novel in the light of the larger issue, as representative of current French fiction.

Between Life and Death is yet another *Portrait of the Artist.* The book consists of a series of perspectives on the career of a writer, in which his relations with the French language and with his parents, idols, peers, critics, the public, and his duplicitous other selves are explored in scenes from which most visual details have been expunged. Everything comes to us as inner or outer dialogue. Fragments of the self appear on the same footing with other characters. With patience we can sort out the pieces of this jigsaw puzzle and assign them to their proper places. But the picture thus formed is both so faint and so familiar that we are left wondering whether the effort was worthwhile. No doubt this is what we are intended to wonder. No doubt Mme Sarraute has in fact done exactly what she wanted to do, and done it carefully and expertly.

But was it worth doing? Is the book worth reading? I have my doubts. Even *Planetarium* seems to me now to have too much form and not enough substance. *Between Life and Death* is even thinner. There is no news in this work—the one thing every novel must provide. The "new" novelists have promised us new forms to express our new realities. But few of them have managed to catch much life in their formal nets.

Paul Brodeur's *Stunt Man* (November, 1969)

Last summer a charming French lady asked me why the Americans and English had no "new novel." I replied that in fact we do have such a thing and that it is much more interesting than the French *nouveau roman,* which is still engaged in exploring a vision of banality and futility bequeathed it by the realists and naturalists. The British and American new novelists, instead of trying to reduce fiction to the level of dull meaninglessness the French seem to find in life, are happily exploring the possibilities of meaning in fictional form itself, and in considering the ways in which life shares qualities with fictional form.

Paul Brodeur's *Stunt Man* is a novel in this new tradition. Being in the new tradition is, of course, no guarantee of genuine excellence. The publishers' lists are getting crowded with pseudo-Vonneguts and quasi-Barths, just as they were once full of little Hemingways and Fitzgeralds. The very fact that one can recognize a new tradition means that its outward characteristics can be imitated by dozens of competent dullards—writers who can catch the form without the spirit which animated those who achieved a new form for themselves.

When I looked at the dust jacket of *The Stunt Man* I feared that Brodeur might prove to be merely a poor man's Pirandello and his book a mediocre *Magus*. In reading the book itself I began to feel that although Brodeur had risked both of these dangers, he had nevertheless achieved a work of his own, highly readable and intellectually rewarding. *The Stunt Man* is a contribution to the new tradition of Anglo-American fiction and not merely an exploitation of it. Any summary of the book's plot would remind one of both Pirandello and Fowles. A young man named Cameron escapes from a bus full of Army recruits and hides out in a seaside resort. On his way to the resort town he is involved in a strange episode during which he apparently causes the death of another young man. As things work out, Cameron finds a hiding place working as stunt man for a film company that is shooting a picture in the resort town, and he discovers that the man whose death he was involved in was his predecessor as the film's stunt man. Disguised as the leading man's stand-in, Cameron is safe from discovery but at the mercy of the director, Gottschalk (God-rogue or God-joker). When the director begins shaping the film into a story about a fugitive from military service, a number of plots begin to thicken at once, and the novel generates a good deal of fictional and intellectual suspense.

These developments also generate a number of meaningful resonances drawn from several areas of human concern. Clearly, Brodeur is working with a Pirandello-like curiosity about appearance and reality, the interpenetration of art and life. He is also working with myths and archetypes. The god-king and his scapegoat son; the Oedipal triangle; the descent into the underworld—these and other mythic motifs are introduced into the story, helping to structure it and, because they sometimes function ironically, to enrich it.

These stratagems are typical of the new tradition in fiction, of course, and can be handled brilliantly or stupidly by authors of varying skill. What makes Brodeur's use of them interesting and valuable is his ability to involve both of them in a third area of concern—all while moving his story along rapidly and lucidly. This third area of concern is in the way that the communications media shape the realities of our existence. Film is, of course, the medium most important in the novel. The film, with its great power to convince, equaled only by its power to lie and distort, is not only the type of all art; it is the type of all perception, too. In this novel the sun continually makes its presence felt, like a great lens focusing upon the earth. Is it a camera or a projector? Recording or shaping? The human eye, too, is a lens. Does it see what is there or create what it sees by projecting outward the mind's hopes and fears? These questions are built deeply into the structure and the texture of *The Stunt Man*. And all during the story we keep getting information through another medium, radio.

Wars and rumors of wars, claims and counterclaims come pouring out upon the characters and the reader. And where, among this welter of material, is truth? Outside the book, in our "real" world, most of us know nothing about events like the American Indochinese adventure except through the media. For us Vietnam, Laos, Cambodia—these things exist only through papers, TV, and other sources which can lie so easily and convincingly. Almost as convincingly as our own eyes and ears can misperceive and misconstrue.

Cameron *is* a camera. And he is on camera. This is his existence. To what extent is it ours also? The book raises the question of whether this existence can be escaped—literally by Cameron in the story, and metaphorically or allegorically by the rest of us in our lives. Can one break through to reality and freedom? Can one pierce through the lenses into some truth that exists on the other side? Important questions, vigorously posed. A good book.

W. S. Merwin's *Miner's Pale Children* (October, 1970)

Things refuse to stay in their places. A category is a challenge. Poets write prose. Philosophy abandons metaphysics for mathematics. And fiction becomes more philosophical. Now W. S. Merwin, along with his latest book of poems, offers us a volume containing eighty-seven little bits of "prose." Bite-sized, they look, like breakfast cereal—but these are not empty calories. Nor are they like peanuts, where the consumption of each makes the next more irresistible. For these bits of prose are magical; they only look more digestible than poetry. Once taken, they grow inside the reader: first filling him comfortably, contenting belly, heart, and brain, then expanding beyond comfort, forcing the eyes toward new perceptions, straining the ears toward unheard questions.

Merwin likes to offer us a simple situation or a plain literal statement, which he then expands into metaphor, stretches further into symbol, and further yet to the point where it is like allegory—but a strange sort of allegory that has forgotten it is supposed to hide some other meaning and is content with its own unearthly existence. Often we are faced at the end with simple situation and plain statement again, but transfigured, no longer of this world but clearly for this world.

It is hard, as you can see, to talk about this achievement in downright critical prose, but perhaps an illustration will help. "Unchopping a Tree" begins with the simple details of the laborious job at hand ("start with the leaves, the small twigs, and the nests"), and moves through an excruciating process of reconstruction until finally the thing is made. It is still dead, of course, and

> You cannot believe it will hold. How like something dreamed it is, standing there all by itself. How long will it stand there now? The first breeze that touches its dead leaves seems to flow into your mouth. You are afraid the motion of the clouds will be enough to push it over.
> What more can you do? What more can you do?
> But there is nothing more you can do.
> Others are waiting.
> Everything is going to have to be put back.

This is not just a lesson in ecology, though it can and no doubt should be read as such. It is a consideration of the nature of Being, a truly metaphysical fiction, which at the same time is resolute in its concreteness and defies reduction to a philosophical formula. The dust jacket quite rightly suggests that we think of the book's contents in relation to Kafka's "Parables" and the *Ficciónes* of Borges. Merwin can stand the comparison. But we should also see his work in relation to his contemporaries in this country, for it is part of a whole movement of prose fiction that is one of the most interesting and hopeful things on the current literary scene. *The Miner's Pale Children* belongs on the same shelf with Robert Coover's *Pricksongs and Descants*, John Barth's *Lost in the Funhouse*, Donald Barthelme's *City Life*, and William Gass's *In the Heart of the Heart of the Country*.

Merwin writes not fiction but metafiction. These bits of prose are not prose-poems, with all the *fin de siècle* preciosity that designation implies: they are visionary fictions, of astonishing range and power. Unlike James Dickey, who deliberately set his poetic talent aside to write a best-selling novel (and succeeded admirably, in my view), Merwin has worked *through* his poetry toward fiction. His prose is formidably spare and lean. It has been everywhere and done everything. Now it speaks austerely and with great authority. Often it adopts a voice of apparently childlike innocence and simplicity. But this voice conceals the other, which speaks through it. Here, perhaps, lies the significance of the title: not the weary, blackened miner himself is addressing us in these metafictions, but his children, who have inherited his weariness and the pallor that hides under his dark face.

The power of Merwin's prose must be experienced to be understood. Of its range one may speak more comfortably, categorizing and illustrating. Some of the pieces are fairy tales that resemble those of tradition. "The Fountain" (which readers of *The New Yorker* may remember) is one of these. "Phoebe" is another. In reading such a tale, one is forced to experience the narrative as something that is happening, like a dream that engulfs the dreamer and then casts him on some shoal of awakening, from which he may contemplate what has happened to him. These tales are almost pure narration, reaching toward myth, where their meanings lie hidden among our unconscious fears and desires. Others in the collection are closer to the essay in form and spirit. One such is "Memorials," in which the essayist's voice considers the way war memorials try to turn the "intentions" of the dead into legends:

Something at last is chosen, which is felt to be, within the practical limitations, suitably sad and suitably noble, to commemorate all these fictions.
And the result, for heaven knows how many years afterwards, graces the little square in all weathers, with the names on its base and the war in which they were called meaning less and less to more and more people. . . .

But throughout this apparent essay discussion always turns toward narration, the general toward the particular, the abstract toward the concrete. The idea of memorials gives way to the image of the square, in which "familiarity and the symmetry of its surroundings before long set about making the object itself grow dim." Finally, the object grows dim so that its meaning may shine more brightly.

A few of these pieces approach topical satire ("The Billboard," for instance) and some lean toward science fiction ("The Remembering Machines of Tomorrow"); some ("Marietta") are daydreams, others ("The First Time") are nightmares. Some contemplate the lives of objects ("Knives" and "Within the Wardrobes"), while others examine aspects of mind and thought ("Memory" and "Dawn Comes to Its Mountain in the Brain"). A number of the most ambitious and impressive seem to take an almost journalistic interest in "real" situations ("The Trembler" and "The Death-defying Tortonis"), only to move inexorably through the world of behavior into the realm of being that transcends it. In "The Death-defying Tortonis" the acrobatic speaker describes himself and the rest of the "family" as they balance in an elaborate tableau on the high wire. He complains, as a poet might, that "less and less people seem to believe in us, to say nothing of understanding our art." But the family's grandfather sees it differently: "He says we are no longer of interest because in fact we are not defying anything real at all. According to him we know too much, and it is all a game. Even if we were killed we would be killed in a game. . . . He watches us seldom, and with scorn, and he says we should turn to something we know nothing about if we are going to talk about defying death."

Perhaps this is why a poet turns to prose. But whatever the reason, the effect is immense. Grandfather Tortoni would be pleased.

Jerome Charyn's *Eisenhower, My Eisenhower* (June, 1971)

Ignorance is the mother of research. The embarrassing fact that Jerome Charyn had written five books of fiction before *Eisenhower, My Eisenhower* without registering on my consciousness led me to Brown's Rockefeller Library (*after* my reading of *this novel,* of course). In libraries, one learns. Here is my report.

Jerome Charyn was born in New York in 1937. His father was a furrier. He admires Dostoevsky and Babel. Four of his books are in this library. His first novel, *Once upon a Droshky* (1964), had been taken out four times. His second, *On the Darkening Green* (1965), only once. His book of stories, *The Man Who Grew Younger* (1967), twice. *Going to Jerusalem* was never acquired; and his last novel, *American*

Scrapbook (1969), is in the library but has not been taken out at all. What does this mean? I'm not sure, but on the surface it does not look like an encouraging record.

Book Review Digest tells a rather different story. In general, Charyn's fiction has been well received. His obscenity has offended *Best Seller*, but in the *Saturday Review* he has been effusively (and ponderously) praised—more than once by the same reviewer. In various places he has been both lauded and damned for his "black humor." His verbal energy, his sensitivity, and his wit—all of which are evident in the *Eisenhower* book—have received their due from the reviewers. He has been favorably compared to John Barth.

Charyn's first fiction was intensely Jewish in its matter and its manner. Local color, Yiddish humor. Moving gradually away from his native ground, he wrote his last novel about Japanese Americans interned during World War II. His latest is about a strange race of gypsies who live in Bedlam on the Marzipan, a nightmare borough much like the Bronx, or Brooklyn. (But it must be said, there is something Jewish about both his Japanese and his gypsies.) These gypsies are most unusual creatures: men with tiny tails, big buttocks, powerful bodies, great wit, and a kinky religion presided over by an irresponsible deity. They are the lowest of the low. Displacing Jews, Italians, blacks, and Puerto Ricans, they are the new niggers. And they rise in their chains against the System. Their great bodily and mental skills (you should see what they can do with their bony little tails) enable them to become great lovers, famous stage personalities, notorious musclemen, corporate wizards, indestructible politicians, superb commando leaders, and Panther-Weathermen revolutionaries. Their women are not much in evidence—that is, the women they have are mostly "Anglos."

This comic distortion of contemporary American reality is certainly amusing. And sometimes the satire bites pleasantly. Why is it, then, that I might not have finished reading the book without the encouragement of a reviewing assignment? And does this have anything to do with what seems to have been a shortage of readers for Charyn's earlier work? If something important is lacking in the work of this admittedly talented young man—what is it? The problem, at least in *Eisenhower, My Eisenhower,* is, in the broadest sense, structural. And it is a problem which turns up in the work of a lot of young writers today. If we think of structure in fiction as being responsible both for moving us through an experience and giving a coherent shape to that experience, then structure is what *Eisenhower* lacks. The inventiveness of the parts is greater than the intelligibility of the whole. There is more ingenuity here than meaning, more display than entertainment. The life of Toby Malothioon flashes forward and backward before our astounded eyes. But to what end? And who cares? The fantastic in fiction must always justify itself by presenting more order or more meaning than we can find in pure reporting. But here we have not fantasy but mere exaggeration, simple distortion.

It is, of course, Charyn's obvious talent which makes all this exasperating. This fuss would be pointless if *Eisenhower, My Eisenhower* were simply a "bad" book. It is not. It is a clever book, which has as much to do with Eisenhower as *The Man Who Knew Kennedy* had to do with Kennedy or *Why Are We in Viet Nam?* had to do with Vietnam. And if it were a first novel it could properly be considered full of promise in its verbal energy and comic humanity. But it is its author's sixth work of fiction. He is still young, but after five books the word "promising" must be an insult. As we age, bones mean more, flesh less. It is time for structure to make itself apparent in Mr. Charyn's work.

Bob Dylan's *Tarantula* (July, 1971)

They tell me that the world's leading Dylan expert actually picks over the bard's garbage to see what interesting tidbits of Dylaniana he can find. No doubt such devotion has its rewards. Reading *Tarantula* has its rewards, too, but one still has a sense of picking over a lot of unlovely stuff in order to find the good things. "Free associating" on various themes in a surrealistic way, Dylan frequently comes up with a telling phrase, a witty image, or a crisp little character sketch like this one: "jack of spades—vivaldi of the coin laundry—wearing a hipster's dictionary—we see him brownnosing around the blackbelts & horny racing car drivers—dashing to & fro like a frightened uncle remus. . . ." But for the most part *Tarantula* is just not interesting enough.

Dylan, who is a true poet in song, a voice with a conscience, is simply a bright, self-indulgent fellow in prose. To his credit, he stopped publication of this book in 1966 after it had reached the galley-proof stage. But with proofs drifting about, and unauthorized

copies being made of them, he and his publishers apparently could
not hold out. So here it is, complete with a coy foreword by "The
Publisher," whose string of little Dick-and-Jane declarative sentences tells you he thinks the book's potential audience is the very
young. But more kids will carry the lightweight *Tarantula* around
with them than will actually read its 137 pages.

Raymond Federman's *Double or Nothing* and J. M. G. Le Clezio's *Book of Flights* (January, 1972)

Q. You are an expert on fiction, Monsieur le Professeur?

A. *Bien sûr, mais . . .*

Q. *En anglais, s'il vous plait.*

A. Oh, pardon me. Yes, I know something of fiction.

Q. And you are a devotee of the so-called experimental novel?

A. I am not devoted to anything that might be called "so-called."
   Nor do I care for experiments. But I am not afraid of things that
   are new.

Q. Well, in the light of these two new works of fiction, do you think
   the experimental novel can succeed in English?

A. My friend, it has a hard enough time succeeding in French.

Q. Quite. But one of these works was written originally in French,
   and the other has passages in French and was produced by a
   professor who has written books on Beckett. These two novels are
   virtually French, then.

A. I am afraid you are right.

Q. Why afraid?

A. Because they are not experiments that have my unqualified admiration. Oh, I admire the intelligence, the perseverance that went
   into them. But this notion of an experimental novel, it seems to
   me, is based upon an analogy with science. Since the scientist
   experiments, then the novelist, if he is to compete, must experiment also.

Q. I hadn't thought of it that way, but yes, I suppose you're right.

A. But in the sciences, if the experiment does not work, the savant
   does not insist on publishing his results in the scientific journals.
   It is only in literature that all experiments are deemed worthy of
   publication.

Q. Then would you say there is no case for experimental fiction?

A. But of course there is a case. The world goes on. Things change. These matters must be dealt with.

Q. You do not feel that Federman and Le Clezio deal with them successfully?

A. Allow me a moment, please. Theirs are very different books, and manage to fail in quite different ways. All this is instructive. Federman's *Double or Nothing* calls itself a "concrete" novel.

Q. Concrete?

A. Yes, its pages are
   pages of typescript
   , and many ingeniou
   s spacings and arra
   ngements of lines a
   ppear upon those pa
   ges.

Q.   This is good?

A. Not   necessarily.   I
   t is possible, howe
   ver, and we live in
   an age where whatev
   er is possible will
   probably be done to
   us sooner or later.
   This too, is an as
   pect of SCIENCE

Q. What is *Double or Nothing* all about?

A. It is about a man recording a story written by a man who intends to shut himself up in a room for 365 days so as to write the story of yet another man whose life bears some vague resemblance to that of the author as it appears on the dust jacket of the book. This advertised life also may be unreal. Federman is perhaps a fiction. At any rate, whoever the author may be, he "creates" what these other characters do. All this seems more interesting when summarized, because no summary can capture the intentional boredom of the original.

Q. Intentional boredom?

A. Did I not say that Federman is a student of Beckett?

Q. Yes, but Beckett?

A. . . . is a genius—a genius of boredom, of course, but very funny too.

Q. And Federman?

A. He is only a little funny.

Q. A pity. And the concrete typography?

A. If the book were more interesting it would be less of a distraction. As things are, it gives one something to look forward to.

Q. What?

A. Blank spaces.

Q. Ah. And what of Le Clezio?

A. He is a more interesting failure.

Q. How is that?

A. He has genius.

Q. And still he is a failure?

A. He has a genius for failure. His book is subtitled "An Adventure Story." But if he had actually produced such a thing, his book would be a failure.

Q. And does he fail?

A. He fails to fail.

Q. You mean . . . ?

A. Precisely what I said.

Q. Tell me about the book.

A. *The Book of Flights* is a dazzling work of prose description, an imaginary landscape realized superbly. It is Sartre's *Nausea* projected in color on multiple screens simultaneously.

Q. It sounds great.

A. If that is the sort of thing you like. . . . But the flight goes on for a long time. I should point out that it contains in addition passages of self-criticism far more clever than any you or I could make.

Q. What is the purpose of this?

A. The purpose is to intimidate us. The book also has an episode that treats the nature of language in a way that makes the essays of writers in the Anglo-Saxon tradition, such as George Steiner, appear both clumsy and old fashioned.

Q. A Gallic prejudice on your part?

A. As you wish. Remember, even I feel that the book goes on too long and is somewhat deficient in variety and development. But read it yourself and see how this brilliant young man fails to fail.

Comedy and Grotesquerie

The Comedy of Extremity

One of the most obvious and permanent qualities of the fable proper—the little brother of the full-scale fabulation—is that it has a moral. It is didactic. Or so it seems, until we look into the matter. In practice we find that many collections of fables include some tales without morals, and that in many other cases well-meaning souls have tacked morals onto tales for which they are absurd or grossly inadequate. For instance, consider this gem from a collection called *A C. Mery Talys (A Hundred Merry Tales*, 1526—this is Paul Zall's modernized version from his Bison paperback edition):

54.

A young man of the age of 20 years, rude, and unlearned, in the time of Lent came to his curate to be confessed—which, when he was of his life searched and examined, could not say his Pater Noster. Wherefore his confessor exhorted him to learn his Pater Noster and showed him what an holy and goodly prayer it was and the effect thereof and the seven petitions therein contained:

"The first petition beginneth, Pater Noster, etc., that is to say—'O Father hallowed be Thy name among men in earth as among angels in heaven.' The second, Adveniat, etc., 'Let Thy kingdom come and reign Thou among us men in earth as among angels in heaven.' The third, Fiat, etc., 'Make us to fulfill Thy will here in earth as Thy angels in heaven.' The fourth, Panem nostrum, etc., 'Give us our daily sustenance always and help us as we give and help them that have need of us.' The fifth, Dimitte, etc., 'Forgive us our sins done to Thee as we forgive them that trespass against us.' The sixth, Et ne nos, 'Let us not be overcome with evil temptation.' The seventh, Sed libera, etc., 'But deliver us from all evil—Amen.'"

And then his confessor after this exposition to him made, enjoined him in penance to fast every Friday on bread and water till he had his Pater Noster well and sufficiently learned.

This young man meekly accepting his penance so departed and came home to one of his companions and said to his fellow: "So it is that my ghostly father hath given me in penance to fast every Friday on bread and water till I can say my Pater Noster. Therefore I pray ye teach me my Pater

Noster and, by my troth, I shall therefore teach thee a song of Robin Hood
that shall be worth 20 of it."

By this tale ye may learn to know the effect of the holy prayer of the Pater
Noster.

This propensity in the fable to point a moral at all costs has been
parodied beautifully by Thurber in such tales as "The Unicorn in the
Garden," with its splendid moral of "Don't count your boobies until
they are hatched." But as readers of fables we can draw, if not a
moral, at least a conclusion, from the existence of these two kinds of
little fables—that is, the Aesopian kind, where the moral really
works, and those such as the one I quoted, which are essentially
amoral and resist violently any attempt to assimilate them as exempla
of an orderly moral world. The moral fable is kin to the larger satire;
the amoral fable to the picaresque tale, which can grow very long
indeed. And both of these large forms have something to do with
that movement in modern fiction—in modern life, really, because it
is not exclusively literary—which is often called black humor. Many
of this country's exciting young writers are connected in some way
with this literary movement. Albee, Barth, Donleavy, Friedman,
Hawkes, Heller, Purdy, Pynchon, Southern, and Vonnegut have all
been stamped with this dark label at one time or another, and,
various as the writings of these men actually are, their works differ
from those of the previous generation in a manner special enough to
justify some common terminology and consideration of what their
work, collectively, implies about the contemporary literary situation.
The term "black humor" is probably too clumsy to be of much use to
criticism, but before discarding it we should do well to milk it of such
value as it may have in helping us to understand this new fiction and
to adjust to it. We can begin with a view from the inside: "They say it
is a critic's phrase, Black Humor, and that whatever it is, you can
count on it to fizzle after a bit. . . . I think they may be wrong on
that . . . count. I have a hunch Black Humor has probably always
been around, always will. . . ."

The quotation is from Bruce Jay Friedman's shrewd and engaging
foreword to an anthology, *Black Humor*, that he edited for Bantam
Books in 1965. The anthology itself is worth looking at, as it includes
work by a number of interesting writers, including Friedman himself. But it is not a really successful book, this anthology, mainly
because some of the best black humorists tend to use larger forms

than the short story, building effects over many pages. Selections from Barth's *Sot-Weed Factor* and Heller's *Catch-22*, for example, hardly begin to work in this format.

But I don't mean to discuss Mr. Friedman's anthology here. I mention it because I want to use his definition as a point of departure for some theorizing of my own. Friedman suggests that we have had a kind of black humor movement in contemporary writing because events "Out There" in the contemporary world are so absurd that the response of the black humorist is the most appropriate one possible. But he also suggests, in the lines just quoted, that black humor is not merely a modern fad but a continuing mode of literary activity. He doesn't say how this apparent contradiction is to be resolved, however, and this is where I want to begin. I think he is right on both counts. Black humor is a modern movement but also a development in a continuing tradition.

Most of the literary kinds and modes are with us all the time, but in every era some are very alive and others quite dormant. If we consider literature as a way of looking at the world, for every age certain modes serve better than others to bring things into focus, to align the ideals of the age with actuality. In a historical perspective, black humor seems allied with those periodic waves of rationality which have rolled through Western culture with continually increasing vigor for over two thousand years. The intellectual comedy of Aristophanes, the flourishing satire of imperial Rome, the humanistic allegories and anatomies of the later Middle Ages, the picaresque narratives of the Renaissance, the metaphysical poems and satires of the seventeenth century, and the great satiric fictions of the Age of Reason—all these are ancestors of modern black humor. Of course, an illustrious pedigree does not guarantee the worth of an offspring. Nevertheless, since understanding and evaluating depend so completely on our sense of genre, pedigree is where we must begin. This is especially important in the case of the so-called black humorists: first, because their immediate point of departure has been the novel, a form which we view with certain realistic expectations; and second, because nearly two centuries of literature dominated by romantic notions of value lie between the modern black humorists and such immediate ancestors as Swift and Voltaire.

Developments in current fiction are very closely analogous to the poetic revolution of a generation or so back, when the rediscovery of the metaphysical poets helped spark a revival of witty, cerebral verse. Current interest in Rabelais, Cervantes, Aleman, Grimmelshausen, Swift, Smollett, and Voltaire is part of the general drift of fiction into more violent and more intellectual channels. The sensibility and compassion which characterized the great novels of the nineteenth century are being modified by the wit and cruelty of black humor. Horace Walpole's epigram about life being tragic for those who feel and comic for those who think is a gross oversimplification, no doubt, but it is useful to us in describing such a massive change in literary climate as the one we are considering here. Such changes, like variations in the weather, are not things one can do much to alter. The question is how to adjust to them.

For us, the question—like most literary questions—becomes one of how to read. What expectations should we bring to this new writing? What benefit can we hope to derive from it? To put it crudely, what's in it for us? I think there is a lot in it for us—it is our literature, speaking to us most immediately. If it seems out of focus, perhaps we must change our lenses to see it clearly. First of all, we must discard the notion that these works are "novels" as novels have been written. They are different from their immediate predecessors. Here the pedigree of black humor will help, for it is surely better to think of Voltaire and Swift when reading Vonnegut and Barth than to think of Hemingway and Fitzgerald. But we must not take the pedigree in too simple-minded a fashion either. If we say, "O yes, satire," we may go just as wrong as if we were to expect another realistic novel. Though these works are offshoots of a family tree we recognize, they are a new mutation, a separate branch with its own special characteristics and qualities. To define the special attributes of this new branch is surely the critic's business. But it is a hard business because the writers are a mixed group, differing in temperament, intellect, and experience; and because they themselves are experimenting with this new, uncrystallized mode of writing, often trying new things from book to book. A writer like John Hawkes seems almost to obliterate his humor with his blackness, while Bruce Jay Friedman makes a nearly opposite emphasis. How can we unite such disparity other than by mere verbal trickery or sleight-of-word?

I am hedging here, warning the reader to take my attempt to define a revolution in progress as necessarily a tentative formulation. But despite the difficulty, I think enough can be said to justify the project. I see black humor as crucially different from its satiric and picaresque ancestors, but also as clearly relatable to these two traditional kinds of fiction. In this section and the following ones I intend to explore certain aspects of these relationships. First, the relationship of Kurt Vonnegut's kind of black humor to the satirical tradition. Then, the relationship of Terry Southern and John Hawkes to the picaresque tradition. This arrangement is not intended to be a neat pigeonholing affair: for, first of all, in practice satire and picaresque are often very hard to distinguish from one another, and second, all three of these writers are clearly inheritors of both traditions. I have divided the genres in this manner mainly for convenience—but not arbitrarily, as I hope to demonstrate.

The satirical kind of black humor is qualified by the modern fabulator's tendency to be more playful and more artful in construction than his predecessors: his tendency to fabulate. Fabulative satire is less certain ethically but more certain esthetically than traditional satire. This causes the special tone that the term "black humor" so inadequately attempts to capture. The spirit of playfulness and the care for form characteristic of the modern fabulators operate so as to turn the materials of satire and protest into comedy. And this is not a mere modern trick, a wayward eccentricity. These writers reflect quite properly their heritage from the esthetic movement of the nineteenth century and the ethical relativism of the twentieth. They have some faith in art but they reject all ethical absolutes. Especially, they reject the traditional satirist's faith in the efficacy of satire as a reforming instrument. They have a more subtle faith in the humanizing value of laughter. Whatever changes they hope to work in their readers are the admittedly evanescent changes inspired by art, which need to be continually renewed, rather than the dramatic renunciations of vice and folly postulated by traditional satire.

The special tone of black humor, often derived from presenting the materials of satire in a comic perspective, is perfectly illustrated in a passage from Vonnegut's *Cat's Cradle*. The narrator in this passage is interviewing the son of a Schweitzer-type jungle doctor on a small Caribbean island:

"Well, aren't you at all tempted to do with your life what your father's done with his?"
Young Castle smiled wanly, avoiding a direct answer. "He's a funny person, Father is," he said, "I think you'll like him."

"I expect to. There aren't many people who've been as unselfish as he has."

"One time," said Castle, "when I was about fifteen, there was a mutiny near here on a Greek ship bound from Hong Kong to Havana with a load of wicker furniture. The mutineers got control of the ship, didn't know how to run her, and smashed her up on the rocks near 'Papa' Monzano's castle. Everybody drowned but the rats. The rats and the wicker furniture came ashore."

That seemed to be the end of the story, but I couldn't be sure. "So?"

"So some people got free furniture and some people got bubonic plague. At Father's hospital, we had fourteen hundred deaths inside of ten days. Have you ever seen anyone die of bubonic plague?"

"That unhappiness has not been mine."

"The lymph glands in the groin and the armpits swell to the size of grapefruit."

"I can well believe it."

"After death, the body turns black—coals to Newcastle in the case of San Lorenzo. When the plague was having everything its own way, the House of Hope and Mercy in the Jungle looked like Auschwitz or Buchenwald. We had stacks of dead so deep and wide that a bulldozer actually stalled trying to shove them toward a common grave. Father worked without sleep for days, worked not only without sleep but without saving many lives, either."

[*After an interruption*]

"Well, finish your story anyway."

"Where was I?"

"The bubonic plague. The bulldozer was stalled by corpses."

"Oh, yes. Anyway, one sleepless night I stayed up with Father while he worked. It was all we could do to find a live patient to treat. In bed after bed after bed we found dead people.

"And Father started giggling," Castle continued.

"He couldn't stop. He walked out into the night with his flashlight. He was still giggling. He was making the flashlight beam dance over all the dead people stacked outside. He put his hand on my head, and do you know what that marvelous man said to me?" asked Castle.

"Nope."

"'Son,' my father said to me, 'someday this will all be yours.'"

In the passage an excess of the horrible is faced and defeated by the only friend reason can rely on in such cases: laughter. The whole episode is a comic parable of our times. Progress, that favorite prey of satirists from Swift and Voltaire onward, means that some people get free furniture and some get the plague. Some get Biarritz and some get Auschwitz. Some get cured of cancer by radiation; others get radiation sickness. But the spuriousness of progress is not seen here with the *saeva indignatio* of the satirist. Progress is seen not as a conspiracy but as a joke. The black humorist is concerned not with what to do about life but with how to take it. In this respect black humor has certain affinities with some existentialist attitudes, roughly distinguishable in terms of the difference between seeing the universe as absurd and seeing it as ridiculous—a joke. The absurd universe is a pretty dismal affair. The best, in fact, that Camus found to offer humanity as a response to the human condition was "scorn." In "The Myth of Sisyphus" he told us that "there is no fate that cannot be surmounted by scorn." The black humorists offer us something better than scorn. They offer us laughter. The scorn of Sisyphus leads finally to resignation—"He, too, concludes that all is well." Beneath the hide of this scornful hero beats the heart of Dr. Pangloss after all. Vonnegut's fictional prophet Bokonon suggests a better posture for man on the mountain top than that of Camus' Sisyphus, who simply starts down again to pick up his burden. At the end of *Cat's Cradle,* with the world nearly all frozen, Bokonon gives one of his last disciples a bit of advice: "If I were a younger man, I would write a history of human stupidity; and I would climb to the top of Mount McCabe and lie down on my back with my history for a pillow; and I would take from the ground some of the blue-white poison that makes statues of men; and I would make a statue of myself, lying on my back, grinning horribly, and thumbing my nose at You Know Who."

What man must learn is neither scorn nor resignation, say the black humorists, but how to take a joke. How should one take a joke? The best response is neither acquiescence nor bitterness. It is first of all a matter of perception. One must "get" the joke. Then one must demonstrate this awareness by playing one's role in the joke in such a way as to turn the humor back on the joker or cause it to diffuse itself harmlessly on the whole group which has participated in the process of the joke. Even at the punch line of apocalypse, feeble man can respond with the gesture prescribed by Bokonon, suggesting an amused, tolerant defiance. Of course, a joke implies a Joker, as Gloucester observed amid the cosmic tomfoolery of *King Lear:* "They kill us for their sport." But I do not think the black humorists mean to present us with a new deity, crowned with a cap and bells in place of thorns. No more than Paul Tillich do they wish to "bring in God as a *deus ex machina*" to fill the great hole in the modern cosmos. To see the human situation as a cosmic joke, one need not assume a Joker.

Some accidents are so like jokes that the two are indistinguishable. Moreover, it is possible to conceive of all human history as part of a master plan without thinking of the Planner in quite the traditional way. In an early science fiction novel, now re-released in paperback, Kurt Vonnegut developed such a view. In *Sirens of Titan* he presented a cosmos in which the whole of human history has been arranged by intervention from outer space in order to provide a traveler from a distant galaxy with a small spare part necessary for his craft to continue its voyage to the other side of the universe. Such purposefulness to entirely extra-human ends is indeed a cosmic joke, but is not intended as such by those superior beings who have manipulated earthly life for their own ends. This novel suggests that the joke is on us every time we attribute purpose or meaning that suits us to things which are either accidental, or possessed of purpose and meaning quite different from those we would supply. And it doesn't matter which of these mistakes we make.

Samuel Johnson, whose *Rasselas* is a rather solemn ancestor of *Cat's Cradle*, picked on just this aspect of the vanity of human wishes in one of his finest works—an *Idler* paper so black and humorous that Johnson later suppressed it. In this essay Johnson presented a dialogue between a mother vulture and her children, in which the wise old bird, looking down at a scene of human carnage from a recent European battle, tells her young that men do this at regular intervals as part of a divine plan which has shaped the best of all possible worlds—for vultures. In presenting this view of life as a joke on all those who think this is the best of all possible worlds for men, Johnson is very close to his modern descendants. For the joke is one key to the fabulative impulse, especially to the impulse behind black humor. To present life as a joke is a way of both acknowledging its absurdity and showing how that very absurdity can be encompassed by the human desire for form. A joke like Dr. Johnson's acknowledges and counteracts the pain of human existence. In the best of all possible worlds there would be no jokes.

Of all the things that men must endure, war is one of the worst. Certainly war brings the contrast between human ideals and human actions to the highest possible degree of visibility. In time of war the drums, the rituals, the rhetoric all collaborate to suppress reason and its ally laughter, to prevent any rational scrutiny of such an irrational process. But satirists and picaresque novelists have subjected these phenomena to their fierce scrutiny nonetheless. Grimmelshausen's *Simplicissimus* is an honored ancestor of Céline's *Journey to the End of Night,* and the king of Brobdingnag's pronouncement on European history still reverberates in our ears with an eerie relevance to modern conditions. The black humorists of today, of course, have found the fields of Mars as fertile as ever. *Catch-22* and *Dr. Strangelove* are among the triumphs of modern comic fiction. Thus it should not surprise us to find that two of Kurt Vonnegut's strongest performances deal with modern war: one with World War II, and one with the scientific discovery of an ultimate weapon.

The Making of a Comedian

Kurt Vonnegut is a vulgar sentimentalist—a quality he shares with Dickens, for instance. He is also a crude humorist—a quality he shares with Mark Twain. Like other writers who have reached a broad spectrum of the populace, he is a difficult case for elitist criticism to confront. Thus he has had the honor of an attack in the *New York Review of Books*, which is radical in its politics but reactionary in its esthetics. Vonnegut is a literary maverick, who runs with no pack and must have been surprised to find himself the darling of the hippie kids while all the time he was just trying to shake some sense into Middle America. He has written short sentences, small paragraphs, tiny chapters, and little books in an attempt to reach busy, unliterary folk with his criticism of life and his help in making it bearable. He is himself, of course, the lovely false prophet Bokonon, the foolish philanthropist Rosewater, and above all the kindly, untrustworthy, honest, quadruple turncoat Howard Campbell of *Mother Night*.

How he got that way is an interesting question, with some of its answers buried in the mysteries of identity but others more accessible, to be found in libraries and other such places. There are some important clues, for instance, in a series of pieces he wrote as an undergraduate for the *Cornell Sun*, in the spring and fall of 1941. They show us a Vonnegut nearly fully formed but still in the process of formation, and they reveal some of the forces that helped to shape him.

Vonnegut began to write pieces under his own by-line for the *Sun* in the spring of his freshman year at Cornell. He started by taking over a column called "Innocents Abroad," which specialized in college humor, reprinting jokes from other magazines and papers, which in turn reprinted from others, so that the same body of material kept busily circulating with virtually no infusion of new blood.

College humor in its great days had spawned a school of excellent
American writers, and there is a sad but interesting story in the
partial failure of such writers as Thurber, White, Benchley, Parker,
and Perelman to move far from the trivial genre which they exploited so thoroughly. But in the spring of 1941, with World War II
looming over the horizon, the task of the college humorist posed
special problems which Vonnegut acknowledged in his first piece:
"With the hilarious nature of this golden age we live in, with Adolph
Hitler, labor riots, and the Cornell Widow, one cannot help but see
the screamingly funny side to everything—or such is the hope of one
dope who spends his time clipping witticisms from exchange papers
and having the gall to demand a by-line for it." Vonnegut then began
his career with this gem, under the heading "Quip Clipped by
Drip":

> Little ear of corn: "Where did I come from?"
> Big ear of corn: "The stalk brought you."
> —*Northeastern News*

His next column was introduced with another personal paragraph:
"Whether anyone else gives a hang or not about keeping out of
World War II, we do, and from now on, readers may rest assured that
material appearing in this column has been carefully edited so as to
exclude anything smacking in the slightest of propaganda."

In these, two of his first published paragraphs, Vonnegut revealed
both his budding talents as an ironist and some of the fundamental
attitudes that have shaped his work. There was no need, in a joke
column, publicly to disclaim propaganda. In fact, the disclaimer itself
was a kind of propaganda: Vonnegut making his own pacifistic
views known. But what he meant by propaganda was talk in favor of
entering the war, not talk against it. Still, "Innocents Abroad" was
not an ideal forum for Vonnegut's serious concerns, however it may
have appealed to his love of jokes. Thus he must have been pleased
to get a chance at the wholly original column "Well All Right," which
also appeared regularly on the *Sun*'s editorial page. On April 22 he
wrote the following "Well All Right" column, under the subhead
"Bayonet Drill at the Rate of Seven in 20 Seconds, or, Oh for a Couple
of Nazis."

A military potentate has recently returned from an extensive tour of the
United States armed forces with the happy news that the general morale is

high and admirable. We recently got a cross-section of military morale of our own—we were the only civilian on a bus ride from Hartford, Connecticut to Ithaca.

We sat next to one of the nation's happy warriors, an enlisted man of eighteen, whose attitude filled us with confidence in the face of the dictatorships.

He described with boyish enthusiasm bayonet drill, which seems to be a hilarious sport. Seven life-like dummies are set up in a realistic trench, and each soldier starts from a given point at a full run, dives into the trench, and maims each of his seven passive enemies as quickly as he can with his bayonet—all timed by stopwatch. Our talkative source of information (these may be military secrets) said that a good man could do the job in twenty seconds, and that there were a number of good books written on bayonet technique if we were really interested.

We thanked him, and recalled a delightfully interesting pamphlet we had seen which covered the subject—translated from the French into English and issued by the War Department in 1917.

He went on to recite a series of actions which he repeats to himself when going into mock action, something like this: "Parry, stab, withdraw, smash (with the rifle butt), etc.," and it's supposed to go faster than the eye can follow.

We asked him what he thought his chances would be if he were pitted aginst a Nazi soldier who had been practicing with a bayonet for five years. His eyes glistened, and he said that he just wished he had the chance. He hates Germans—all of 'em.

We were going to ask him what he had against Beethoven but decided that we probably wouldn't get a very good answer.

At this time, of course, Vonnegut was having an experience rare for white Protestant Americans. He was a member of a minority group which was feeling the active antagonism of others. Before and during World War II anti-German feeling in the United States was not as virulent as it had been at the time of World War I, but it was there, and the German-American Vonnegut was very sensitive to it. And of course, all the time that great joker History was holding a reservation for this young man in Slaughterhouse Five, Dresden, from which he would be privileged to emerge after the British/ American bombing of that open city—an unscathed prisoner of war surveying a smoking ruin that had once been a center of German civilization. How can art hope to compete in irony with a life which arranges such intricate absurdities? But back in Ithaca, New York, in the spring of '41, young Vonnegut continued clipping jokes for "Innocents Abroad," never getting far from thoughts of the war. On

May 9 he began with some words addressed "To the Cornell Military Department":

We, along with the chemical engineers and those boys in advanced drill, are smug about the important and lucrative part we will play when war comes. Uncle Sam needs zoologists and plenty of them—that's us.

Up in the front lines our commanding officer will say, "Vontegal" (that's the way Bool's Flowerdale addresses its bills to us—should we pay them?), "what the hell kind of a butterfly is that," and we'll be the only man in the trench that can tell him. That's the sort of thing that wins wars.

It's a waste of our time and yours, boys, trying to teach us how to blow things up. We don't know a fuse-setter from Lieutenant Wilcox and never will. We're cut out for bigger things. And we're not just being a sorehead because we didn't get a blue and gold medal like the rest of the fellows.

As the spring semester came to its end, Vonnegut kept up the jokes, but he also got a few opportunities at "Well All Right." He devoted one of these to that perennially pressing problem, fraternity financing. But even on this subject he found his own way of propagandizing, for the financial problems of fraternities in his view were caused partly by "defense taxation" which was likely to increase "as the war fever heightens." After a chillingly detailed forecast of the growth of financial difficulties, he opened his last paragraph this way: "It's a nasty picture no matter how you look at it. From an abstract point of view it will be interesting to watch, just like bombing." Another "Well All Right" column he devoted to a lengthy and serious study of the way newspapers slant events. His examples were drawn mainly from the current invasion of Crete, which he felt was being reported from a strictly pro-British point of view. His sober last advice was, "We must know the shortcomings of the British—and of ourselves—as well as of the Germans if we would create any kind of lasting remedy when the dangers of the moment are averted." Vonnegut regained his comic touch with his last "Well All Right" piece of that semester, subheaded, "We Impress *Life* Magazine with Our Efficient Role in National Defense":

Life Magazine was at drill to take our pictures Tuesday afternoon, and we were sorry that we didn't have a more impressive and less scratchy uniform. We were delighted to show them what we were doing for national defense which was the object of the photographer's mission.

Lieutenant Wilcox and Colonel Metcalf were pretty upset and excited by the visit. Lieutenant Wilcox's voice cracked twice while trying to calm us down over the public address system. It was a terrific strain, with the marvelous showing that Harvard made three weeks ago hanging over our heads.

We had never considered that we were doing anything for national defense before. As a matter of fact, one of the officers had told us that we were a detriment to that cause and that we'd better have a necktie next time. Everybody was trying to look like they were keyed up to the national emergency. Some looked blood-thirsty, some pensive—we looked square into the lens of the camera and grinned. The cheerful optimism of a soldier, we figured, will do wonders for American morale when it beams out on *Life*'s millions.

After spoiling a couple of plates, the cameraman told us to look natural which we did in spite of the good name of Cornell. They made us pose in what they thought were typical attitudes. We all leaned forward in the bleachers, gazing at a French 75 as if it was the most wonderful little gadget ever designed. Lieutenant Wilcox conducted a mock class for the sake of the photographs, asking us to identify several parts of a breech-block which were laid out on a table. To impress the visitors we yelled out such phoney technical terms as "flathatcher" and "biffle-block," which had its desired effect and seemed to sound OK to the officers, too.

They had us read maps. With shutters clicking over our shoulders we would plot mysterious curves over charts. Some fellows got pretty bitter about Lieutenant Wilcox being in all the pictures, but nobody said anything to his face.

We predict that *Life*'s circulation will jump by 7,000 for the Cornell issue, and that America will rip into national defense with redoubled enthusiasm when they see what a deadly bunch of artillerymen from Ithaca are working hand in hand with them.

The following autumn, as a mature sophomore, Vonnegut regularly wrote "Well All Right." He managed to keep the war and all that out of his column most of the time, except for one splendid outburst in defense of a fellow German-American, subheaded, "We Chase a Lone Eagle and End Up on the Wrong Side of the Fence":

Charles A. Lindbergh is one helluva swell egg, and we're willing to fight for him in our own quaint way. Several sterling folk, *Sun* members not excluded, have been taking journalistic pot-shots at the Lone Eagle, effectively, too. The great work is spreading. Give the stout, red-blooded American—the average mental age is fourteen, we're told—a person to hate, tell him to do so often, and he and his cousin Moe will do a damned fine job of it, providing there are plenty of others doing the same.

The mud slingers are good. They'd have to be good to get people hating a loyal and sincere patriot. On second thought, Lindbergh is no patriot—to hell with the word, it lost its meaning after the Revolutionary War.

What a guy! Look at the beating he takes. Why on God's green earth (we think He's sub-let it) would anyone lay himself open for such defamation if

he wasn't entirely convinced that he must give the message to his country at
any cost? To offer an obstacle to the premeditated Roosevelt foreign policy is
certainly to ask for a kick in the face.

There was another bum who stood in the way of America's divine destiny
during the shambles of 1917. Hughes, that's the guy, former Chief Justice
Charles Evans Hughes. That's the sort of louse that makes trouble.

Crusades, not that they're not worth twice the cost, cost about five million
men these days. It's America's purpose to defend its way of life, to bankrupt
itself rather than let Hitler take our South American trade—a farce which
ends in red ink every time—and to send the best crop of young technicians
the country has ever known, who could make this fabulously wealthy nation
self-sufficient within itself, into battle.

Charles A. Lindbergh has had the courage at least to present the conserva-
tive side of a titanic problem, grant him that. The United States is a democ-
racy, that's what they say we'll be fighting for. What a prize monument to
that ideal is a cry to smother Lindy. Weighing such inconsequential items as
economic failure and simultaneous collapse of the American Standard of
Living (looks good capitalized—it'll be fine for chuckles in a decade), and
outrageous bloodshed of his countrymen, the young ones, is virtual treason
to the Stars and Stripes—long may it wave.

Lindy, you're a rat. We read that somewhere, so it must be so. They say
you should be deported. In that event, leave room in the boat for us, our
room-mate, Jane, mother, that barber with the mustache in Willard Straight,
and those two guys down the hall—you make sense to us.

Editor's Note: The opinions expressed above are those of the author and
do not necessarily reflect the views of the *Sun.*

The Editor's Note was printed in heavy type. Obviously, the rest of
the staff did not share Vonnegut's views. His connection with the
Sun seems to have been severed at around that time, and Pearl
Harbor put an end to most American protests against the war. But
the unmistakable emotional intensity of that last editorial suggests
how powerfully events were conspiring to crystalize the attitudes
that have shaped Vonnegut's mature work. At the end of the year he
left Cornell and joined the American army. As it turned out, he had
an appointment with the R.A.F. in Dresden on February 13, 1945, for
the completion of his education in pacifism.

Vonnegut's *Cat's Cradle* and *Mother Night*

These two works will serve well to indicate the range and quality of Vonnegut's achievement to date and also will help to reinforce the distinction I have been trying to make between the modern fabulator's comedy of extremity and the method of traditional satire. The need to insist on this distinction is demonstrated continually, but I can illustrate it by citing a retrospective review of Vonnegut's work which appeared in the *New Republic* at the time when he was first beginning to attract serious critical attention: "And so goes Vonnegut's most powerful writing. All the anger, the shame, the shock, the guilt, the compassion, the irony, the control to produce great satire are *there*. . . . Why, then, does Vonnegut settle for such lovely, literate amusing attacks upon such simple targets as scientists, engineers, computer technicians, religion, the American Legion, artists, company picnics?" These words are a comment on a passage from the introduction to *Mother Night*, which will be quoted below, but they are meant as a reaction to all of Vonnegut's work, and could serve as a typical reaction to much of black humor. The review from which I have taken this criticism is long and favorable, but the reviewer is finally baffled by Vonnegut's refusal to turn his material into satire. Such a reaction, it seems to me, is clearly better than assuming either that Vonnegut has produced works of satire or that he is trying to and failing. But it is still an unfortunate reaction and, in a word, wrong. It is based, I should judge, on the assumption that satire is "better" than comedy. Why anyone should assume this, I do not know, though I suspect such an assumption goes along with a belief that the world is sick and that the satirist can cure it by rubbing its nose in the filth it produces. This assumption is one that I want to reject. The world, in any fair historical perspective, is about as sick or healthy as it has been. These times are perhaps more dangerous than some moments in the past, because man's weapons are stronger, but that goes for his weapons against disease as well as for his weapons against life. But whether the world is especially sick, now, or not, there is no evidence that satire ever cured any human ailment, or any social disease either. In fact the whole notion of "great satire" seems rather suspect from this point of view. What *are* the great satires? And what are the hard targets they attack? Is Dr. Pangloss a hard target? Or Stalinist Communism? Even Jonathan Swift's finest achievement, the fourth book of *Gulliver's Travels,* is hard to call a great satire, precisely because its greatness is problematic and not satiric at all.

If I tried to pin down the nature of Vonnegut's fabulation—to find a phrase more descriptive than black humor, and more precise—I would, borrowing a phrase Hugh Kenner used in another connection, call Vonnegut's work stoical comedy. Or perhaps I would go one step further and call it Epicurean comedy—if I could take my definition of Epicureanism from Walter Pater's elaborate fabulation on that subject. Like Pater's *Marius,* Vonnegut's works exhibit an affection for this world and a desire to improve it—but not much hope for improvement. (In making this suggestion toward a name for Vonnegut's fabulation, I do not mean to suggest that it resembles Pater's work in any respect. The slow, dreamy movement of *Marius* is a far cry from Vonnegut's crisp deftness. If we can call Vonnegut's work Epicurean comedy, let us be sure to put the emphasis on the noun—he is a comic artist first and last.)

In *Cat's Cradle* Vonnegut brings his comic perspective to bear on contemporary aspects of the old collision between science and religion. The book is dominated by two characters who are offstage for the most part: a brilliant scientist and the founder of a new religion. The scientist, "Nobel prize physicist Felix Hoenikker," is presented as a child-like innocent who is finally as amoral as only an innocent child can be. He is a "father" of the atomic bomb (rather more of a father to it than to his three children) and he finally develops a much more potent device—*ice-nine*—which can (and does) freeze all the liquid on this watery globe. One of his children tells the narrator this anecdote about him: "For instance, do you know the story about Father on the day they first tested a bomb out at Alamagordo? After the thing went off, after it was a sure thing that America could wipe out a city with just one bomb, a scientist turned to Father and said, 'Science has now known sin.' And do you know what Father said? He said, 'What is sin?' "

This anecdote parallels that told of the jungle doctor by *his* son, which I quoted earlier. The contrast between the aware humanity of the one and the terrible innocence of the other is pointed up by the parallel structure of the anecdotes. The doctor, however, is a minor figure, almost eclipsed by the major opposition between the sinless scientist and the distinctly fallen religious prophet, Bokonon. As the scientist finds the truth that kills, the prophet looks for a saving lie. On the title page of the first of the *Books of Bokonon,* the "Bible" of this new religion, is the abrupt warning: "Don't be a fool! Close this book at once! It is nothing but *foma!*" *Foma* are lies. Bokonon, a Negro from Tobago in the Caribbean, has invented a religion for the island of San Lorenzo (where he arrived, a castaway, after considerable experience of the world). His "Bible" includes some parable-like anecdotes, some epigrams, and many psalm-like calypsos, such as this one:

> I wanted all things
> To seem to make some sense,
> So we all could be happy, yes,
> Instead of tense.
> And I made up lies
> So that they all fit nice,
> And I made this sad world
> A par-a-dise.

The epigraph to Vonnegut's book reads this way:

> Nothing in this book is true.
> "Live by the *foma** that make you brave and
> kind and healthy and happy."
>> *The Books of Bokonon,* 1:5
>> *harmless untruths

The author's disclaimer is partly a parody of the usual "any resemblance to actual persons . . ." hedge against libel suits. But it is also a way of encircling Bokononism and making *Cat's Cradle* a repository of religious untruth itself. The very confrontation in the book between science and religion is aimed at developing the "cruel paradox" that lies at the center of Bokononist thought as it lies at the center of our world: "the heartbreaking necessity of lying about reality, and the heartbreaking impossibility of lying about it."

The ideas I have been trying to sketch out briefly here are only the string for Vonnegut's cat's cradle. The life of the book is in its movement, the turns of plot, of character, and of phrase which give it vitality. Vonnegut's prose has the same virtues as his characterization and plotting. It is deceptively simple, suggestive of the ordinary, but capable of startling and illuminating twists and turns. He uses the rhetorical potential of the short sentence and short paragraph better than anyone now writing, often getting a rich comic or dramatic effect by isolating a single sentence in a separate paragraph or excerpting a phrase from context for a bizarre chapter-heading. The apparent simplicity and ordinariness of his writing mask its efficient power, so that we are often startled when Vonnegut pounces on a tired platitude or cliché like a benevolent mongoose and shakes new life into it: "Son . . . someday this will all be yours."

Despite his mastery of the prose medium, and a sense of the ridiculous which is always on duty, Vonnegut never abandons himself to relentless verbal cleverness of the Peter De Vries sort. Sometimes we may wrongly suspect him of this kind of self-indulgence, as in the opening sentence of *Cat's Cradle*—"Call me Jonah"—which seems like a gratuitous though delightful parody of the opening of *Moby-Dick*, until we realize that by invoking Jonah and *his* whale, along with the biblical Leviathan, Vonnegut is preparing us for a story on the Job theme, with the anti-Joblike conclusion provided by Bokonon's advice to the narrator on the proper posture for death in response to the plague of *ice-nine* (quoted on p. 147 above).

Vonnegut's prose always serves his vision and helps to make narrative structures of that vision. This process is illustrated nicely by a longish passage from the introduction he wrote in 1966 for the new edition of *Mother Night*. In it he speaks of his actual experience as a prisoner of war in Dresden, in prose which has the lucidity of the best journalism enriched with the poetic resources of a born storyteller. (One falls naturally into the word "speaks" in discussing this prose, which gives a strong sense of a voice behind the words.)

There were about a hundred of us in our particular work group, and we were put out as contract labor to a factory that was making a vitamin-enriched malt syrup for pregnant women. It tasted like thin honey laced with hickory smoke. It was good. I wish I had some right now. And the city was

lovely, highly ornamented, like Paris, and untouched by war. It was sup-
posedly an "open" city, not to be attacked since there were no troop concen-
trations or war industries there.

But high explosives were dropped on Dresden by American and British
planes on the night of February 13, 1945, just about twenty-one years ago, as
I now write. There were no particular targets for the bombs. The hope was
that they would create a lot of kindling and drive firemen underground.

And then hundreds of thousands of tiny incendiaries were scattered over
the kindling, like seeds on freshly turned loam. More bombs were dropped
to keep firemen in their holes, and all the little fires grew, joined one
another, became one apocalyptic flame. Hey presto: fire storm. It was the
largest massacre in European history, by the way. And so what?

We didn't get to see the fire storm. We were in a cool meat-locker under a
slaughterhouse with our six guards and ranks and ranks of dressed cadavers
of cattle, pigs, horses, and sheep. We heard the bombs walking around up
there. Now and then there would be a gentle shower of calcimine. If we had
gone above to take a look, we would have been turned into artifacts characteristic of fire storms: seeming pieces of charred firewood two or three feet
long—ridiculously small human beings, or jumbo fried grasshoppers, if you
will.

The malt syrup factory was gone. Everything was gone but the cellars
where 135,000 Hansels and Gretels had been baked like gingerbread men. So
we were put to work as corpse miners, breaking into shelters, bringing
bodies out. And I got to see many German types of all ages as death had
found them, usually with valuables in their laps. Sometimes relatives would
come to watch us dig. They were interesting, too.

So much for Nazis and me.

If I'd been born in Germany, I suppose I would have *been* a Nazi, bopping
Jews and gypsies and Poles around, leaving boots sticking out of snow-
banks, warming myself with my secretly virtuous insides. So it goes.

The admission at the end of this passage suggests one reason why
Vonnegut and other black humorists write the way they do. And in
this respect they are close to the traditional satirists. They would like
to prevent us from "warming ourselves with our secretly virtuous
insides" while we condone the freezing of others. And as long as we
persist in fire-bombing other human beings, they would like to blow
our cool for us. Comically but relentlessly they seek to make us
thoughtful—in all the senses of that most sensible word.

Mother Night is the autobiography of a fictional hero/criminal of
World War II, Howard W. Campbell, Jr. This Campbell is a hero or
criminal depending on how one looks at him. He is an American
who stayed in Germany during the war to broadcast for the Nazis a
special line of virulent anti-Semitism and other hateful stuff: a Nazi

hero, an American traitor. But in his broadcasts he was secretly sending back coded messages for American intelligence: an American hero, a Nazi traitor. The novel begins with Campbell in prison— "a nice new jail in old Jerusalem"—awaiting trial along with Adolf Eichmann. As Campbell unravels his life story, we begin to find out how he got there and to worry about what will happen to him. These affairs are managed very skillfully. With perfect aplomb, Vonnegut juggles three distinct time schemes: the present, the past of the war period, and the past of the post-war period; and three distinct settings: Israel, Germany, and New York. The effect of this juggling is superbly controlled. It operates not so as to call attention to the juggler himself but so as to combine the narrative suspense involved in resolving these actions with a moral and intellectual suspense generated by them. From *what* and *how,* we progress to *why* and *why not*—but without ceasing to care about *what* and *how.* I am not going to give away the lines of narrative development here. The reader deserves the pleasure of experiencing them firsthand, without warning. But I will give away one of the morals because Vonnegut himself mentions it in the first paragraph of his new introduction: "This is the only story of mine whose moral I know. I don't think it is a marvelous moral; I simply happen to know what it is: We are what we pretend to be, so we must be careful about what we pretend to be."

In Vonnegut, as in his contemporaries, we do not find the rhetoric of moral certainty, which has generally been a distinguishing characteristic of the satirical tradition. The writers of modern dark comedy do not seek the superior position of the traditional moralists. Nor do they point to other times and customs as repositories of moral values, or to any traditional system as the Law. Even in essaying to abstract a moral from his own book, Vonnegut makes no special claim for its virtues, or his. The book itself must be the test. Our experience of it must be satisfying and healthy. If this is so, then it may nourish our consciences without requiring reduction to a formula. My feeling is that, far from manifesting sickness (as some critics seem to feel it does), black humor is a sign of life and health.

Vonnegut, in his fiction, is doing what the most serious writers always do. He is helping, in Joyce's phrase, "to create the conscience of the race." What race? Human certainly, not American or German or any other abstraction from humanity. Just as pure romance provides us with necessary psychic exercise, intellectual comedy like Vonnegut's offers us moral stimulation—not fixed ethical positions which we can complacently assume, but such thoughts as exercise our consciences and help us keep our humanity in shape, ready to respond to the humanity of others.

Black Humor in Hawkes and Southern

John Hawkes is perhaps the most consciously traditional of all the modern fabulators. He is also the most experimental, the most avant-garde. I suspect this is no coincidence, and I take it as confirmation of my suspicion that when asked by the late John Enck whether he was an avant-garde writer, Hawkes replied in terms of tradition:

My own concept of "avant-garde" has to do with something constant which we find running through prose fiction from Quevedo, the Spanish picaresque writer, and Thomas Nashe at the beginnings of the English novel, down through Lautréamont, Céline, Nathanael West, Flannery O'Connor, James Purdy, Joseph Heller, myself. This constant is a quality of coldness, detachment, ruthless determination to face up to the enormities of ugliness and potential failure within ourselves and in the world around us, and to bring to this exposure a savage or saving comic spirit and the saving beauties of language. . . . A writer who truly and greatly sustains us is Nabokov.

The line traced by Hawkes, here, from Spanish picaresque through French surrealism to such modern fabulators of the last generation as West and O'Connor is first of all a perfect piece of literary genealogy by a writer who sees his own family tree as clearly as the most gifted of critical heralds could hope to. And, unlike most writers, Hawkes has no desire to conceal—from himself or anyone else—his true ancestry. This may be because his work remains so unequivocally his own. As he put it in the same interview, discussing the one writer whose name really needs to be added to complete a Hawkesian genealogy,

as a matter of fact, while I was reading from *The Lime Twig* last night, I became quite conscious again of echoes of a Faulknerian use of inner consciousness and expanded prose rhythms. The echoes are undeniable, I think—Faulkner is still the American writer I most admire—though at this point I ought to insist again that my work is my own, and that my language, attitudes, and conceptions are unique.

In speaking thus of the writers he admires, Hawkes has not only traced for us his own literary pedigree, he has also pointed to one of the principal strands in the fabric of modern fabulation. In Durrell we saw the romantic strand, enriched by techniques learned from the novelists, but aiming at a return to the source of all fiction, the marvelous well-spring of pure story. In Vonnegut we saw the satiric strand, tempered by modern Epicureanism to a dark comedy of ideas. In Hawkes we have the picaresque strand, with its traditional cruelty and violence modified by its passage from a proto-realistic form to a surrealistic one. In this line of development Céline is a crucial figure and his *Journey to the End of Night* a crucial book. This work is so important because in it Céline seemed to recognize, more deeply than anyone before him, a natural tendency in picaresque toward a grotesque exaggeration of misfortunes: an intensification of everyday troubles into an ironic vision of a distorted cosmos, where a poetic injustice reigns, which destroys all who do not learn to accommodate themselves to it. Céline's surrealism gets to the black heart of the picaresque tradition and finds there an existential despair of the human condition as far removed from satire in one direction as the stoical or Epicurean comedy of Vonnegut is in the other. Content with this discovery, Céline preserved virtually intact the loose and episodic picaresque form which allowed his despairing imagination such freedom as it needed to range from scene to scene and topic to topic. From this point in the picaresque/surrealistic tradition, modern fabulation departs in a number of directions: some writers (and I would number Heller, in *Catch-22*, and Hawkes among them) move toward a tighter narrative structure; Purdy (in *Malcolm*) toward allegory; Terry Southern toward what we might call revenge comedy.

Such distinctions may seem like arid pedantry, but I want to insist on them. That term "black humor," which can be helpful up to a point, also tends to obscure both minor generic differences and the individual qualities of particular writers, leading us to such positions as an insistence that since Hawkes and Vonnegut are both doing black humor and doing it differently, then one must be right and the other wrong. To avoid this sort of critical absurdity we must resist such lumping in some way. The only legitimate way to approach "intention" in a literary work is through a highly discriminated sense of genre. Our reactions to such an immediately enjoyable and "popular" work as Terry Southern's *Magic Christian*, even, will inevitably be enhanced if we are able to "place" the work in some way—if we are able, quite literally, to "get with it."

The Magic Christian has the loosest of narrative structures. It is truly episodic, in some ways resembling a rudimentary ancestor of picaresque more than picaresque itself. In its fundamental narrative pattern *The Magic Christian* is like those Renaissance jest books which string a sequence of quite separate practical jokes and witty replies on a thread consisting of a single central character: the merry pranks of Till Eulenspiegel or his English descendant Howleglass. There was a touch of Robin Hood in Howleglass, in that most of his pranks were directed at people of some substance or authority, but Guy Grand is fabulously rich and enjoys "making it hot" for rich and poor with equal vigor. He is no Robin Hood. What, then, is he? If *The Magic Christian* were an attack on anything, it would be an attack on the human condition. (I avoid the term "human nature" for the same reason the existentialists do. Southern is not satirizing man for his weaknesses. The object of his attention is not a string of human frailties such as the seven deadly sins. It is the total situation which makes for those forms of behavior which at one point in man's history seemed adequately described by the notion of seven deadly sins.) As I said, if this book were an attack, the human condition would be its object. But it is not an attack. Southern's attitude is beyond satire. It reminds us of H. L. Mencken's attitude toward the United States. Mencken's harshest criticisms of American life were always balanced by his feeling that such a rare zoo provided much too amusing a spectacle to abandon merely because it was a bit nauseating. Some such combination of horror and amusement at American life must lie behind all of Southern's work—even the pornoparodical *Candy* and the peacenikky *Dr. Strangelove*. The traditional satirist is always in the awkward position (for an artist) of trying to obliterate his material. If things or people really change, he will have to write something else. But there is in picaresque fiction—from its earliest beginnings—a special relish for the grotesque details of contemporary life and an appreciation of the fact that there is always a catch; which makes its tone rueful but not revolutionary. The satirist often has his vision of Utopia. The picaresque writer expects that there will be catches even there.

The hero of Thomas Nashe's sixteenth-century quasi-picaresque tale, *The Unfortunate Traveller,* thinks of himself on occasion as a divinely appointed minister of justice: "I think confidently I was ordained God's scourge from above." So does Hamlet think of himself at times, for that matter, and so do most revengers in early fiction and drama. The central character in *The Magic Christian,* Guy Grand, who seems partly to be designated by the title (which also refers to an ocean liner, the *S.S. Magic Christian*), is a scourge. He goes around "making it hot" for people, playing somewhat the role assigned to devils in Christian tradition. Like Satan, he is tempter and punisher, and the righteous (or those who feel righteous) must take pleasure in his actions. Thus, in this story Southern not only distorts satiric materials into a comedy of excess, he also imposes on the picaresque world an unlovable but effective kind of poetic justice, which adds another dimension to the comedy—a Dantesque dimension. But the inhabitants of Southern's inferno are not full-blooded sinners paying the penalty for their willful crimes against God's law. They are automata, governed by stock responses to various stimuli—mainly economic.

The man who behaves with rigid, mechanical actions in a world where most men act with some spontaneity is the archetype of the comic figure, Bergson tells us. But what happens when the world turns mechanical and all men behave according to banal and predictable patterns? Guy Grand, a sadist with a sense of humor, is the only "free" individual in the world of *The Magic Christian*—the only "individual" in fact. If we were truly automated ourselves, his actions could not amuse us. The fact that they do suggests that things are not completely hopeless. The mirror is distorted after all. One tiny episode, one of the least amusing in the book but handy because of its brevity, may serve as an example of Southern's technique of vengeful comic distortion:

Speaking of upsets though, Grand upset the equilibrium of a rather smart Madison Avenue advertising agency, Jonathan Reynolds, Ltd., by secretly buying it—*en passant,* so to speak—and putting in as president a pygmy.

At that time it was rare for a man of this skin-pigmentation or stature (much the less both) to hold down a top-power post in one of these swank agencies, and these two handicaps would have been difficult to overcome—though perhaps could have been overcome in due time had the chap shown a reasonable amount of savoir-faire and general ability, or the promise of developing it. In this case, however, Grand had apparently paid the man to behave in an eccentric manner—to scurry about the offices like a squirrel and to chatter raucously in his native tongue. It was more than a nuisance.

An account executive, for example, might be entertaining an extremely important client in his own office, a little tête-à-tête of the very first seriousness—perhaps with an emissary of one of the soap-flake kings—when the door would burst open and in would fly the president, scrambling across the room and under the desk, shrieking pure gibberish, and then out he'd go again, scuttling crabwise over the carpet, teeth and eyes blazing.

"What in God's name was that?" the client would ask, looking slowly about, his face pocked with a terrible frown.

"Why, that . . . that . . ." But the a.e. could not bring himself to tell, not after the first few times anyway. Evidently it was a matter of pride.

Later this a.e. might run into one of his friends from another agency, and the friend would greet him:

"Say, hear you've got a new number one over at J.R., Tommy—what's the chap like?"

"Well, as a matter of fact, Bert . . ."

"You don't mean the old boy's got you on the *mat* already, Tommy. Ha-ha. *That* what you're trying to say?"

"No, Bert, it's . . . well I don't know, Bert, I *just don't know.*"

It was a matter of pride, of course. As against it, salaries had been given a fairly stiff boost, *and* titles. If these dapper execs were to go to another agency now, it would be at a considerable loss of dollars and cents. Most of the old-timers—and the younger ones too, actually—had what it took to stick it out there at J.R.

Like most of the book, this episode draws some of its strength from the validity contained within its distortion. The flabby quality of American life, and in particular our tendency to respond automatically to economic stimuli and the pressures of status, are certainly being illustrated here. But they are not being satirized so much as chastised. Criticism and punishment are so closely fused in this episode that no residue of indignation remains when it is over. The pygmy punishes the venality of the flacks who work at Jonathan Reynolds even as he exposes that venality. And the flacks accept their lot—titles and fat paychecks in return for a purposeless and degrading existence. They "had what it took to stick it out there at J.R." What it took, of course, was "pride of status without pride in function" (Lionel Trilling's phrase)—an empty snobbery which one rejoices to see taking its appropriate punishment.

As I suggested earlier, the title seems to point in part to Guy Grand himself, whose penchant for making things hot for people suggests a devilish figure doing God's work of punishment in a wicked world. The whole book flirts with allegory of this sort. Even the pygmy episode is readily interpretable as a view of an affluent society, a prosperous but aimless state where everyone is well enough paid not to care about the direction of the enterprise. Or this same episode may be seen as an even grander scheme: a cosmic vision of a world which worships a figurehead divinity who talks gibberish while fronting for a real power concerned only with amusing itself at the expense of its creatures. This modern allegory, like Dante's, is interpretable on several levels, though it is neither so serious nor so consistent as his. The picaresque forms of fabulation, like the romantic forms, however fantastic or grotesque their surfaces, continue to be concerned with reality in their depths. And this is nowhere more evident than in the work of John Hawkes, to which we now must turn.

John Hawkes's Theory of Fiction

Considering Hawkes as a picaresque writer, we can begin with the obvious fact that his affinities with the picaresque tradition are not mainly formal. He has accepted some of the dark premises of the picaresque attitude, but he has moved very far indeed from the loose and episodic picaresque form, with its simple, chronological string of events in the life of a roguish individual. In addition to Céline and the early picaresque writers, Hawkes admires Nathanael West, Flannery O'Connor, Faulkner, and Nabokov. His admiration for the last two, in particular, suggests the kind of delight in formal and verbal dexterity that is the essence of fabulation. For a modern writer, such care for form almost inevitably involves the rejection of any too easy adoption of the forms of his predecessors. Alain Robbe-Grillet, for example, in defending himself against charges that his writing is a kind of empty formalism, has responded with a counter-charge that the imitators of Balzacian realism are the true formalists because they slavishly copy the forms devised in another era by another sensibility to represent another reality. The artist who wants to capture modern life, this argument runs, must care for form, because only appropriately new forms will be capable of representing contemporary life. This is a powerful argument; though it does not guarantee that every experiment will succeed. Still less does it convince us that experiment and success are really the same thing. But it does put the argument for newness about as strongly as it can be put. Literary forms have a way of becoming stereotyped, especially successful ones, as anyone can tell who looks through the dreary history of "popular" English fiction. The novelists of the third rank and lower imitated their betters in much the same way that commercial television shows imitate a successful formula.

In the twentieth century it has become increasingly apparent that realism itself, instead of being simply the truest reflection of the world, was simply a formal device like any other, a tool to be put aside when it had lost its cutting edge. In making their revolt against the realistic novel, different writers have resorted to different stratagems. Some have paid lip service to realistic premises while calmly going their own way. Others have taken up polemical positions and publicly challenged representatives of the Old Guard. This latter method is more characteristic of the new French novelists than of their English and American counterparts. But John Hawkes is closer to the French in these matters than any other modern writer I can think of. He has written more criticism than most first-rate American writers do, and he has been readier than most to explain his work seriously in interviews and discussions. In doing this sort of thing, Hawkes has created something like a polemical position for himself. Perhaps because he has done it in this piecemeal and roundabout way, his statements seem unusually free of the self-serving public relations gimmicks that one associates with Robbe-Grillet's frequent position papers. At any rate, I have selected for some serious consideration a statement about his work that Hawkes made in the same interview for *Wisconsin Studies in Contemporary Literature*, from which I quoted his remarks on picaresque above. This statement should help us to see how Hawkes situates his work against the background of previous fiction, and where he would wish us to find the "unique" qualities he mentioned in acknowledging Faulkner's influence on his work.

My novels are not highly plotted, but certainly they're elaborately structured. I began to write fiction on the assumption that the true enemies of the novel were plot, character, setting, and theme, and having once abandoned these familiar ways of thinking about fiction, totality of vision or structure was really all that remained. And structure—verbal and psychological coherence—is still my largest concern as a writer. Related or corresponding event, recurring image and recurring action, these constitute the essential substance or meaningful density of my writing. However, as I suggested before, this kind of structure can't be planned in advance but can only be discovered in the writing process itself. The success of the effort depends on the degree and quality of consciousness that can be brought to bear on fully liberated materials of the unconscious. I'm trying to hold in balance poetic and novelistic methods in order to make the novel a more valid and pleasurable experience.

This statement tells us a good deal, and there are aspects of it which I believe we can accept without reservation as illuminating.

There are others about which I feel we should have some reser-
vations. (I am always suspicious, for instance, of suggestions that
fiction can get along without plot. Both Robbe-Grillet and Hawkes
sometimes claim to have eliminated or suppressed this element in
their fiction, but when I read them I find myself responding to an
intense, forward-moving pressure, a real narrative flow. And this, I
say, is what makes their works stories rather than poems. They may
have abandoned certain conventions of plotting, but I do not think
they have abandoned plot.) But the statement is certainly as good a
way into Hawkes's special world as any other, especially if we
understand all its implications. What I propose to do is examine
three parts of the statement in some detail, working out some of their
implications, in hopes that they will serve to illuminate our later and
more specific consideration of Hawkes's practice as a fabulator. One
is the question of plot *vs.* structure. A second is the notion that
structure is developed by a process in which consciousness works on
materials liberated from the unconscious. A third is the notion that
this structure (which can be seen as a balance between poetic and
novelistic methods) should lead the reader to a valid and pleasurable
experience.

Each of these three parts of the statement points toward a different
object. Structure directs our attention to the internal coherence of the
works themselves, and beyond that to the art with which they have
been put together. The relationship between consciousness and unconsciousness emphasizes both the connection of the works to the
psychological processes of the author—along with his understanding
of them—and, by extension, to all mental processes; Hawkes means
to use conscious thought and art to illuminate the unconscious, to
show us things about ourselves which may be locked in our own
unconscious minds, avoiding the scrutiny of our consciousness. Finally, the notions of pleasure and validity point directly to our
experience as readers—in two different ways. Hawkes feels that his
aim is to produce a "more" valid experience. More valid than what?
More valid, I should think, than that of the "conventional" novel,
and perhaps more valid than our experience of day-to-day living as
well. But why "valid" in particular, rather than "real" or "true"—
more common words for the rational content of fiction? The word has
interesting implications. "Real" would point to an absolute and
empirically verifiable sort of truth—scientific, the truth of "realism."

"True" would also suggest an absolute, not physical but metaphysical. "Valid," on the other hand, introduces a less comprehensive kind of accuracy, suggesting an internal coherence rather than a correct statement about something outside the work itself. In logic, a proposition is valid if its conclusion is correctly derived from its premises. But validity, precisely because of its self-checking characteristic, is never relative. It is a logical absolute. No proposition is *more* valid than another. Thus when Hawkes uses the expression "more valid" he is removing the quality of validity from its precise application in logic and employing it in another context. In what sense can a fiction have qualities analogous to logical validity? In the sense of internal consistency, one supposes, but Hawkes seems to be aiming here at a consistency beyond the internal.

He is suggesting that the validity he is aiming for—and the pleasure he hopes to give—are functions of his attempt (a) to balance poetic and novelistic methods, and (b) to apply conscious consideration to materials from the unconscious. Thus "validity," in this context, becomes both a matter of art and of life, of form and of content. It involves discovery and creation simultaneously. The artist, by his method of composition, which is as unplanned as possible, proceeding by recurrences and correspondences rather than logical or chronological sequence, seeks to induce a sort of dreamlike state—first in himself, last in his audience. Durrell's Arnauti, we remember, wanted to set his book "free to dream." Hawkes wants to keep his esthetic superego sufficiently dormant to allow dark materials to well up from his subconscious. Then—when they are "fully liberated"—he will turn the machinery of his consciousness—tuned as delicately as possible—upon these materials. The ideal reader of Hawkes should probably participate in a reciprocal fashion: his delicately tuned consciousness will lead him finally into the ideal dreamlike state; but if he reads with inert incomprehension, he will never experience the book at all. As the writer moves from unconscious materials to conscious deployment of them, the reader must move from conscious reception to an awareness of the unconscious.

A notion something like the old surrealistic method of "automatic writing" seems to lie behind Hawkes's formulation here. Except that André Breton and the surrealists would have been horrified at the thought of allowing consciousness to work on these precious materials. Hawkes, on the other hand, insists that a valid structure in

fiction depends on the combination of conscious thought with materials from beyond consciousness—just as a successful psychoanalysis
depends on the analyst's skill in first helping the patient expose and
liberate the sources of his anxieties or neuroses, and then (almost
simultaneously) in making a valid interpretation of the symbols
through which these materials are manifested. Hawkes has modeled
his manner of proceeding as a fabulator, apparently, on the techniques of psychoanalysis. Thus his works are most likely to find their
justification in terms of psychic value. Not, like pure romance, in
terms of the pleasures of wish-fulfillment; nor, like intellectual comedy, in the joy of perceiving the world as ordered and rationalized by
a comic vision; but in terms of the psychic relief of facing our fears
and anxieties, to grapple with them rather than flee from them.

Now, the last thing I wish to do here is suggest a hierarchy of
values for the different modes of fabulation. I believe we need them
all—need all our dreams and all our laughter. But at this point I must
emphasize our need for the kind of nightmare experience which
Hawkes is most concerned with giving us. One need not be a Jungian to see how important it is for man to face his "shadow." Conrad
was thinking of this need when he worked out that extraordinary
fabulation, *The Heart of Darkness*. In Conrad's view, if man does not
face and acknowledge the dark in him in order to struggle with it, he
will become its victim. Kurtz is "hollow" because he thinks he has
reached a pitch of civilization safely beyond savagery. This is why he
is such an easy convert to the bestial. Hawkes, in virtually all of his
fabulations, seems in search of ways to liberate images from the heart
of darkness so that they may awake in the reader an emotional
consciousness of evil along with a shock of recognition.

At this point we have considered—perhaps as extensively as one
should without a text in front of him—two of the three aspects of
Hawkes's statement. We have yet to consider the distinction between plot and structure. This is a very slippery area in narrative
theory, and it will probably be well to set out a few guidelines
before plunging into it. There is a sense, of course, in which we
immediately understand the point Hawkes is making about his fiction. He has certainly turned away from orthodox plotting. And he
has turned in the opposite direction from a writer like John Barth,
who has chosen to emphasize plot more than the realistic novelists
did, rather than to reduce its role in his fabulations. But there is a

kind of counter-movement in both these turns. By his exaggeration of "plottiness" in a work like *The Sot-Weed Factor*, Barth finally causes us to take his plot more lightly than we might take a less rococo arrangement of events. A sort of esthetic inflation operates, which makes such plotting—as in *Tom Jones*—less serious as it becomes more energetic. A highly plotted novel *wants* to become comic. This has always been an esthetic problem for the writer of romance. Fielding and Barth, in the works mentioned, take advantage of this comic momentum by making the tone and decor of their works enhance this comic plotting.

Similarly, by reducing the overt plottiness of his fiction, Hawkes generates an intense reaction to such elements of plot as remain there. If Barth gives us the sense of being on a great roller-coaster ride, in which we move up and down—but always safely on a track, Hawkes seems to place us in an emotional quicksand where we struggle painfully for every inch, and finish with a sense of great achievement when we lie gasping on firm ground a few steps from where we began. Thus by driving his plot underground Hawkes has made it less visible but no less important. His work *is* poetical, in his sense, of course. That is, it is a tissue of recurring and corresponding images and verbal patterns which are emotionally and intellectually meaningful. But his fabulations are not poems; they always depend on some sort of narrative impetus to keep the reader moving. The recurring beads are held together by a string of plot. The buried string of events attracts our attention and draws us toward it, so that we prize it all the more when we have discovered it and experienced it. The dislocations of time and space in Hawkes's work serve the same purpose that they do in Conrad, Ford, and Faulkner. They involve the reader in the constructive process, making him help to create the story.

I have been writing with all of Hawkes's fiction in mind—to the extent that I could hold it there—but this is not a really satisfactory way to proceed. It is time to look at specific works. I have chosen *The Lime Twig* for fairly extended treatment because it seems to me representative of the controlled wit and power which animates Hawkes's mature work. But before turning to it, I wish to pause a moment over an early and somewhat neglected piece: his first long fiction, *Charivari*.

Charivari is militantly avant-garde, not in the philosophical sense employed by Hawkes in speaking of a perpetual avant-gardism, but

in the more trivial sense of formally shocking. After appearing in a
New Directions anthology it long remained unprinted—the only one of
Hawkes's fabulations not published in book form. It seems at once
more aggressive and more tentative than the nearly contemporary
Cannibal: more certain of what it is not, less certain of what it is;
closer to Nathanael West, more overtly surrealistic and psychoanalyti-
cal, but less richly and deeply imagined. Perhaps we have in this
work an excess of conscious effort working on an insufficiency of
materials liberated from the unconscious. It is, then, not a great
performance, but it has a special importance for us because it reveals
so much about the roots of Hawkes's fiction. It also has the special
charm that often accompanies youthful precociousness. I, for one,
should like to see it reprinted in a separate volume. But because of its
relative inaccessibility, I will assume my readers have not read it.

The book's aggressiveness begins with its title: a word to be
looked up. Unlike Hawkes's other titles which are words to be
understood in context, this word provides a context for understanding the book. "Charivari. . . . A serenade of 'rough music,' with
kettles, pans, tea-trays, and the like, used in France, in mockery and
derision of incongruous or unpopular marriages. . . .   The *OED*."
This particular *Charivari* is a surrealistic examination of the
marriage of two "typical" well-to-do modern people. The married
couple are a pair of forty-year-old children, faced with the fact that
the "bride," after fourteen years of marriage, has become pregnant.
The ground plan of the narrative covers two days in the lives of the
married couple—two days mainly devoted to a houseparty of West/
Fitzgerald and Waugh/Huxley tone and dimensions. In the course of
these two days both husband and wife make forays away from their
home, where the party is in progress. The husband rides a bus into
town, considers picking up a woman who resembles his wife, and is
finally brought back home like a runaway child in his father's
limousine. The woman drowns in a wild storm. The wife too makes a
child-like limousine voyage—accompanied by her mother—to have
her pregnancy verified (with overtones of abortion) by a doctor who
finds it hysterical (or aborts it) much to everyone's relief. When she
returns, miraculously restored to youth by the doctor's discovery, the
party continues with fun and games:

When she ran across the lawn, hair loose and flying, colored skirt whirling
about her knees, he knew she was not going to have a child. The flowers

around her neck were white with dew, and as she ran she laughed, and her
face was momentarily bright.

"My goodness," thought Henry, "she *does* look younger." She ran quickly
towards him.

Gaylor blew loudly on his whistle. "All right," he called, "it's time to
play."

The two excursions from the party are used by Hawkes as ways of
illuminating the suppressed fears and desires of Emily and Henry.
These two, racked by a fear of growing up, of living as adults and
hence of dying, represent aspects of the modern cult of youth. And
the entire work, borrowing its hallucinatory technique from surrealism and such originals as the Circe episode of Joyce's *Ulysses*—
where hallucination is employed mainly to act out sexual fantasy—
can be seen as a bitter satirical fantasy of the Nathanael West variety.
It also has a good deal in common with the early Albee play *The
American Dream*. Both Hawkes and Albee, in these early works, seem
to have found surrealism a handy vehicle for attacking contemporary
mores. Later on, one suspects, they became dissatisfied with using
such a powerful weapon on such easy targets. Both the Albee play
and *Charivari* are full of delightful exuberance and joy in the mastery
of technique—the joy of the fabulator realizing his skills. But their
display of skill invites us to question their employment of it. In many
writers—one thinks of Jane Austen's parodies or some of Joyce's
supercilious epiphanies—the easy satirical victories of youth pave
the way for more searching and problematic achievements later on.
To realize this, however, is not the same as to wish such works
unwritten. In addition to such interest as they have in themselves,
they are often of special value as ways into the mind and art of their
authors. The cruder values and more blatant displays of the early
work may help us to understand the more complex values and more
subtle techniques of mature work. *Charivari* is in itself quite good
indeed—more interesting than Albee's *American Dream*, I should
say—and in it we can find some clear examples of the attitudes and
techniques which, in more refined form, shape the later works. One
of the most important attitudes, one, in fact, which seems to be a
governing attitude throughout all of Hawkes's work, is the attitude
toward cruelty in fiction which the narrator of *Charivari* formulates
with a bold directness and simplicity that we shall not find elsewhere
in his fiction: "And have you heard, or do you think we are likely to

hear what very private shames and resentments and misgivings these people are harboring? May we be cruel enough?"

Something like this purpose seems to animate all of Hawkes's fabulation. The cruelty and brutality of the work are there in order to expose private shames and resentments. But this statement in *Charivari* is a bit too complacent about locating the shames and resentments in the characters only—"these people." A sense is established of reader and narrator conniving to expose "them." In the later works the exposure involves *us* as well as *them*. Here the reader's psyche is insulated from emotional complicity by a curtain of satiric detachment which Hawkes drops between reader and characters. To me, this sort of detachment is an aspect of the special kind of youthful idealism one encounters in modern student rebellions. The word at Berkeley during the free-speech demonstrations was, "Don't trust anyone over thirty." The pathos of this slogan lies in its acceptance of the connection between this kind of idealism and immaturity. The old have "sold out." They have what Hawkes has called here "private shames and resentments" which inhibit their devotion to the ideal. The characters of picaresque are usually "them." Rogues and whores, outcasts and outlaws. But picaresque depends for its effect on our sense of some common conditions uniting us and them: common outlandish impulses, perhaps, and a common suspicion of the way things happen—a sense of the unfitness of things. *Charivari*, however, is less picaresque in spirit than Hawkes's later work. It is a satire of manners, really. And Hawkes's growth as a writer has involved developing beyond satire. His cruel and clever wit finds its true scope in works like *The Lime Twig* and *Second Skin*, where it functions more circumspectly and humanely.

The view of himself presented by Hawkes in the interview I quoted earlier emphasizes the quality of cold wittiness present in his work. It does not direct our attention to the delicate sensibility which is married to that wit in the later works, and in isolated passages even of *Charivari*. Here, I suspect, we may have a blind spot in the writer's self-scrutiny. He may be unaware of—or reluctant to recognize—the extent to which his work depends not on wit alone, but on wit and tenderness interacting. The source of his narrative power, it seems to me, is located at the point where his cruel wit and delicate sensibility converge to generate the special tonal qualities which mark his best work. I think we have some of his best work in *The Lime Twig*, and I propose to examine some of it here in detail.

The Lime Twig

To trace the interconnections between cruelty and tenderness in *The Lime Twig*, I must try to concentrate closely on the texture of particular passages, but in the context of the work's total structure. To do this I am going to consider a fairly large block of narrative, Chapters 6 and 7 (pp. 123-62 in the New Directions paperback). In dealing closely with so much material, I am necessarily going to assume a reader who has his copy and can follow my references back and forth, but I shall try to quote the really vital passages as well. These chapters do not provide the most dazzling verbal pyrotechnics of the book. There are other passages and episodes more brilliant in themselves—the superb unloading of Rock Castle from the barge, for instance, with the Faulknerian rhythms Hawkes acknowledged (see above, p. 163). But these two chapters will serve quite well to illustrate the way Hawkes qualifies and controls the cruel vision of his later works. They will also provide a narrative unit sizable enough for some consideration of the way plot and structure operate in this work. And finally, since brutality and cruelty are not only matters of the novelist's vision in these chapters but their subject matter as well, this discussion can be the occasion to face the special problem of responding to the brutal in Hawkes's work.

The problem is apparently a real one, since it seems to bother reviewers and ordinary readers alike. It is related to similar responses to quite different writers, however, those writers who can be lumped with Hawkes as black humorists. For certain readers and reviewers black humor is apparently a synonym for "offensive"; thus it can be applied indiscriminately to the excremental gaiety of Barth's *Sot-Weed Factor,* the jolly stoicism of Vonnegut's *Cat's Cradle,* or the chilling cruelty of *The Lime Twig.* Against such blanket indictments there can be no rational defense, but there is a more serious and pointed charge which is sometimes made specifically against

Hawkes. This is worth some attention. A convenient statement of this charge happened (as it was meant to, no doubt) to arrive in my mailbox in the form of a review of Hawkes's novel, *Second Skin*. The editor-in-chief of *Salmagundi* charges Hawkes with playing "to the expectation of an audience which is if anything too ready to embrace violence and madness as a norm, at least insofar as 'artistic' reflections of experience are concerned." And he adds the following two strictures, which seem fairly to sum up a whole line of argument against the kind of thing Hawkes is doing:

> The appallingly violent character of the experience depicted in *Second Skin*, while it washes over our sensorium, is not something to which we can intellectually attest. It is not a truth I can affirm from the experience I know, and is therefore not creditable as a viable representation of our common situation. . . .
>
> That a John Hawkes should feel compelled to dwell on morbidity and perversion because it is expected of him, because to do so is somehow part of his function, is indeed lamentable.

These criticisms, though directed at *Second Skin*, could apply equally well to *The Lime Twig*, which is just as well stocked with materials this reviewer would call appallingly violent, morbid, and perverse. As I understand this line of attack, it makes two related charges against Hawkes: (a) that his work is not a valid record of common experience, and (b) that it is morbid, indulging in excesses of brutality when it could be persuading us to some sort of uplifting social commitment. The first point can be disposed of briefly. Extremes of violence such as those given us in Chapter 6 of *The Lime Twig* are not common experiences, but they are frequent enough for such scenes in fiction to have innumerable counterparts in journalism. In war and in peace, man is often a brutal animal. Furthermore, even those who have never been personally involved in external violence (surely not a large majority in these militant decades) must find in their responses to fictional cruelty and brutality genuine psychic echoes of these fictional events. The second point is both harder and easier to answer. As for the writer's responsibility to make the world better rather than worse, I certainly acknowledge it. But the writer of fiction is concerned with his reader as an individual. His aim is to exercise the separate sensibilities of his readership, not to weld them into a great society. But even if this is so, point (b) is not fully answered until we have considered the uses of what the reviewer calls "morbidity and perversion." To deal with this question fairly, we must have a text in front of us. Chapter 6 of *The Lime Twig* ought to be a fair test.

The central event of this chapter is the beating of innocent Margaret Banks by the brutal mobster Thick. Margaret's attempt to escape has given this sadist an excuse to go to work on her with his rubber truncheon:

His arm went up quivering, over his head with the truncheon falling back, and came down hard and solid as a length of cold fat stripped from a pig, and the truncheon beat into her just above the knee; then into the flesh of her mid-thigh; then on her hips; and on the tops of her legs. And each blow quicker and harder than the last, until the strokes went wild and he was aiming randomly at abdomen and loins, the thin fat and the flesh that was deeper, each time letting the rubber lie where it landed then drawing the length of it across stomach or pit of stomach or hip before raising it to the air once more and swinging it down. It made a sound like a dead bird falling to empty field. Once he stopped to increase the volume of the radio, but returned to the bedside, shuffling, squinting down at her, his mouth a separate organ paralyzed in the lower part of his face, and paused deceptively and then made a rapid swing at her, a feint and then the loudest blow of all so swiftly that she could not gasp. When he finally stopped for good she was bleeding, but not from any wound she could see.

We know why Thick does this; the question is why does Hawkes feel obliged to devote a chapter to it, why does he present it so elaborately, why, in fact, does he present it at all? Is this a perverse indulgence, a wallowing in brutality for its own sake?

These questions should be considered from two aspects. One has to do with the function of this chapter in the narrative as a whole: the degree to which it can be accounted for in terms of specific contributions to the larger scheme. The other has to do with the way brutality and cruelty are presented here; in comparison with other works which present us with the cruel and brutal, to what extent does this work seem wantonly sadistic? The second question, if answered satisfactorily, should help us to answer the first. The more clearly we see what is going on when Thick beats Margaret, the better we will be able to understand the relationship of this scene to the rest of the book.

First of all, we need to remind ourselves that there are beatings and beatings—many ways of actually hurting people and many ways of describing or representing any such occurrence in literature. An examination of some scenes from other works of fiction may help us to put this one in perspective. First of all, consider this familiar episode:

Stephen closed his eyes and held out in the air his trembling hand with the palm upwards. He felt the prefect of studies touch it for a moment at the fingers to straighten it and then the swish of the sleeve of the soutane as the pandybat was lifted to strike. A hot burning stinging tingling blow like the loud crack of a broken stick made his trembling hand crumple together like a leaf in the fire: and at the sound and the pain scalding tears were driven into his eyes. His whole body was shaking with fright, his arm was shaking and his crumpled burning livid hand shook like a loose leaf in the air. A cry sprang to his lips, a prayer to be let off. But though the tears scalded his eyes and his limbs quivered with pain and fright he held back the hot tears and the cry that scalded his throat.

This beating is not finished. There is another hand to come. But we have enough to see what Joyce is up to. His main effort is to render the physical pain undergone by Stephen and the associated emotional pain: the "hot burning stinging tingling blow," the "fierce maddening stinging tingling pain," followed by "a palsy of fright" and the "scalding cry" and "scalding tears" which well up in Stephen to his "shame" and "rage." Joyce's rendering of physical pain here should help us see how little Hawkes is concerned to render it: in fact, how carefully he avoids it. It is not Margaret's pain but her situation as helpless victim which Hawkes is rendering. Joyce's simile of Stephen's hand crumpling like "a leaf in the fire" is just one detail in a whole sequence of high-temperature imagery Joyce uses as the most potent means of evoking pain. (Hell is fiery for the same reason.) Hawkes, however, emphasizes the coldness of the weapon and its ugly sexuality ("hard and solid as a length of cold fat stripped from a pig") and in his most elaborate image compares the sound of the blows to "a dead bird falling to empty field." This image is telling us more about Margaret's situation as lonely victim than about the sound it is ostensibly aimed at rendering. Sympathetic fear, not empathetic pain, is the emotional effect actually sought by the prose in this passage.

For another perspective on cruelty, consider this passage from a less familiar work:

The air immediately resounds to the whistle of lashes and the thud of stripes sinking into lovely flesh; Octavie's screams mingle with the sounds of leather, the monk's curses reply: what a scene for these libertines surrendering themselves to a thousand obscenities in the midst of us all! They applaud him, they cheer him on; however, Octavie's skin changes color, the brightest tints incarnadine join the lily sparkle; but what might perhaps divert Love for an instant, were moderation to have direction of the sacrifice, becomes, thanks to severity, a frightful crime against Love's laws; nothing stops or slows the perfidious monk, the more the young student complains, the more the professor's harshness explodes; from the back to the knee, everything is treated in the same way, and it is at last upon his barbaric pleasures' blood-drenched vestiges the savage quenches his flames.

This is the real thing, Sadism with a capital S, from *Justine*. The obvious parallels with the scene in *The Lime Twig* should be noted: the innocent female victim, the brute who takes pleasure in her pain, the viciousness of the beating itself. But the differences in the two scenes far outweigh their surface similarities. In Sade, the effects of the beating are themselves described in voluptuous terms: "the brightest tints incarnadine join the lily sparkle"; and the subject, though finally beaten to a pulp, is afterward a fit object for further abuses: "The rest of the *soirée* would have resembled all the others had it not been for the beauty and the touching age of this young maiden who more than usually inflamed those villains and caused them to multiply their infamies; it was satiety rather than commiseration that sent the unhappy child back to her room and gave her, for a few hours at least, the rest and quiet she needed." This orgy makes an hour with Thick and his truncheon seem like a pleasant massage in comparison—yet no permanent damage is done. Sade's characters are inexhaustible and indestructible. They are exactly skin deep. His fantasies are truly erotic because he separates pain from destruction, making it a mere sensation rather than an expression of bodily malaise. We do not sympathize with the objects of Sade's voluptuous fantasies because they are so indestructible, like some special kind of doll which not only wets its panties and says "mamma" but bleeds when whipped—all without in any way suggesting actual human life. But Margaret Banks is hurt by her beating—not just pained but damaged, physically and psychologically:

Thick had been too rough with her, treated her too roughly, and some things didn't tolerate surviving, some parts of her couldn't stand a beating. She hadn't even her free hands with which to rub them. [p. 130]

. . . a wetness under the eye exposed to the wash of light and the sobs just bubbling on the lips. Margaret inert, immobile, young woman with insides ruptured and fingers curling at the moment of giving sound to her grievance. [p. 131]

We are a long way from Sade here. But we are not with the sentimentalists, indulging in a "good cry" over a poor victim. Hawkes has worked in a number of ways to frustrate any attempt we make to descend into mere sentimentality here. He is, as in all his best work, trying to construct what Rilke called a "bridge barely curved that connects the terrible with the tender." And even in this scene, the bridge of his sympathetic perception is braced and stiffened by his cold and grotesque wit. Margaret's relief (p.128) at the thought that Thick has his truncheon and will not be reduced to his favorite substitute is—even under the circumstances—comic: "she thought that a wet newspaper would be unbearable." The pitiful inadequacy of this response to her situation, which is unbearable in any case, is pathetic. But Margaret's maintenance of her own prim perspective under these terrible circumstances, the incongruous rigidity of her mental processes, qualifies the pathos of her situation. Her perception of Thick as a sort of naughty child also has in it a bizarre mixture of appropriateness and incongruity. His truncheon makes "her think of a bean bag, an amusement for a child," which is partly just an inadequate response to the threat in the instrument, derived from Margaret's innocence, and partly a very shrewd perception of Thick's childishness. This sort of complication, which prevents any easy sentimental response to these brutal events, is also in evidence in the complicity of understanding (as between mother and naughty child) between her and Thick. The paragraph just preceding the actual beating is an extraordinary one:

Then something happened to his face. To the mouth, really. The sour sweat was there and the mouth went white, so rigid and distended that for a moment he couldn't speak: yet all at once she knew, knew well enough the kinds of things he was saying—to himself, to her—and in the darkness and hearing the faint symphonic program, she was suddenly surprised that he could say such things.

Innocent Margaret is surprised that Thick can think the things she attributes to him. He does not speak aloud, but she understands whatever sadistic ravings are implied by that white, rigid, distended mouth. And so do we. She is surprised that Thick "could say such things." We are surprised that Margaret can find words for thoughts that so surprise her. But we know what she means he means. By her understanding she becomes a kind of accomplice to this crime of sadism. And by ours we share that guilt.

A further dimension, also partly comic, is added to these events by the matter-of-factness Margaret maintains throughout. A touch of pride enters into the way she conceives of her experience. She is "like a convent girl accepting the mysteries . . . and no matter how much she accepted she knew it now: something they couldn't show in films." To conceive the inconceivable elements of her experience she tries to frame it in religious or cinematic terms. It is like an initiation into inconceivable "mysteries," and it is too outlandish to be put on the screen. These terms, again both pitifully inadequate and curiously appropriate, make Margaret's situation both poignantly accessible to us and ironically distanced from our own situations. Thus Hawkes, by intertwining comic and pathetic elements, has generated a situation so fraught with tones and attitudes that no simple emotional reaction is adequate to it. And when we consider the relationship between the events of this chapter and the rest of the story, we find further important lines of connection sufficient to dispel any notion we might still have that the brutality we have been considering is gratuitous or indulged in for its own sake.

Margaret's destruction, of course, is "undeserved." In the picaresque world this is the way things happen; rewards and punishments are incongruous and inappropriate. But this is not a purely picaresque world. Things happen in a curiously dislocated way, but there is also a kind of logic at work, a kind of plotting behind the apparently random sequence of events which makes the events more meaningful than they could be in a merely episodic structure. In the chapter we have been considering, Margaret suffers because of Michael's involvement with the people who make her suffer. Not only does she become hostage and victim so that the gang will have maximum control over Michael, but, specifically, some of what she suffers has been directly and immediately caused by Michael's actions of the same night—actions which are presented to us *after* we see their results so that we apprehend them colored by their consequences. We are forced to see them ethically.

In Chapter 7, Hawkes chronicles Michael's activities of the same night we have been considering in Chapter 6, and in his presentation he takes care to give us a number of ways to synchronize the two chapters and understand their interrelationship. Actually, Chapter 7 overlaps Chapter 6 chronologically. Chapter 6 begins at "4 A.M.," after Margaret's partial recovery from Thick's violence (which is narrated in a flashback). The chapter ends with Larry's additional violence. He slashes Margaret's wrists as he cuts the ropes that have tied her to the bed:

"You've wounded me," she whispered, eyes to the ceiling and in darkness. "You cut me."

He said only: "I meant to cut you, Miss. . . ."

So sometime after 4 A.M. she tried to use her numb and sleeping arms, twice struck out at him, then found her hands, the bleeding wrists, the elbows, and at last her cheek going down beneath and against the solid sheen of his bullet-proof vest.

This rape of Margaret is the final violence of the sixth chapter. And among our other reactions it leaves us wondering whether there might have been any particular reason for Larry's cruelty here; we wonder why he "meant" to cut Margaret. The next chapter provides our answer, but not at first. It begins earlier, at "2 A.M. of the last night he spent alive," with Michael cavorting in bed with Larry's girl Sybilline. Her task has been to keep Michael docile and amused until the race is over, but she has apparently exceeded the call of duty, having "given a single promise and three times already made it good." And this is only the beginning of a night of surrealistic sexual activity for Michael. Before the evening is over he also contents the widowed landlady; Annie, the girl next door; and finally even Dora. After Annie, he returns to the parlor while Dora and the others are stripping Larry down to his bullet-proof vest:

The pearl buttons came off the shirt and Banks stepped no closer, though Sybilline was there and laughing on one of Larry's arms. "Oh, do what Little Dora says," he heard her cry, "I want you to!" And there was a bruise, a fresh nasty bruise, beneath Syb's eye. [p. 158]

The bruise is the first part of Larry's reaction to Sybilline's behavior with Michael. The rape of Margaret is the final part: "he was cock of this house." Thus after Michael retires to engage in his final sexual activity of the evening—this time with Dora—Larry, with his torso bare except for the bullet-proof vest, visits Margaret. By giving us the timing of the two chapters so precisely—one beginning at

four, the other at two—Hawkes helps us to make the necessary
synchronization. But he also uses another device, which reaches out
beyond synchronization for the book's larger implications. In each
chapter we have a bird on a branch. In Chapter 6 Margaret hears it
just before Larry enters:

> Outside on a branch above the garbage receptacle, an oven tit was stirring:
> not singing but moving testily amidst the disorder of leaf, straw sprig,
> remnant of gorse, fluttering now and then or scratching, making no attempt
> to disguise the mood, the pallidness, which later it would affect to conceal in
> liveliness and muted song. A warbler. But a sleepless bird and irritable.
> Through drowsiness and barge-heavy pain she noticed the sounds of it and
> did not smile; saw rather a panorama of chimneys, fine rain, officers of the
> law and low yards empty of children; farther off there was a heap of tile and a
> young woman in rubber shoes, an apron and wide white cap, and there were
> bloodstains on the ticking.

In Chapter 7 Michael hears its mate:

> The mate of the oven tit had found a branch outside his window and he
> heard its damp scratching and its talk. Even two oven tits may be snared and
> separated in such a dawn. He listened, turned his head under the shadows,
> and reflected that the little bird was fagged. And he could feel the wet light
> rising round all the broken doors, the slatted crevices, rising round the fens,
> the dripping petrol pump, up the calves and thighs of the public and de-
> serted visions of the naked man—the fire put out in the steam-bath alley,
> the kitchen fire drowned, himself fagged and tasteless as the bird on the sick
> bough.

The birds serve to link the two chapters and the two characters.
This evening with its bizarre and strenuous activities has seen them
both receive initiation "into the mysteries." In their separate beds
they have explored the world of violence and sensuality. Margaret's
excess of pain and suffering has been ironically balanced by Michael's excess of "pleasure." But they are both doomed. It is the
last night for both. They are like birds lured to a lime twig and stuck
fast for destruction. The two chapters end almost simultaneously.
Little Monica discreetly runs out of Margaret's room as Larry begins
his assault, only to be shot by the absurd constable. Michael, pricked
by one of the pearls Sybilline lost in his bed, fingers it idly and drops
it ("lost the pearl for good") just as the constable's shot explodes in
his ears.

Michael has become like one of those characters in folk literature
(often doomed), who have their wishes granted. Annie's appearance

at the orgy is simply the result of Michael's having lusted after her
—the girl next door—at one time or another. The whole involvement of Michael and Margaret with Larry and the gang is the result of
another wish fulfilled—a dream: "his own worst dream, and best,
was of a horse which was itself the flesh of all violent dreams."
Hencher is the fairy godmother who grants Michael his wish. The
destruction that ensues has been lurking in Michael's dream all
along. "If wishes were horses, beggars would ride," our folk wisdom
tells us. And when Michael's wish takes on the form of horseflesh,
Michael rides out to his destruction. He "rides" sexually throughout
that long pre-race orgy. And he races out across the track on the day
of the Golden Bowl to throw himself in the path of the destructive
energy he has unleashed, to bring to a halt the terrible motion of his
dream fulfilled. This act of self-destruction redeems Michael, returns
him from the brutal dream world of Larry and Syb to the ordinary
world of humanity. He atones for the crimes he has helped set in
motion, and especially for what his dream has done to Margaret—
that suffering of which we readers are so well aware. At the moment
of Michael's death a voice—it must be half-dead Margaret's—asks
"take me out to him, please," ratifying with this loyalty and care
Michael's decision to break the hold of the dream upon him by
meeting it head-on.

In *The Lime Twig* Hawkes has gone well beyond the easy satire of
Charivari to a richer, more complex mode of narrative. By pruning
somewhat his surrealistic exuberance, and coming to terms (even if
somewhat ironic and parodic ones) with fiction's need for plot, he
has achieved a controlled intensity of effect which bridges beautifully the gap between terror and tenderness. This effect is based
partly on the balance he maintains between the delicately serious
and the grotesquely comic, and partly on the way he has ordered the
flow of information about the events of the story as they enter our
consciousness. He demands a resolutely alert reader, willing to pay
close attention to detail and piece out from dislocated hints the real
fabric of events: what has happened, what is happening, and what is
going to happen.

In the two chapters which I have been discussing, the order in
which the fictional events enter our consciousness has much to do
with our attitude toward them and toward the whole narrative. We
know why Thick beats Margaret, but we have to wonder about why

Larry cuts her, finally reaching understanding through an inference based on the fresh bruise under Sybilline's eye. Our discoveries about the timing of events also serve to enrich our attitude toward them. At 4 A.M. Margaret is recovering from the beating she received "several hours" earlier. At 2 A.M. Michael has finished his third "commotion" with Sybilline. So we must conclude that Thick's sadistic performance and Michael's more normally erotic one were cruelly synchronous.

In *The Lime Twig* the very language in which events are described conspires to suggest connections and correlations with other events. Thick's truncheon, sounding like "a dead bird falling to empty field," is subtly and ironically connected to Michael's flinging aside the widow's whalebone stay "as he might a branch in a tangled wood." Birds and branches are woven all through *The Lime Twig*, making a tapestry of images which elaborates on the motif of the title. Michael is ominously greeted by a "tiny black bird" (p. 30) as he stands near his and Margaret's bed at the beginning of the day in which he becomes involved in "this crime." Lying in bed and plotting, Hencher hears "a little bird trying to sing on the ledge where the Kidneys used to freeze" (p. 28). This interweaving of images around the title motif (which one could follow at much greater length than I have here) must be the sort of thing Hawkes had in mind when he spoke of introducing a poetic structure into his work in place of the traditional plot. But this structure in *The Lime Twig* is subordinated to the more peculiarly narrative structure of multiple suspense which gives the story its driving force.

One of the things I am trying to suggest here is that this kind of book, which seems so foggy and dreamlike, is actually as neatly and tightly put together as the electrical circuitry of the human nervous system. In his perceptive introduction to the book, Leslie Fiedler makes one emphasis which I should like to reverse. He suggests that Hawkes "does not abandon all form in his quest for the illusion of formlessness." I should like to go much further, to say that not only are there what Fiedler calls "occasions for wit and grace" in the book, but that it has been plotted with a grace and constructed with a wit that makes the whole story not a "random conjunction" but a true fabulation—a more satisfying piece of work than any casual construct, no matter how full of occasional graces, might be. The revulsion inherent in facing the shadow of terror is turned into a pleasurable experience for Hawkes's readers precisely by means of his care for form. It is the form—and the sense it gives us of connections and correspondences, along with the feeling of controlled movement from tension to stability—which makes such terrible materials not merely bearable but beautiful. This is what makes Hawkes a fabulator like the one described in the fable: capable of rejoicing us when we are heavy. The joy that goes into the fabulation is returned to us in the reading. And it is for this joy that we must be grateful, even to the darkest of fabulators.

A Portrait of the Artist as "Escape-Goat": Malamud's *Fidelman*

Bernard Malamud's *Pictures of Fidelman* is his *Portrait of the Artist*. In each of its six pictures (or stories) Arthur Fidelman is caught, frozen in some crucial posture, on his way to an esthetic Calvary. The stories are, in a sense, six comic Stations of the Cross. We can trace Fidelman's progress through these Stations, as he plays the roles of both Judas and Jesus, betrayer and betrayed, until the ultimate betrayal, which is his salvation. It is safe to say these rather ponderous and academic things about Malamud, because his readership is established and knows that he never fails to communicate in a simple and humane manner. In this respect he resembles that quite different novelist, Kurt Vonnegut, Jr. Both men have tried to write really serious and modern fiction for a broader audience than that reached by some of their contemporaries. It may be no accident that they also share a comic and compassionate vision of the world, although Vonnegut is primarily, like John Barth and John Leonard, a novelist of ideas, whereas Malamud is primarily, like Saul Bellow and Philip Roth, a more traditional novelist of social and psychological behavior. And, like the Bellow of *Herzog* and the Roth of *Portnoy*, Malamud is forthrightly and gratefully a Jewish novelist. However, it seems to me (and I write from a *goyische* perspective) that Malamud is the best of these Jewish novelists, that he has been more successful than the others in universalizing his Jewishness.

The WASPish parody of *Portnoy* that appeared in the *New York Times Book Review*—a mock review of "Peabody's Complaint"—was possible because *Portnoy* is ostensibly so exclusively Jewish. (As if only Jews have Jewish mothers!) But Malamud's Arthur Fidelman, who also has a mother and a sister whom he spies and sponges on, passes through as universal a rendition of the artist's progress as the Catholic Stephen Dedalus or the Protestant Gulley Jimson. *Pictures of*

Fidelman, an allegory of the artistic and moral life, is clearly an achievement. The story, in its panel of pictures, is reminiscent of Hogarth; but whereas Hogarth's Rake and Harlot progress downward to destruction, Fidelman progresses down and out—to salvation. He becomes (to coin formally an expression I have seen on high school English themes) an "escape-goat."

When we first see Fidelman in "Last Mohican," he is making a false start on his career—the first of many. He plans to be an art critic and has come to Italy with the opening chapter of a book on Giotto already completed. In Rome he encounters the *schnorrer* Shimon Susskind, who steals his manuscript and finally burns it, offering in defense the statement: "I did you a favor. . . . The words were there but the spirit was missing." Saved by the grace of Susskind from the hideous fate of becoming a critic, Fidelman seems on his way. After all, how could an artist fall lower than to repudiate art for criticism? Fidelman could and does. In the second picture, "Still Life," he rents part of a woman artist's studio in Rome, only to pursue her more assiduously than his work. After a sequence of bizarre misadventures, he unlocks the young *pittrice*'s heart and door inadvertently by donning a priest's garb to attempt a self-portrait "of the Artist as Priest." Annamaria confesses to him what she cannot tell her own confessor, and he finally makes love to her, still wearing, at her request, part of his costume:

"Not the cassock, too clumsy."
"At least the biretta."
He agreed to that.
Annamaria undressed in a swoop. Her body was extraordinarily lovely, the flesh glowing. In her bed they tightly embraced. She clasped his buttocks, he cupped hers. Pumping slowly he nailed her to her cross.

In the next picture, "Naked Nude," Fidelman has "progressed" from a false priest and lover to janitor of a whorehouse. Here he forges a Titian nude in order to escape from his despicable position. As a forger, he paints his best work, and he ratifies this criminal deed by stealing his copy instead of the original when he has the chance. In "A Pimp's Revenge" Fidelman does not merely sink to pandering. The subject of his one continuing painting-in-progress sinks from "Mother and Son," to "Brother and Sister," to "Prostitute and Procurer." (Alexander Portnoy would understand.) Even the artist's name in this tale dwindles from Fidelman to F. When he completes this new and truer portrait of himself, the artist as pimp, he cannot let it alone and finally ruins the picture by trying to make it "truer to life."

The fifth picture presents, in a mosaic of fragmented episodes, Fidelman's descent to the underworld: the artist as huckster peddling holes in the ground as sculpture with a pseudo-esthetic pitch about form being the content of art; the artist as Judas, trying to win fame by painting Christ-Susskind's portrait, then spending his traitor's reward of silver on "paints, brushes, canvas"; and finally the artist as a brother too preoccupied with his work to speak to his dying sister. Through a comic miracle, Fidelman finally says hello to Bessie on her deathbed, preparing the way for his salvation in his sixth picture.

Salvation works in queer ways. In "The Glass Blower of Venice" Fidelman has given up painting and lives by performing menial errands. Then he seduces—or is seduced by—the wife of Beppo, a glass-blower. One day Beppo, who prefers men to women anyway, catches Fidelman in the act of adultery and gently sodomizes him. "Think of love," the glass-blower murmurs. "You've run from it all your life." Apprenticed to Beppo, Fidelman learns to invent life instead of art. He discovers love, and he becomes a glass-worker. Ultimately he returns home. "In America he worked as a craftsman in glass and loved men and women."

This sometime critic, impostor, forger, pimp, and Judas is saved by giving love rather than taking it, and by abandoning the pretenses of art for the honesty of craftsmanship. Salvation through sodomy sounds like an outrageous and almost blasphemous notion. But, as presented by Malamud, it is only sufficiently shocking to wake us into awareness. Malamud is writing about love: and love, which is never "normal," is not an automatic thing like heterosexuality. In the iconography of these pictures, Fidelman's submission to Beppo symbolizes the acceptance of imperfections in existence. Craft, not art; love of men and women, not Love. This wise and kindly vision concludes a work in which we find Malamud the craftsman at his wry and comic best, a gentle fabulator, whose allegory shines through a surface which is itself deceptively realistic. In his other recent work, where he has approached historical and social problems more directly, the results have been less happy.

Ishmael's Black Art

Whoever called him Ishmael picked the right name. His hand is against every man's—and every woman's, too. Or so it seems. He is a black Juvenal, a man to whom satire comes as naturally as breathing. And, like Juvenal, he might well ask who could consider the last decade and not be a satirist. Especially if he concentrated on the San Francisco Bay area. So Ishmael Reed is a black satirist, which is not exactly the same thing as a black humorist. Oh no. Though his prose wickedly parodies everything from street talk to academic rhetoric, he is not to be confused with those who use their art as a bulwark against the horrors of existence. Ishmael Reed is a committed man, a satirist with a specific point of view. Beneath that funky façade beats the heart of a preacher.

Since his first novel, *The Free-Lance Pallbearers,* appeared in 1967, he has been recognized as a writer of extraordinary facility. His prose has been compared to works by such masters of other media as Hieronymus Bosch and John Coltrane. With each new novel—*Yellow Back Radio Broke-Down* in 1969 and *Mumbo Jumbo* in 1972—his reputation has increased. In fact, people have been laughing at him so hard and praising him so indiscriminately that little attention has been paid to what he is saying. In his fourth novel he is as funny as ever, but the message is coming through clearly, and not all those who understand it are going to find it palatable. For Reed is offering his own weird fiction as an antidote to certain elements of black mythology dear to the hearts of liberal sociologists. And he is doing this from a political position somewhat to the right of Booker T. Washington.

The world of *The Last Days of Louisiana Red* is a cartoonist's version of the last decade in Berkeley, California. And the cartoonist who has given us this picture is closer in spirit to Al Capp than to Herblock. Major figures in this satirical gumbo are Street Yellings, Maxwell

Kasavubu, the Rev. Rookie, Big Sally, Cinnamon Easterhood, and Rusty. Street is an escaped murderer who "had his 'consciousness raised' in prison and was immediately granted asylum in an 'emerging' African nation." Maxwell Kasavubu is a white literature instructor "on loan" to Berkeley from Columbia University. He is "writing a critical book on Richard Wright's masterpiece, *Native Son.*" His "startling thesis, now being circulated in literary and political circles," is "that Richard Wright's Bigger Thomas wasn't executed at all but had been smuggled out of prison at the 11th hour and would soon return." Max has this recurring nightmare in which he is a blond woman about to be raped or murdered (or both) by Bigger Thomas, and by the end of the book he thinks he himself is Bigger.

The Rev. Rookie of the Gross Christian Church preaches "a powerful jumpy sermon replete with strobes, bongos, and psychedelic paraphernalia." At a meeting of leaders of the Moocher Movement, the Rev. Rookie, who shouts in capital letters, comes out with things like "MY UKELELE AND PETE SEEGER RECORDS ARE OUT IN THE VW," plus a lot of "TELL IT, SISTER, TELL IT" and things like that. Big Sally has "a Ph.D. in Black English." She talks like this: "I ain't through. Now I ain't through. Let me finish what I'm saying and then you can have your turn to talk, cause ain't no use of all us talking at one time, and so you just sit there and let me finish." Cinnamon Easterhood, "hi-yellow editor" of the *Moocher Monthly*, comes to the meeting "all tense and hi-strung in a nehru suit, clutching a wooden handbag which the men were wearing or carrying these days." Easterhood smiles at Sally's talk but really wants to crawl out of the room. "He didn't mind all that downhomeness, but, shit, he had an M.A." Accompanying Easterhood is Rusty, "his dust-bowl woman of euro descent, wearing old raggedy dirty blue jeans, no bra, and no shoes." Rusty admires Street Yellings. "She remembered his Wanted poster in the post office. The girls would go down there and get all fired up." But, deep down, Rusty has ambitions. She wants "to play tennis, express myself, visit motels."

Ishmael Reed has a shrewd eye, a mean ear, a nasty tongue. The main object of his satire is the organization called The Moochers. Moochers are "people who, when they are to blame, say it's the other fellow's fault for bringing it up. Moochers don't return stuff they borrow. Moochers ask you to share when they have nothing to share. Moochers kill their enemies like the South American insect that kills its foe by squirting it with its own blood. God do they suffer." And finally, the highest order of this species of Moocher is the President, who "uses the taxpayers' money to build homes all over the world where he can be alone to contemplate his place in history when history don't even want him." This is the unkindest cut of all, seeing Nixon and his enemies on the New Left in the same light, as Moochers, whining and grabbing, talking poverty but living high. Reed attacks self-serving hypocrisy wherever he finds it.

These thrusts at Moochism hit the mark, but they are not the ultimate end of the book, which is a rewriting of black history and black sociology—a sort of lowering of consciousness. After all, if blacks got into the Moocher Movement it was only because the Movement wanted to use them, as whites have used blacks since this country began. The hero of *The Last Days of Louisiana Red* is the old hoodoo detective, Papa La Bas, who comes out to Berkeley from New York to solve the murder of Street Yellings's father, Ed, and to save Ed's Solid Gumbo Works from destruction. Ed Yellings had been fighting Louisiana Red—the way exploited people "oppressed one another, maimed and murdered one another"—fighting it with Solid Gumbo, a mysterious antidote to the psychological poison of Louisiana Red. In solving Ed's murder, La Bas also exposes the false history of blacks in America, a history concocted and supported by white men and black women—who have always gotten along together very well. This false history fosters the myth that black women have been the only force holding families together over the years. La Bas tells Ed's radical daughter Minnie (the Moocher) that this belief is an insult to "the millions of negro men who've supported their families, freemen who bought their families freedom, negro men working as parking-lot attendants, busboys, slop emptiers, performing every despicable deed to make ends meet against tremendous odds." And through La Bas's words we hear the voice of Ishmael Reed, preaching up a storm.

Like his hero, Papa La Bas, Reed admires "pros." He, too, is against "Louisiana Red: insolence, sloppiness, attitude, sounds from the reptilian brain." As a preacher, Reed is addressing other members of the Afro-American persuasion, telling them pretty much what Booker T. told them a while ago. He is not really speaking to the white middle-class citizens who will buy most of the copies of this book. But he knows we are listening, and every now and then lets fly a verbal arrow in our direction. Still, he saves his most barbed shafts for blacks, especially black women. Which puts us somewhat in the position of bystanders at a family quarrel. We may be horrified or amused—or both. But we are too fascinated to go away. So there we are, caught between outrage and hilarity, trying to follow an alien idiom, and worrying about whether we should really be enjoying all this so much. And this amusement is not without its risks. Bystanders at a family quarrel often get hurt. Look out!

But also learn. Reed's combination of fabulation and satire, of surrealism and caricature, has roots in Ralph Ellison and strong affinities with other socially engaged fabulators like Robert Coover, William Burroughs, and J. G. Ballard. Yet Reed also seems gifted with a kind of fundamental high-spiritedness and good humor that keep his satire close to comedy and prevent his black art from sinking into the futilities of literary rage.

Epilogue

In the past decades two parallel movements of mind have characterized our society. In academic circles a philosophical sense of the inevitable disparity between words and things has led to a "deconstructivist" attitude toward all texts. Every text is seen as a pretext to be plumbed for repressed attitudes and latent meanings. The only interesting readings are misreadings. The best books are the least readable. At the same time, a popular or vulgar version of this attitude has grown even more widely. This takes the form of cynicism and skepticism about all public statements. The more people understand media, the more conscious they are of mediation. When skepticism reaches a certain point, persuasion fails. And when persuasion fails, can coercion be far behind?

There are deep and troubling political problems here for a society founded on persuasive processes, but our present concern is with only the literary dimensions of the problem. Specifically, what can writers do to confront this skepticism in their audiences and in themselves? Can one be suspicious of all "facts" and still have a care for "truth"? Or should one rejoice in freedom from "truth" and revel in the mendaciousness of "facts"? One response to this situation has been a "new" journalism that frankly asserts the personality of the journalist and focuses our attention on the process of mediation itself, as the writer struggles to make sense of the world with words, often through a haze of booze or drugs, sometimes in the throes of personal crisis, mental instability, anger, and shame. I do not mean to mock the real achievements of such writers, often purchased at great psychic cost. As a literary form, however, this genre is very volatile, and seems more a symptom of our predicament than a solution to it. But the writer of fiction who would deal with historical realities (as opposed to journalistic immediacies) must confront many of the same philosophical doubts without recourse to the solution of personality. For the novelist, personality is not enough.

History as Fabulation: Malamud and Vonnegut

The Fixer and *Slaughterhouse-Five* represent two approaches to the problem of writing fiction about historical events. It seemed to me when each of these books came out—and it still seems to me—that Vonnegut's more fabulative approach to history solved the problems better than Malamud's attempt to be more "faithful" to fact and probability. You may feel otherwise. But here are my arguments.

By one of those coincidences so common in the world of ideas, two books were published in the fall of 1966, both "based" on the long-neglected trial of the Jew Mendel Beiliss for ritual murder of a Christian boy. The trial took place in Kiev, Russia, in 1913. It seems, in retrospect, to have been a curious affair, brought on by a uniquely Russian combination of medieval and modern anti-Semitism. Coming so shortly after the Dreyfus case, the final acquittal of Beiliss seemed to mark a new and more enlightened era—distinguished by the absence of hysterical anti-Semitism. As Hitler and Stalin taught us, the Beiliss case was not an epilogue but a prelude.

Here, however, we are concerned not with history but with a literary event: the publication of a fourth novel by one of our better novelists. This event has been properly celebrated by a multitude of reviewers in the daily and weekly press. But in the general rejoicing over the appearance of a new work by this very gifted writer, only a few critics have remembered to be critical; only a few have tried to take the measure of the work itself and relate it to Malamud's other work. In attempting to do this myself, I have come to the melancholy conclusion that the book is Malamud's weakest novel; that, despite a few flashes of the unique Malamud wit and sensibility, this is an ordinary book. Not a bad book or a stupid one, mind you—there is a lot of territory between *The Valley of the Dolls* and Malamud country—but an undistinguished book.

In attempting to understand the reasons for what I judge to be a poor performance, I reviewed in my mind this novel's three predecessors, *The Natural*, a wonderfully grotesque baseball fantasy; *The Assistant*, a strong and problematic drama of human relationships; and *A New Life*, a delicate blend of comedy and pathos, again concentrating on relationships—especially the most intense: love—but in a different setting and a different key from the tragic notes touched in *The Assistant*. A beginning—and more than a beginning —of great promise and considerable achievement in these three novels, I should say. Considerable variety of subject and treatment, unified by that indispensable quality, a unique perspective—an individual style or tone. Whether serious or clowning, Malamud's wry and delicate grotesquerie is his special quality. Tamed, after the fantastic flights of *The Natural*, this sense of the grotesque was placed by Malamud in the service of a revitalized realism, making for the very substantial achievement of his next two novels.

This quality is not altogether lacking in *The Fixer*, yet *The Fixer* seems a distinct falling off from its predecessors. In trying to account for the relative failure of this novel, I began with its most obvious difference from its predecessors: the fact that it is a "historical" novel. The almost simultaneous appearance of another work "based" on the same historical event—Maurice Samuel's *Blood Accusation*— led me to consider the two works together. It was an instructive experience.

I have been keeping the word "based" in quotation marks as a precaution. Obviously, a work of history and a work of imagination are not "based" on an event in the same manner. The imaginative writer moves from the base of specific events toward some satisfying artistic shape and some universal aspect of the human situation. He seeks to make a myth. The historian, of course, is after another kind of truth. He is concerned with what really happened: his truth must be, first of all, factual. Thus, it would be absurd to judge Malamud's novel as a history of the Beiliss case. But it is not absurd to use a history of the case as a way of examining just what Malamud has done in moving from his factual base to his imaginative myth. This is what I tried to do.

I was, first of all, astonished to discover how closely Malamud followed the actual pattern of events leading up to the trial. He chose not to include the trial itself—though it is certainly the most dramatic thing in the case history—but he accepted the general pattern of the actual events and he used, with some ingenious compression and modification, quite a few of the historical personages involved in the Beiliss case. He rejected the trial, I should judge, as material for his novel in order to shift the focus from the outcome of events to the character at the center of those events. And he modified history so as to isolate his fictional hero and make his situation more poignant. Beiliss seems to have been a dull little man, respectably married, father of five, legally employed, with some friendly acquaintances outside the Jewish community of Kiev, including a local priest. But the fictional Yakov Bok is childless; his wife has run off with a goy; he is illegally employed under an assumed name in a forbidden area; and he is absolutely friendless. Bok is also a homespun philosopher of sorts, a reader of Spinoza, and a pretty shrewd fellow with a quip or humorous reflection on life. All these departures from fact seem appropriately imaginative. And there are other purely fictional things, especially in the first part of the novel, which seem to me quite convincing and compelling.

It is not, in fact, the departures from history but the intrusions of it and the restrictions it generates which weaken the novel as a work of art. A particularly flagrant case of intrusion is the lawyer Ostrovsky's visit to Bok in prison, where we find the visitor saying, "Your case is tied up with the frustrations of recent Russian history . . ." and going on for two pages with facts about the Tsar, the Duma, and the Constitution, while Bok says, "Yes, but go on." Such undigested gobbets of history represent Research rather than Art. Moreover, the whole action of the novel has been keyed to the pattern of events in the historical Beiliss episode in an unfortunate way. Beiliss was imprisoned for two years without a trial. And so is Bok. After his arrest on page 69, Bok spends most of the book's remaining 265 pages in prison, and much of this in solitary confinement. This must have been the major technical problem Malamud faced in writing the book—a self-imposed problem carried over from history into fiction. Malamud chose to restrict himself rigidly to the point of view of Yakov Bok during a period when he was mainly an imprisoned victim with almost no scope for action. All of the bizarre and fascinating activity around Beiliss, which makes *Blood Accusation* such absorbing reading, comes to us, if at all, through the awkward device of expositors like the lawyer Ostrovsky.

Through works of literature we have already had considerable experience with the Russian penal system. From autocracy to communism, from Dostoevsky to Koestler, we have learned about what to expect from this system. Malamud has no surprises for us here. He has only his hero's character to work with. So much time in jail—a limited character in a limiting environment—so many pages. The problem is to find appropriate action to explore and develop the character of Yakov Bok. Here Malamud is quickly reduced to some obvious melodrama, numerous dreams and hallucinations, and discussions with a string of curiously implausible visitors including relatives, well-wishers, and policemen. And he does what he can with the prisoner's guards. But history and imagination are obstructing one another at this point, with factual research intruding awkwardly into imaginary conversations, and imaginative material clashing with our sense of actual probabilities. The central problem of the historical novel—how to make fact and imagination reinforce one another—is one which Malamud has not solved in *The Fixer*. On this central failure rest most of the weaknesses in this disappointing work.

Kurt Vonnegut speaks with the voice of the "silent generation," and his quiet words explain the quiescence of his contemporaries. This is especially true of his sixth novel, *Slaughterhouse-Five*, in which he looks back—or tries to look back—at his wartime experience. In the first chapter he tells us how for over twenty years he has been trying to re-create a single event, the bombing of Dresden by American and British pilots. Vonnegut had an unusual perspective on that event. Safe, as a prisoner of war in a deep cellar under the stockyards, he emerged to find 135,000 German civilians smoldering around him. Dresden had been an open city. We closed it. We. We Anglo-Saxons, as a recent ruler of France liked to term us.

For twenty years Vonnegut has been trying to do fictional justice to that historical event. Now he has finished, and he calls his book a failure. Speaking of the biblical destruction of Sodom and Gomorrah (like Dresden, subjected to a firestorm), Vonnegut writes:

Those were vile people in both those cities, as is well known. The world is better off without them.
And Lot's wife, of course, was told not to look back where all those people

and their homes had been. But she looked back, and I love her for that, because it was so human.

So she was turned to a pillar of salt. So it goes.

People aren't supposed to look back. I'm certainly not going to do it anymore.

I've finished my war book now. The next one I write is going to be fun. This one is a failure, and had to be, since it was written by a pillar of salt.

The connection between that biblical act of God and the destruction of Dresden is not accidental. Vonnegut's book is subtitled "The Children's Crusade." The point is a simple one, but it is important. The cruelest of deeds are done in the best of causes. It is as simple as that. The best writers of our time have been telling us with all their imaginative power that our problems are not in our institutions but in ourselves. Violence is not only (as Stokely Carmichael put it) "as American as apple pie." It is as human as man. We like to hurt folks, and we especially like to hurt them in a good cause. We judge our pleasure by their pain. The most dangerous people in the world are those with an unshakable certainty that they are right. A man *that* certain of his cause will readily send a bunch of kids off to rescue his Holy Land. His rectitude will justify any crimes. Revolution, wars, crusades—these are all ways of justifying human cruelty.

It may seem as if I have drifted away from considering Vonnegut's book. But I haven't. This is what his book keeps whispering in its quietest voice. Be kind. Don't hurt. Death is coming for all of us anyway, and it is better to be Lot's wife looking back through salty eyes than the Deity that destroyed those cities of the plain in order to save them.

Far from being a "failure," *Slaughterhouse-Five* is an extraordinary success. It is a book we need to read, and to reread. It has the same virtues as Vonnegut's best previous work. It is funny, compassionate, and wise. The humor in Vonnegut's fiction is what enables us to contemplate the horror that he finds in contemporary existence. It does not disguise the awful things perceived; it merely strengthens and comforts us to the point where such perception is bearable. Comedy can look into depths which tragedy dares not acknowledge. The comic is the only mode which can allow itself to contemplate absurdity. That is why so many of our best writers are, like Vonnegut, what Hugh Kenner would call "Stoic Comedians." Vonnegut's comic prose reduces large areas of experience to the dimensions of a laboratory slide. Consider how much of human nature and the nature of war he has managed to encompass in this brief paragraph: "Billy . . . saw in his memory . . . poor old Edgar Derby in front of a firing squad in the ruins of Dresden. There were only four men in that squad. Billy had heard that one man in each squad was customarily given a rifle loaded with a blank cartridge. Billy didn't think there would be a blank cartridge issued in a squad that small, in a war that old." The simpleminded thought processes of Billy Pilgrim are reflected in those ultra-simple sentences. But the wisdom and verbal skill of the author shaped the final, telling phrases: "in a squad that small, in a war that old." That deceptively simple prose is equally effective when focused on peacetime American life. In speaking of Billy's mother (who acquired an "extremely gruesome crucifix" in a Santa Fe gift shop) Vonnegut says, "Like so many Americans, she was trying to construct a life that made sense from things she found in gift shops." The pathos of human beings enmeshed in the relentless triviality of contemporary American culture has never been more adequately expressed.

Serious critics have shown some reluctance to acknowledge that Vonnegut is among the best writers of his generation. He is, I suspect, both too funny and too intelligible for many, who confuse muddled earnestness with profundity. Vonnegut is not confused. He sees all too clearly. That also is the problem of the central character of *Slaughterhouse-Five*, Billy Pilgrim, an optometrist from Ilium, New York. Billy sees into the fourth dimension and travels, or says he does, to the planet Tralfamadore, in a distant galaxy. Only Billy's time-warped perspective could do justice to the cosmic absurdity of his life, which is Vonnegut's life and ours. Billy's wartime capture and imprisonment, his ordinary middle-class life in America, and his visionary space-time traveling are reference points by which we can begin to recognize where we are. The truth of Vonnegut's vision requires its fiction. That is what justifies his activity as a novelist and all imaginative writing, ancient, and modern. Art, as Picasso has said, is a lie that makes us realize the truth. Kurt Vonnegut is a true artist.

Fabulation as History: Barth, García-Marquez, Fowles, Pynchon, Coover

It has happened while we were unaware. The major novels of the past decade or so have tended strongly toward the apparently worn-out form of the historical novel. John Barth's *Sot-Weed Factor*, Gabriel García-Marquez's *One Hundred Years of Solitude*, John Fowles's *French Lieutenant's Woman*, Thomas Pynchon's *Gravity's Rainbow*, and Robert Coover's *Public Burning* are all historical novels. But they are not novels based upon the empirical concepts of history that dominated Western thought in the nineteenth century. The North American works, in particular, bristle with facts and smell of research of the most painstaking kind. Yet they deliberately challenge the notion that history may be retrieved by objective investigations of fact.

These are fabulative histories that mix fact with fantasy in ways unique to this time. We might speculate endlessly—and fruitlessly—about why this is so. But that it *is* so, is incontestable. The fabulative impulse has achieved its most impressive results when it has worked most closely with the raw material of history. *The Sot-Weed Factor* is based upon a real poem of that name by a real Ebeneezer Cooke, and is more full of history than a DAR clambake. Yet it is frankly fabulous, delighting in stories for their own sake and outrageously inventing totally implausible "documents" to fill the lacunae in the historical record. Plugging the gaps in the record in this way amounts to a rape of history by imagination: an idea that reaches its literal culmination at the end of Coover's *Public Burning* when a fabulous Uncle Sam buggers a historical replica of Richard Nixon.

Even less ambitious works—more popular, more readable—like E. L. Doctorow's *Ragtime* share this impulse. When a historical Emma Goldman gives a historical Evelyn Nesbit a quite implausible rub-down with a totally fictional voyeur masturbating in the closet, so that his ejaculation "traced the air like bullets and then settled slowly over Evelyn in her bed like falling ticker tape," we have a similar intrusion of fantasy upon the historical record. Where Stephen Dedalus found history to be a nightmare from which he was trying to awake, the verbal artists of *our* time find it readily adaptable to the artifices of daydream and fabulation.

Part of the justification for this strange procedure is put in the mouth of Coover's narrator, Richard Nixon, as he ponders the mysteries of the Rosenberg case:

what was fact, what intent, what was framework, what was essence? Strange, the impact of History, the grip it has on us, yet it was nothing but words. Accidental accretions for the most part, leaving most of the story out. We have not yet begun to explore the true power of the Word, I thought. What if we broke all the rules, played games with the evidence, manipulated language itself, made History a partisan ally? [*Public Burning*, p. 137]

The fact is that an "innocent" history, a collection of facts and deeds, is itself a myth—and a myth that has lost its power to command belief. Art enters the scene even before the turning of deeds into words. The Rosenberg trial, for instance, is a theatrical event:

Not only was everybody in this case from the judge down—indeed just about everyone in the nation, in and out of the government, myself included—behaving like actors caught up in a play, but we all seemed moreover to be aware of just what we were doing and at the same time of our inability, committed as we were to some higher purpose, some larger script as it were, to do otherwise. [p. 117]

Saypol had even managed to arrange a complete dress rehearsal—sort of like trying the show out in New Haven—in the thematically similar, though less serious, Brothman-Moskowitz trial four months earlier, in which virtually the entire cast—including the Judge and excepting only the accused—was the same. Thus the Rosenbergs and their lawyers were the only ones not rehearsed, and were in effect having to attempt amateur improvisation theater in the midst of a carefully rehearsed professional drama. Naturally they looked clumsy and unsure of themselves . . . and so, a bit like uneasy liars. [p. 121]

Not only is the trial a public event, but some of the evidence itself is pure fabulation. One of the key witnesses, Harry Gold, is a very strange fellow indeed:

. . . as a boy—probably now in prison, still—he played these weird baseball games with decks of cards, inventing a whole league of eight teams with all

their players, playing out full seasons, keeping all the box scores and statistics, even taking note of what they looked liked! It's a wonder one of his ace
pitchers didn't turn up in the trial testimony as a contact or something.
Maybe one did. And vice versa. [p. 124]

Robert Coover once played a baseball game like that, as does his
tetragrammatical protagonist, J. Henry Waugh, in *The Universal
Baseball Association*. Like Coover, like Waugh, Gold is a fabulator,
and, as Nixon observes, the attorneys at the trial feel they just can't
"trust a fabulator like Gold": "A preposterous tale; but who could
say? More than once what looked like a complete Gold fantasy had
resulted in arrests and confessions almost as though he were dreaming the world into being. Maybe *he* was the real playwright here" (p.
126).

Coover's point is that fabulation is not simply something that
happens after events, distorting the truth of the historical record.
Fabulation is there *before*, making and shaping not merely the record
but also the events themselves. So how can any historian hope to
record events that are themselves "preposterous" or interpret a trial
which is a drama based on fabulation? The question is rhetorical. Let
it hang there, unanswered.

A similar situation exists in *Gravity's Rainbow*, which is documen-
tarily accurate to an extraordinary degree but calmly intersperses
outrageous and impossible events among its historical details. *One
Hundred Years of Solitude* mixes history and fabulation in a different
manner: with much less documentation and a more obviously legendary style of presentation. But it is a history all the same, in the form
of a modern, fabulative epic narration. Only the English novel in this
group of five stands out as less obsessed with the dilemmas of
historiography. And even Fowles, in *The French Lieutenant's Woman*,
engages in metafictional manipulations, allowing his narrator to
burst through the frame and rupture the surface plausibility of the
fiction by setting his watch back and giving us a second ending. For
all these writers history is important. It offers the temptation of truth,
a temptation they find irresistible. But they seek the truth in dimensions of experience beyond the factual and documentary. And the
North Americans in particular are obsessed with their own history—perhaps because they live in a country which was itself a
fabulous fiction that grew in the minds of men like Columbus,
Hudson, and John Smith before they found it and founded it—and in

the minds of other men like Paine, Jefferson, and Franklin, who invented its political and social structures out of their ideals and hopes, and then sought as actors on the stage of history to make a real nation out of their fabulous dreams.

In America myth has always been stronger than reality, romanticism stronger than realism. What Barth, Pynchon, and Coover have tried to give us in these books is nothing less than the kind of realism this culture deserves. We have always pretended to be pragmatical—and so we have been, in a sense. We accepted whatever worked and invented myths of all kinds to justify it, including myths of freedom, equality, and justice which we have never succeeded in achieving in fact. No matter if we have more of these things than many other nations. We had a dream. We have always had a dream. And we pretended it was real until we believed the pretense. *The Sot-Weed Factor*, *Gravity's Rainbow*, and *The Public Burning* are offered as atonement for the guilt of having created a fabulation and pretended it was real. After his rape by Uncle Sam the narrator of Coover's book says essentially what Winston Smith said of Big Brother in *1984* after his torture and destruction as a person: *"I . . . I love you, Uncle Sam!"*

All these books remind us—or *should* remind us—of one other dimension of *1984*. In Orwell's world humanity is finished precisely because reality itself has been destroyed and replaced with fictions. If the appeal to truth is denied, then all that is left is power. And surely the energy and inventiveness of Barth, the obsessive ingenuity of Pynchon, and the shame and anger of Coover are themselves signs of faith in something. If the truth is that our whole history is a mess of fabulation and deception, then this at least *is* the truth, and it can be told, or at least suggested, in books like these. But for how long? These books are marvelous monsters, like leviathans and pachyderms. The environment grows more hostile to them every day. They may indeed go the way of the woolly mammoth, preserved only as skeletons in the display cases of college lit courses, to be marveled at for having ever existed but not suggested as models for emulation. Fabulation itself will last as long as humanity, for we have need of it; but these great and gaudy creatures seem already part of an era that is drawing to a close.

Imagination Dead Imagine: Reflections on Self-Reflexive Fiction

Imagine a literary conference. It might have actually taken place somewhere in Wisconsin not too long ago, but imagine it anyway. The same road—imagination—leads to both fable and history. There is no other way to go. At this conference there might be people like Raymond Federman, W. H. Gass, Ihab Hassan, Jerome Klinkowitz, and Robert Scholes. Imagine them, too. And finally, imagine that at a panel on self-reflexive fiction the final speaker, whose time has been restricted by the length of other panelists' reflections, gets up and extemporizes for a few minutes along the following lines:

In the two minutes that are left I have a few profundities to utter, with diagrams that I hope you will all carefully copy and take home. Among the various critical postures (and impostures) being voiced at this conference, I suppose that I represent Ye Olde Literarye History—a traditional branch of criticism frequently assumed to be defunct, but just as frequently phoenix-like rising to function again. I invoke this specter (or perhaps have been myself invoked by it) because we obviously need the perspectives of literary history here to put self-reflexive fiction in its place among other narrative strategies.

If we look at the history of narrative literature, as we must to discover where we are, it makes a great deal of difference how long we look and how far we see. The following diagrams, which I offer somewhat more seriously than Lawrence Sterne's diagrams in that most self-reflexive fiction, *Tristram Shandy*, should illustrate this point. If we assume that the history of narrative began somewhere at a point in time which we may call alpha, and is moving toward some future point, the end of the world, perhaps, called omega, we can visualize the history of narrative as a line $\alpha\omega$.

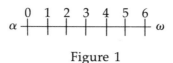

Figure 1

Now most of us who have investigated the history of narrative would find any graphic representation of this history unsatisfying, because history has more dimensions than admit of graphic representation. And a simple linear view, such as that in Figure 1, is particularly subject to this objection. A presentation in two dimensions, though still unsatisfying, is much better, because it allows us to suggest, however crudely, some of the dialectic which informs actual literary history. Consider, then, a representation of narrative history as a zigzag line superimposed on the straight line of our first diagram:

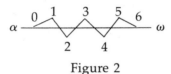

Figure 2

Ridiculously simple as this is, it can preserve us from some even simpler errors in historicizing literature. Let us suppose arbitrarily that we are presently located somewhere between points 3 and 4 in this scheme. (We might be between points 334 and 344 on some more refined scale, but no matter, for the present.) And let us say that the segment from 2 to 4 represents the history of realistic fiction: the rise, flowering, and decadence of the novel as a literary form. For some writers, some critics, and some students of fiction, this segment will itself appear as the whole history of fiction, from alpha to omega—a single line, perhaps curved, waving, or spiral, but nevertheless a line which is nearing its end point. To others, and I count myself among them, we seem only to be nearing the end of a segment, preparing for a movement in new directions. The first group will feel as if the apocalypse is at hand, while the others will be anticipating the new dispensation. Admittedly, these views are related, but the consequences of them are very different. If you take a short view of narrative literature, limited by the life of the novel as a form, you may well feel that we are close to the end of it, about to disappear up the fundament of fiction. If you take the longer view, however, you see simply that we are at a point where turning is necessary and likely, where changes will have to be made so that this does not turn out to be point omega in actuality. And the changes will be made. The system of narrative is self-regulating and will not tolerate a fictional vacuum.

Starting from the view, then, that we are not at the end of the fictional world but simply at a turning point in the history of narrative, I wish to consider with you the position of self-reflexive fiction in the larger perspective of narrative history. My discussion will necessarily be general. I will not be concerned with individual writers, whose behavior is as unpredictable as the behavior of sub-atomic particles. An individual writer may well be moving with the general zig or zag of his time, or he may be working through some maneuver of his own which will put him apparently in the opposite direction to the larger mass—and there is no reason why he shouldn't be there and doing that thing. I for one have no intention of criticizing someone for not conforming to some grand scheme of the history of literature. But I do believe that history is real and that we are in it. Some of its processes are cyclical and some are irreversible. We don't understand them all, but we have good insights into some of them. In my view of the historical process, what we have been calling self-reflection in fiction is essentially a short-term trend which is nearing its end.

Having said that, I am obliged to say something about new directions. I don't know the future. I don't even know exactly how to look for it. But I know some of the considerations we have to deal with in thinking about the future—and we have to think about the future all the time. When we get up in the morning, we have to think about the rest of the day. When we put down a word, we have to think about the rest of the sentence. We can't get away from thinking about the future. As readers of writers, we have to think about the future of ourselves and our fellow readers. I suppose the critic takes himself as a representative reader. He generalizes himself frequently as the ideal reader or the common reader, however un-ideal or uncommon he may be. But we have to think about the needs of actual readers, because writers need them. Writers need actual readers, not just critics playing the roles of readers, and reading because it is their métier, which they must practice to live. Writers need readers because writing is, among other things, communication, employing language which is common property but in uncommon ways—which readers recognize as uncommon precisely because they have a store of common notions and common usage against which to measure the writer's performance. The future of this act of communication which we call fiction depends upon the responses of actual readers to the fictions that writers produce. Thus we must ask ourselves what the needs of readers are—what writing, what fiction does for readers.

If reading is simply a chore for readers, if it does not reward their attention sufficiently, they won't bother with it. Too often, now, this seems to be the case. The problem of fiction's disappearing audience was considered by Charles Newman in *TriQuarterly 26*: Newman saw the trouble with contemporary fiction as being a matter of poor distribution, and blamed this on money-grubbing publishers (who can be blamed for lots of things, and it's always fun to blame them). But I think the problem is bigger than that. There is a lot of writing going on today which is technically admirable and in accordance with all of the standards for literary excellence that have been established over the past generation. But not many people want to read this fiction. Not many people find this admirable work rewarding enough to justify whatever expenditure of time or energy it takes to read it. This is a crucial aspect of the situation of contemporary fiction, so that when Jerry Klinkowitz says that self-reflexive fiction can be fun, I would answer that it had *better* be fun. It has to be. When it isn't fun, it is as dead as any kind of writing that has ever appeared—deader, perhaps. "Fun" is a homely word, perhaps too homely to encompass all the pleasures of fiction, but if we are not ready to insist that fiction be fun, we must still ask what its value is to actual readers, what function it plays in the lives of human beings.

From the reader's point of view, fiction is characterized by its ability to fulfill two functions. Some fictions accomplish both, some only one, but a work which accomplishes neither is either no fiction or bad fiction. We may call these functions sublimation and feedback. As sublimation, fiction is a way of turning our concerns into satisfying shape, a way of relieving anxiety, or making life bearable. Sometimes this function of fiction is called a dirty and degrading word: "escapism." But it is not exactly that, any more than sleep is an escape from being awake, or a dream is an escape from not being in a dream, from being wherever we are when we are not dreaming.

Sleeping and dreaming are aspects of life which are important and necessary for our functioning as waking beings. A healthy person sleeps and dreams in order to wake refreshed. As sublimation, fiction takes our worst fears and tames them by organizing them in a form charged with meaning and value. Even the label "escapist" acknowledges that fiction is connected to our actual existence precisely by offering us relief from its problems and pressures. The flimsiest fairy tale plays with our fears of death and failure by offering us vicarious triumph over both of these terrors. And the tale of terror, like the nightmare, offers us finally the relief of escaping back from fiction into an actuality which seems sweet in mere contrast to the horrors of dream or fiction. But the sublimation of anxiety and fear is only one of fiction's major functions. The other is feedback.

As feedback, fiction is a means toward correcting our behavior in the world. The fictions of feedback help us to perceive actual situations, situations that we are in, have been in, might be in, could be in. This may be done by some sort of replication of actuality or through analogies of actuality which are deliberately distorted to emphasize one aspect or another of their analogues in the world of experience. But however it is done, such fiction gives us material for correcting our perception of things and our actions in the world as a result of our experience with simulated situations. Fiction as a corrective of our vision and our behavior is certainly as important as the fiction of sublimation, though it is a rather different thing. It is a daytime, daydream fiction, as opposed to a nighttime, nightdream fiction. Both of those functions are important—are necessary to humans, in fact—and so will go on, in one form or another. And in the greatest works of literature, the products of our most powerful imaginations, they may be combined.

Which brings me to the subject of the fictional imagination itself. I've been suggesting ways that we may consider the fictional imagination from the reader's point of view. But if we shift to the writer's point of view, other aspects of imagination come into relief. Raymond Federman has presented an interesting discussion of imagination as plagiarism—which I would agree is an important aspect of imagination. Imagination feeds on previous imagination. For my own sins against imagination, no doubt, I have just been required to read a book on this subject, called *The Anxiety of Influence*, which would reduce our contemplation of poetry primarily to a study of the way one poet has been anxious about his dependence on prior poets. This book by Harold Bloom presents the situation of the poet or creative artist (Bloom is thinking especially about the poet as poet, a maker of poems) as an aspect of Freudian romance. The poet has a literary father, regrets that he has a father, kills the father, but must also keep the father alive, and so on. All poetry, seen in this way, becomes a struggle of the poet with his great predecessor, upon whom he is dependent, with a dependency he would rather not acknowledge; so that the poet's growth may be charted in terms of his changes of attitude toward this predecessor and the confidence with which he is able to plagiarize and finally to allow his predecessor to re-enter and repossess their joint poems, the predecessor, in a Borgesian manner, seeming to become a plagiarist of his follower or a ghostly voice speaking through him. This is an extreme but very instructive way of perceiving the whole process of imagination in terms of plagiarism. Raymond Federman's position, if I understand it, goes one step further. Since plagiarism is inevitable, he says, relax and enjoy it. Away with anxiety, he says; let us manipulate the old counters with confidence that there is nothing new under the fictional sun. But what if there is something new under that yellow dwarf from which we draw our energy and our life? The elements of the universe, whatever they are, may be fixed, but that they get rearranged into new structures which perform new functions cannot be contested.

These two attitudes toward the possibilities of fiction can be related to a greater problem, not only in the situation of writers at the present time, but also in the entire human situation. The word "alienation" has been fashionable for so long that we have begun to assume it as a necessary state of affairs; we define our humanity by the extent of our alienation from everything, and the more alienated we are, the more human we are. It seems to me that alienation, as a way of describing the situation of a writer, a reader, or any person, is again a paradigm with some truth value for this situation, but only for a part of it. The opposite of alienation—"integration," as it might be called—is just as true of our situations as people, readers or writers or whatever, as alienation is. We inherit the notion of alienation, I suppose from Descartes, or we like to think we do. Poor Descartes gets blamed for nearly everything that has gone wrong in the past several centuries. I don't think any man should be credited with that much power, but he is convenient for people who want to talk about alienation, who want to insist on a divorce between mind and matter, between the subject and the object. (More specific kinds of alienation, such as that discussed by Marx, are another matter, not under consideration here.) It seems to me that both self-reflexive fiction itself and the critical rhetoric of self-reflexive fiction accept the Cartesian split with far too much alacrity and acquiescence. Accepting it frees one to do certain things, of course, and it prevents one from doing other things. In order to perceive this more clearly, I suggest that as an exercise we try to alter the usual Cartesian arrangement, and instead of thinking of man merely as a subject forced to deal with objects that are "out there" or "other," we try for a moment to think of man as an object among other objects—or, if you wish, a subject among other subjects. This alteration of our habitual mode of perception will take a certain amount of imaginative extrapolation to achieve, but it will be a very healthy thing for us if we can manage it.

That it is not impossible is demonstrated by its achievement in certain works of modern fiction, among them some of such humble status as to seem invisible to the orthodox critical eye. Just last night at about 1:30 in the morning I was finishing a book which I found very satisfying, a work of fiction called *Earth Abides*, by George Stewart. The book was written in 1949, and reprints of it still turn up on the science fiction shelves of bookstores. It presents us with a situation in which the world is almost totally devastated, not by the expected atomic holocaust which haunted the fiction of the 1950's, but by a virus which sneaks up on man while he has been watching for an atomic bomb. This virus kills virtually everyone in the world, leaving a few scattered survivors around. But the things of the world are not destroyed, not radioactive; they are still there, just the way they were, being acted upon by all the physical forces of the universe. The book is a chronicle, so severe as to seem almost unimaginative, of the things Stewart imagines as likely to happen to a few people living in this world, as the processes of ecology which have been controlled and subdued by man for so long begin to operate with virtually no human input.

Granting the book its slightly fantastic premise, the reader then finds himself involved in an imaginative process of a severely realistic, even naturalistic, kind. What happens, with an impressive inexorability, is that in a few generations (and people breed very quickly because they are afraid of dying off if they don't) virtually everything that we cherish as civilization—written language, ability to handle complex tools, elaborate social structures—virtually all of this is gone. And it is sobering to realize how much of what we recognize and cherish as civilization depends upon the specialized labor of massive numbers of individuals. To watch civilization slipping from the grasp of man is in some ways horrifying, but there are compensations which Stewart develops with considerable skill. For instance, near the end of the story its principal protagonist, Isherwood Williams, now an old man, called Ish by later generations and thought of as a kind of god, is confronted by one of his greatgrandchildren. They have a sort of conversation—across the generations and through the old man's weakening grip on the reality of his own situation. In the course of this dim conversation, Ish, in his senile way, asks the young man if he is happy. And the young man answers, "Yes, I am happy. Things are as they are and I am part of them." That, of course, is integration, the opposite of alienation. But it has been bought at a very high price.

The lesson is clear, and I find it convincing. Man and nature are not divided in essence. Alienation is simply the price we pay for civilization. This is not news, you may say; Freud told us something very similar over half a century ago in *Civilization and Its Discontents*. Yes and no, for there is no question of guilt or repression in Stewart's vision. Alienation is a function of the complexity of human systems and the way that they twist and thwart natural systems for human ends. Alienation has been willed, desired by man. Having reached the point where we understand this, we can see that the great task of the human imagination for the present time is to generate, in literature and in life, systems that bring human desires into closer harmony with the systems operating in the whole cosmos. For this we need a cosmic imagination. We need to be able to perceive the cosmos itself as an intricate, symmetrical, cunningly contrived, imaginative entity in which we can be as much at home as a character in a work of fiction. We must see man as himself imagined and being re-imagined, and now able to play a role in the re-imagination of himself. It is now time for man to turn civilization in the direction of integration and away from alienation, to bring human life back into harmony with the universe.

For fiction, self-reflection is a narcissistic way of avoiding this great task. It produces a certain kind of pleasure, no doubt, this masturbatory reveling in self-scrutiny; but is also generates great feelings of guilt—not because what it is doing is bad, but because of what it is avoiding. Readers need imaginative help from writers. If all they get are muffled cries of "Go 'way, I got my own problems," they will indeed go away. But this will not lead to the death of imagination. A certain kind of imaginative self-reflection may indeed be going through a death which is a kind of metamorphosis. But imagination dies as the caterpillar, to be reborn with wings.

The question to be asked here is simply whether fabulation will play a part in this necessary, this inevitable rebirth of imagination. My answer is, Yes, it will; it is playing, has played such a part. For this rebirth is indeed under way around us. If one dimension of fabulation has become too self-involved, and another is threatened by over-elaboration of its own complexities, there is still another dimension that has renewed its vigor by touching the earth of popular narrative. From the field of science fiction, in particular, new writers have been emerging to join the ranks of literary fabulators, bringing both a concern for the traditional values of story-telling and a fresh vision of human problems and aspirations. From this point on, anyone interested in studying fabulative literature will have to consider writers like Ursula Le Guin, John Brunner, Philip K. Dick, Kate Wilhelm, Samuel R. Delany, Algis Budrys, Joanna Russ, Gene Wolfe, Gregory Benford, and a host of others who have matured and flourished all around us while our attention was focused on more "reputable" authors. It has always been this way. From its beginnings prose fiction has emerged from the despised world of popular culture to challenge established literary forms. The modern novel itself arose in just this way. That the process still continues is in itself a most heartening sign.

Fabulation lives.

Index

Aeschylus, 16
Aesop, 3, 142
Albee, Edward, 142; *The American Dream*, 176
Alemán, Mateo, 144
Alfonce (Petrus Alfonsus), 1–2
Apollonius (of Rhodes): *Argonautica*, 34, 36
Aristophanes, 143
Aristotle, 24, 109
Arnold, Matthew, 23
Auerbach, Erich, 109–10
Austen, Jane, 176

Barth, John, 4, 28, 56, 110–11, 128, 134, 142, 144, 173–74, 190, 209; *The Sot-Weed Factor*, 45, 93, 143, 174, 206, 209; *Giles Goat-Boy*, 45, 75–102; *Lost in the Funhouse*, 114, 118–23, 131 ("Frame-Tale," 119; "Night-Sea Journey," 119)
Barthelme, Donald, 105; *City Life*, 114–18, 131 ("Kierkegaard Unfair to Schlegel," 115, 117; "Brain Damage," 116, 119; "Bone Bubbles," 119; "The Glass Mountain," 122)
Beckett, Samuel, 31, 123, 137
Bellow, Saul: *Herzog*, 190
Benchley, Robert, 151
Benford, Gregory, 218
Bergson, Henri, 166
Best Seller, 134
Bloom, Harold: *The Anxiety of Influence*, 214–15
Book Review Digest, 134
Borges, Jorge Luis, 4, 9–20, 123; *Other Inquisitions*, 9–10, 20; *Labyrinths*, 10–18 ("Avatars of the Tortoise," 10; "The Circular Ruins," 14; "Parable of Cervantes and the Quixote," 16; "The Witness," 18; "Pierre Menard, Author of the Quixote," 15); "The Modesty of History," 16; "Límites," 18; *Ficciónes*, 131
Bosch, Hieronymus, 193
Bourjaily, Vance: *The Man Who Knew Kennedy*, 135
Breton, André, 172
Brodeur, Paul: *Stunt Man*, 128–30
Brontë, Emily: *Wuthering Heights*, 64
Brown, Norman O., 89
Brunner, John, 218
Buchler, Justus: *Philosophical Writings of Peirce*, 7–8
Budrys, Algis, 218
Burgin, Richard: *Conversations with Borges*, 13, 18

Campbell, Joseph, 101
Camus, Albert: *The Stranger*, 56; "The Myth of Sisyphus," 147
Capp, Al, 193
Carmichael, Stokely, 204
Caxton, William, 1–3
Céline, L. F., 163, 169; *Journey to the End of the Night*, 149, 164
Cervantes, Miguel de, 144; *Don Quixote*, 30
Charyn, Jerome: *Eisenhower, My Eisenhower*, 133–35; *Once Upon a Droshky, On the Darkening Green, The Man Who Grew Younger, American Going to Jerusalem*, 133; *Scrapbook*, 134
Chesterton, G. K., 11, 19
Coleridge, S. T., 56

Coltrane, John, 193
Comte, Auguste, 52
Conrad, Joseph, 36, 174; *Heart of Darkness*, 173
Coover, Robert, 4, 105; *The Public Burning*, 4, 206–9; *Pricksongs and Descants*, 114, 118–23 ("The Door," 121), 131; *The Universal Baseball Association*, 208
Cornell Sun, 150

Dante, 11, 49–50, 52, 81–82, 100, 110; *Divina Commedia*, 89
Darwin, Charles, 80
Delany, Samuel R., 218
Descartes, René, 215–16
De Vries, Peter, 159
Dick, Philip K., 218
Dickens, Charles, 150
Dickey, James, 132
Dinesen, Isak: *Seven Gothic Tales*, 56–57
Doctorow, E. L.: *Ragtime*, 4, 206–7
Donleavy, J. P., 142
Donne, John: "The Exstasie" (quoted), 45
Dostoevsky, Fyodor, 89, 203
Durrell, Lawrence, 41, 164, 172; *Alexandria Quartet*, 24–25, 29–36, 54, 77 (*Justine*, 32); *The Black Book*, 35
Dylan, Bob: *Tarantula*, 135–36

Eichmann, Adolf, 161
Einstein, Albert, 87
Eliot, George: *Middlemarch*, 34
Enck, John Jacob, 163

Faulkner, William, 36, 163, 169, 170, 174
Federman, Raymond, 210, 214–15; *Double or Nothing*, 136–38
Fiedler, Leslie, 188
Fielding, Henry, 30, 45, 109, 112, 174; *Tom Jones*, 174
Fitzgerald, F. Scott, 129, 144, 175
Flaubert, Gustave, 15
Ford, Ford Madox, 174
Forster, E. M., 26; *Alexandria, a History and a Guide*, 33–34
Fowles, John, 28, 110; *The Magus*, 25,

37–45, 127, 129; *The Collector*, 37; *The Ariostos*, 37; *Daniel Martin*, 37; *The French Lieutenant's Woman*, 37, 44–45, 206, 208
Franklin, Benjamin, 209
Freud, Sigmund, 50, 52, 80, 87; *Civilization and Its Discontents*, 217
Friedman, Bruce Jay, 144; *Black Humor*, 142–43

García-Marquez, Gabriel: *One Hundred Years of Solitude*, 206, 208
Gardner, John, 4
Gass, William H., 4, 105, 210; "Philosophy and the Form of Fiction," 113; *In the Heart of the Heart of the Country*, 114–18, 131 ("Order of Insects," 115; "The Pederson Kid," 117–18; "Mrs. Mean," 120)
Gide, André, 29
Gogarty, Oliver, 54
Grimmelshausen, Hans, J. C. von, 144; *Simplicissimus*, 149

Hadas, Moses: *Three Greek Romances*, 33
Hassan, Ihab, 210
Hawkes, John, 101, 142, 144, 145, 163–64, 167–77; *The Lime Twig*, 59, 174, 177–89; *Charivari*, 174–77, 187; *Cannibal*, 175; *Second Skin*, 177, 179
Hawthorne, Nathaniel, 11
Heliodorus: *Ethiopica*, 34–36, 44
Heller, Joseph, 142, 163; *Catch-22*, 143, 149, 164
Hemingway, Ernest, 128, 144
Herblock, 193
Hitler, Adolf, 200
Hogarth, William, 191
Homer, 118; *The Odyssey*, 34
Horton, Chase, 3
Hundred Merry Tales, A, 141
Huxley, Aldous, 175

Ibsen, Henrik: *The Pillars of Society*, 70

James, Henry, 112; "The Figure in the Carpet," 94
James, William, 15

Jameson, Fredric: *The Prison House of Language*, 9
Jefferson, Thomas, 209
Johnson, Samuel: *The Idler*, 19, 148; *Rasselas*, 148
Joyce, James, 31, 36, 100, 112, 161, 176; *Stephen Hero*, 52, 53; *Finnegans Wake*, 52, 53–54, 79; *A Portrait of the Artist as a Young Man*, 53, 128, 181; *Exiles*, 53; *Ulysses*, 53; "The Dead," 116–17
Jung, C. G., 50, 52, 53, 87

Kafka, Franz, 34, 131
Kant, Immanuel, 70
Kennedy, John F., 87
Kenner, Hugh, 157, 204
Kierkegaard, Sören, 38, 57
Klinkowitz, Jerome, 210, 213
Koestler, Arthur, 203

Langbaum, Robert: *The Gaiety of Vision*, 56
Lautréamont, Isidore, 163
Lawrence, D. H., 25, 35, 84; *The Man Who Died*, 89
Leary, Timothy, 89
Leavis, F. R., 112
Le Clezio, J. M. G.: *Book of Flights*, 136–38
Le Guin, Ursula K., 218
Leonard, John, 190
Levi-Strauss, Claude, 122
Longus: *Daphnis and Chloe*, 34
Lukács, Georg, 51, 53, 112

Mailer, Norman: *Why Are We in Viet Nam?*, 135
Malamud, Bernard: *Pictures of Fidelman*, 190–92; *The Fixer*, 200–202; *The Natural, The Assistant, A New Life*, 210
Malory, Sir Thomas: *Morte d'Arthur*, 3
Marx, Karl, 216
Melville, Herman: *Moby-Dick*, 159
Mencken, H. L., 165
Merwin, W. S.: *The Miner's Pale Children*, 130–33
Miller, Henry, 165
Milton, John: "Lycidas," 84

Mosley, Nicholas: *Impossible Object*, 125–27
Murdoch, Iris, 28, 50, 52, 55, 111; *The Unicorn*, 56–74; *Sartre, Romantic Rationalist*, 94

Nabokov, Vladimir, 4, 163, 169
Nashe, Thomas, 163; *The Unfortunate Traveller*, 165–66
New Republic, The, 156
New York Review of Books, The, 150
New York Times Book Review, The, 37, 190
New Yorker, The, 132
Newman, Charles, 213
Nietzsche, F. W., 70
Nixon, Richard M., 124, 195, 207

Oppenheimer, J. Robert, 87
O'Connor, Flannery, 163, 169
Orwell, George: *1984*, 209
Ovid, 34, 36

Paine, Thomas, 209
Pater, Walter, 18; *Marius the Epicurean*, 157
Parker, Dorothy, 151
Peirce, C. S., 7–8, 20
Perelman, S. J., 151
Picasso, Pablo, 127, 205
Pirandello, Luigi, 129
Plato, 13, 23, 24
Poe, Edgar Allan, 34, 57
Propp, Vladimir: *Morphology of the Folk Tale*, 112
Proust, Marcel, 25, 29, 35, 36; *Swann's Way*, 31–32
Purdy, James, 142, 163; *Malcolm*, 164
Pynchon, Thomas, 4, 142; *Gravity's Rainbow*, 4, 206, 208–9

Quevedo, Francisco, 9, 163

Rabelais, François, 144
Raglan, Lord (Fitzroy James Henry Somerset): *The Hero*, 101
Reed, Ishmael: *The Last Days of Louisiana Red*, 193–96; *The Free Lance Pall-Bearers, Yellow Back Radio Broke-Down, Mumbo Jumbo*, 193

Index 222

Rilke, Rainer Maria, 183
Robbe-Grillet, Alain, 76, 169, 171;
 Jealousy, 56; *For a New Novel*, 127
Roth, Philip: *Portnoy's Complaint*, 190
Rousseau, Jean-Jacques, 53
Russ, Joanna, 218

Sade, Marquis de, *Justine*, 181–82
Saintsbury, George, 35
Salmagundi, 179
Samuel, Maurice: *Blood Accusation*,
 201–2
Sarraute, Nathalie: *Between Life and
 Death*, 127–28; *Planetarium*, 128
Sartre, Jean-Paul, 57, 94; *Nausea*, 56,
 138; *Being and Nothingness*, 118
Saturday Review, 124, 134
Scholes, Robert, 210; *The Fabulators*,
 1, 124
Schopenhauer, Arthur, 10
Schorer, Mark, 109
Scudéry, Georges and Madeleine de,
 108
Shakespeare, William: *King Lear*, 147
Shelley, Percy Bysshe, 13
Sidney, Sir Philip, 13
Smollett, Tobias, 30, 45, 144
Southern, Terry, 142, 145, 164; *Dr.
 Strangelove*, 149, 165; *Candy*, 165;
 The Magic Christian, 165–67
Spenser, Edmund, 49, 54
Spinoza, Baruch, 202
Stalin, Josef, 200
Steinbeck, John: *The Acts of King
 Arthur and His Noble Knights*, 3–4
Steiner, George, 138
Stendhal, 13, 32
Sterne, Lawrence, 112; *Tristram
 Shandy*, 210
Stewart, George: *Earth Abides*,
 216–17
Suzanne, Jacqueline: *The Valley of
 the Dolls*, 200

Swift, Jonathan, 143, 144, 146; *Gulliver's Travels*, 157
Swinburne, A. C., 84

Thurber, James, 151; "The Unicorn
 in the Garden," 142
Tillich, Paul, 147
Tolkein, J. R. R., 125
Tolstoy, Leo: *Anna Karenina*, 34
Trilling, Lionel, 167
TriQuarterly, 213
Twain, Mark, 150

d'Urfé, Honoré, 26, 44; *Astrée*, 38

Valéry, Paul, 15
Vergil, 34
Verne, Jules, 12
Voltaire, 143, 144, 146
Vonnegut, Kurt, 128, 142, 144, 145,
 164, 190; *Cat's Cradle*, 145, 147,
 156–62, 178; *The Sirens of Titan*,
 148; *Mother Night*, 150, 156–62;
 Slaughterhouse-Five, 200, 203–5

Walpole, Horace, 144
Warhol, Andy: *a*, 124–25
Watt, Ian, 37
Waugh, Evelyn, 175
West, Nathanael, 163, 169, 175, 176
Wells, H. G., 20
White, E. B., 151
White, T. H., 68
Wilde, Oscar, 56
Wilhelm, Kate, 218
Wittgenstein, Ludwig, 50
Wolfe, Gene, 218

Yeats, W. B., 84; "The Trembling of
 the Veil," 75

Zall, Paul, 141
Zola, Emile, 23